The Blind Decades

The Blind Decades

Employment and Growth in France, 1974–2014

Philippe Askenazy

Translated from the French by Susan Emanuel

Foreword by Richard Freeman

UNIVERSITY OF CALIFORNIA PRESS

University of California Press, one of the most distinguished university presses in the United States, enriches lives around the world by advancing scholarship in the humanities, social sciences, and natural sciences. Its activities are supported by the UC Press Foundation and by philanthropic contributions from individuals and institutions. For more information, visit www.ucpress.edu.

University of California Press
Oakland, California

Library of Congress Cataloging-in-Publication Data

Askenazy, Philippe, author.
[Décennies aveugles. English]
The blind decades : employment and growth in France, 1974–2014 / Philippe Askenazy ; foreword by Richard Freeman ; translated from the French by Susan Emanuel.
pages cm
Includes bibliographical references and index.
ISBN 978–0-520–27799–1 (cloth : alk. paper)—
ISBN 0–520–27799–6 (cloth : alk. paper)—
ISBN 978–0-520–95995–8 (e-book)—
ISBN 0–520–95995–7 (e-book)
1. France—Economic conditions—1945–
2. France—Economic policy—1945- I. Emanuel, Susan, translator. II. Title.
HC276.2.A7813 2015
330.944'083—dc23

2014017516

Manufactured in the United States of America

24 23 22 21 20 19 18 17 16 15
10 9 8 7 6 5 4 3 2 1

In keeping with a commitment to support environmentally responsible and sustainable printing practices, UC Press has printed this book on Rolland Enviro100, a 100% post-consumer fiber paper that is FSC certified, deinked, processed chlorine-free, and manufactured with renewable biogas energy. It is acid-free and EcoLogo certified.

CONTENTS

FOREWORD

Tout arrive en France

RICHARD FREEMAN

The way workers and employers interact in the labor market and the way governments regulate labor markets are highly idiosyncratic. The institutions and rules that govern labor reflect the culture and history of a country more than product markets, where multinationals dominate sales worldwide; financial markets, where banks and brokers operate similarly around the world; or international trade, where global agreements set the rules for all countries. In the world of labor, the Nordics are famous for high rates of unionization and collective bargaining, active labor market policies, and low levels of inequality, while the United States is famous for the opposite conditions; Japan is renowned for its lifetime employment practices and seniority and bonus systems; Germany, for its works councils, employees on boards of directors, and apprenticeship systems.

What about labor institutions and policies in France? To analysts outside the Gallic world, the French labor system has long been a riddle wrapped in a mystery inside an enigma. France combines the lowest union density with the highest collective-bargaining coverage among advanced countries; the highest and most far-reaching minimum wage in the world with a work force that has only middling educational attainment;[1] legally mandated profit-sharing that links worker pay to an employers' financial performance; and a publicly funded retirement system based on high social insurance contributions which governments use at times to stimulate employment.

Notwithstanding the occasional rant of foreign executives about French work effort; perennial *Economist* criticisms of France's economic failings; labor policies and practices that diverge from the centralized-bargaining, social-partner or flexible-market models that entrance experts as "peak labor systems";[2] and even a collectively bargained right for staff to disconnect from work calls and emails after working hours,[3] France's unique labor system is associated with good economic performance. French productivity is among the highest in the world. In 2013 GDP per hour in France exceeded GDP per hour in Germany, the United Kingdom, Canada, and Japan, among other countries. France has the fifth-largest economy in the world.[4]

How, then, does the French labor system operate? What are its strengths and weaknesses? What lessons should persons outside of France draw from French experiences?

Phillipe Askenazy's *The Blind Decades* provides an insightful and fascinating picture of the way France's labor system works from the perspective of an economist steeped in French economic and political events, angered by the country's mistakes in the labor sphere, and committed to the country's performing better. Given the importance of the French government in labor and economy, much of the book focuses on national policies and the ideological and factual premises or beliefs that motivated those policy choices. In an era when industrial policy is out of style, French governments intervene regularly to encourage firms to modernize and reach full employment—the latter which Askenazy calls the "French theme in the concert of industrialized countries"[5] with respect to economic policy.

The book is chock-full of facts and insights about the political economy of labor policies and practices, from which readers of different disciplinary backgrounds, perspectives, and bases of knowledge will learn different things that will illuminate labor issues in their own countries. I was struck by three in particular.

1) The divergence between France's policy choices and those of other advanced countries facing the same global challenges. The book contrasts policies in the 1970s oil crisis, when France chose restrictive deficit-reducing financial and monetary policy while Germany and other European economies ran deficits to recover employment; in the late 1970s, when the Barre government sought full employment through "revalorization of manual labor" by encouraging "industrial jobs while European deindustrialization was proceeding inexorably" instead of preparing youth for new white-collar and service-sector jobs or investing in science and technology; in the early 1980s, when the Mitterand government's expansionary economic policies of increasing social benefits and minimum wage was based on misreading the U.S. Federal Reserve's commitment to restrictive monetary policy;[6] and in the late 2000s, when the Sarkozy government decided to lower taxes on extra hours worked while Germany and many other economies encouraged part-time jobs to spread work in the Great Recession

period. In its labor policies (as in much else), France marches to its own drummer. Askenazy explains some of the labor policies as resulting from being "partially hidebound by the reading of the labor market" from the 1970s.[7]

2) The efforts of conservative governments to alter labor contracts and social insurance charges in the hope that this would create enough jobs to resolve joblessness among young and less skilled workers. Micro-economic policies that reduce costs of labor can increase employment by moving firms down their demand curves. But policies have to be drawn carefully to avoid having employers and workers substitute tax-advantaged activities for similar activities that do not get the tax break, with little net effect on employment. If a government offers tax breaks for R&D, firms may declare marketing expenses to be research. If a government offers tax breaks for "performance-based pay" for executives, as the United States does, firms will shift executive pay from salaries to bonuses, stock grants, and options that fit this tax code without evaluating whether the grants, options, and bonuses actually improve performance. As Askenazy reports, France's late 1970s–early 1980s Employment Pacts to reduce youth unemployment through tax exemptions for hiring young people less than a year out of school exemplified this problem. Following introduction of the policy, "employers performed a rational fiscal and social optimization: they replaced young people who were just past a year out of school with newly graduated young people recruited into initial training schemes." This amounts to "employees being

replaced by cheap interns."[8] By contrast, he cites evidence that the "Aubry laws" to establish a 35-hour workweek appear to have had some success in expanding employment.[9]

3) France's distinctive tax policies to redistribute income. The wealthy and super-wealthy in all countries use their money and influence with policymakers to obtain tax breaks for themselves or for their businesses. Normal citizens use their voting power to press governments toward progressive tax and expenditure policies that improve their economic well-being. Both sides often justify their favored distributive policy in terms of its impact on employment. Conservatives say that tax breaks to the rich incentivize "job creators" to create jobs. The Left says that tax breaks to lower-income persons increase consumer demand, which stimulates employment. Some of France's tax breaks are innovative: changes in the rules on unemployment compensation to give higher-paid workers unemployment benefits closer to their salaries; tax breaks to persons who hire helpers in their homes, including 1992 legislation that gave taxpayers a break on income equal to half of salaries and contributions for jobs working at home.[10] The Hollande government famously sought to raise taxes on the wealthy but then endorsed tax cuts for firms in the hope that this would stimulate jobs, which Askenazy views critically.

A good economics book does more than educate a reader about some economic phenomena. It stimulates them to want to know more about certain issues. My want-to-know-mores from *The Blind Decades* are these.

1) What are the ways private-sector actors—unions, employers, and others—influence or seek to influence government policies in France? How do they use lobbying, contributions to candidates, networking with persons from the same Hautes Élysées, public demonstrations or strikes to move politicians in their direction? To what extent are some firms connected more to left or conservative political parties—or do all firms establish links across the political spectrum so they have influence on all governments (as in the United States)? In particular, Askenazy reports that French businesses managed to delay far longer than the businesses in other countries regulations restricting the use of asbestos, despite its scientifically proven horrific effects on human health. How did the industry lobby accomplish this?

   Looking outside of the political world, to what extent do French unions and firms seek to solve labor problems through private discussions, as is common in many other countries, and how do they interact with the government agencies and local officials that carry out policies? The book's concentration on national policies and politics reflects the importance of the central government in the French system, in contrast to Nordic countries, say, where social partners often guard their independence from governments in the labor area—or the United States, where state and local policies matter greatly. But private and local arrangements must have some impact on outcomes in France as well. How much and in what ways?

2) How does France's mandatory profit-sharing system operate? De Gaulle introduced this system in the late 1950s. French governments of all political persuasions have

maintained it ever since, while making sometimes substantial legal changes to improve its uptake and effectiveness.[11] The Left seems to have accepted profit-sharing grudgingly. It never sought to remove this unique aspect of French wage-setting policy nor to modify it in a major way to make it more favorable to lower-paid workers. Chapter 5 reports on the 2001 "Fabius" Law designed to promote investment of employee savings in small-and-medium businesses through fiscal advantages, which would seem connected to profit sharing but which is not examined in depth. In 2011 the French government enacted legislation that required companies meeting specified conditions to pay annual profit-sharing bonuses to employees. Given economic studies that indicate that French profit-sharing has been reasonably effective in raising productivity and reducing absenteeism,[12] economists outside of France would benefit from learning more about this distinct French policy, its link to other French labor and tax legislation, and the political economy that surrounds it. Should other countries consider adopting similar legislation? And if so, what would a detailed analysis of the French experience tell them about the best directions to go and dangers to avoid?

3) Askenazy criticizes French labor policies for weaknesses ranging from failure to undertake social experiments to determine what works to making decisions based on erroneous prognostications of the changing global economy. The criticisms seem well-deserved, but as I read his analysis of French policy blunders, I wondered what comparable volumes would tell us about the labor policies of other major countries. The United States is no paragon of evidence-based

> rational policymaking. The Bush administration backed away from assessing Labor Department programs in the belief that firms would invariably spend public training and adjustment assistance ideally. National Labor Relations Board rulings have invariably favored employers when Republicans had a majority on the board and unions when Democrats had a majority. The Obama administration expected (or hoped) that the flexible U.S. labor market would bounce back quickly from the Great Recession and thus never pushed for active labor-market policies of the type that most other advanced countries tried. In the EU, Danish "flexicurity" failed the test of the Great Recession as well, with Denmark suffering substantial unemployment and a weak jobs recovery. When Germany reunited, it set wages and benefits in the East at West German levels despite the lower productivity and living standards in the former communist state. The result was job loss, high social insurance costs, and slower economic convergence than might otherwise have occurred.[13]

Finding the institutions and policies that are best for workers in advanced countries when billions of people have joined the global capitalist economy from developing countries and former communist states and when emerging digital and artificial-intelligence technologies are altering work is a massive challenge to labor policy and to economic policy more broadly. For all of France's idiosyncrasies, there are lessons for economists, other social scientists, and policymakers in its experiences with labor policies and practices, as told in *The Blind Decades*. With eyes open to the evidence, analysts and policymakers in France and other countries can and will hopefully do better in the next decades.

NOTES

1. Union density of 7.8% in 2010: http://stats.oecd.org/Index.aspx?DataSetCode = UN_DEN. Collective-bargaining coverage of 90%: *Rapport sur la négociation collective et sur les branches professionnelle*, Rapport au premier ministre, Jean-Frédéric Poisson (La Documentation Française, April 28, 2009). In 2014 the *salaire minimum de croissance* was €9.53 per hour (about USD 13.15 at the present exchange rate, compared to the U.S. minimum wage of USD 7.25).

2. In the 1970s analysts cited the Nordic economies and Germany as "peak labor systems" for their centralized bargaining; in the 1980s many proclaimed Japan's lifetime employment and company unions the best way to structure labor; in the 1990s and 2000s the U.S.'s flexible market was the ideal. See Richard Freeman, "War of the Models: Which Labour Market Institutions for the 21st Century?" Labour Economics 5, no. 1 (March 1998): 1–24.

3. For the CEO complaint see http://www.businessinsider.com/titan-ceo-letter-to-montebourg-2013-2. For the *Economist* view as of 2014, see http://www.economist.com/news/leaders/21593456-president-talking-reform-it-his-interest-and-his-countrys-he-should-carry-it?zid = 295&ah = 0bca374e65f2354d553956ea65f756e0. For the new agreement on securing minimum rest periods after hours, see http://www.theguardian.com/money/shortcuts/2014/apr/09/french-6pm-labour-agreement-work-emails-out-of-office.

4. http://www.businessinsider.com/largest-economies-world-gdp-2013-6.

5. Chapter 2.

6. Chapter 3.

7. Chapter 2.

8. Chapter 2.

9. Chapter 5.

10. Chapter 4.

11. http://www.intercentar.de/fileadmin/files/PEPPER_IV/PEPPER_IV_France.pdf.

12. Pierre Cahuc and Brigitte Dormont, "Profit-Sharing: Does It Increase Productivity and Employment? A Theoretical Model and Empirical Evidence on French Micro Data," *Labour Economics* 4, no. 3

(1997): 293–319. Sarah Brown, Fathi Fakhfakh, and John G. Sessions, "Absenteeism and Employee Sharing: An Empirical Analysis Based on French Panel Data, 1981–1991," Industrial and Labor Relations Review 52, no. 2 (1999): 234–51. Fathi Fakhfakh and Virginie Perotin, "The Effects of Profit-Sharing Schemes on Enterprise Performance in France," Economic Analysis 3 (2000): 93–112.

13. Andrew K. Rose, George A. Akerlof, Helga Hessenius, and Janet L. Yellen, *East Germany in from the Cold: The Economic Aftermath of Currency Union,* Brookings Papers on Economic Activity, no. 22:1 (Washington, DC: Brookings Institution, 1991).

Introduction

France has long been presented as a curiosity, with its workweek of only 35 hours and its 36,700 *communes*—organized into an elaborate state apparatus. In the image of its museum-like capital, many of its institutions seem to exist outside of time. Though it produces the Airbus and serves as the headquarters of many multinationals, its economy is said to escape the logics of globalization even now. France is usually seen as vulnerable, in the middle of a European continent stuck in crisis. The *Economist* devoted an issue to France (November 17, 2012), with the headline "The Time-Bomb at the Heart of Europe," concluding that France will have to come to terms with reality or risk falling and taking Europe with it. *Newsweek* even announced "The Fall of France" (January 3, 2014).

Actually, Cassandras have regularly predicted a somber destiny for France due to its uncoupling from the great European economies. Back in 1987, Stephen Greenhouse reported in the *New York Times*:[1]

> While their neighbors are managing to find reasons to feel good about their economies, the French are in the grip of a malaise. The

> Italians are exuberant because of what they see as an "industrial miracle" that has made their country a competitive force in Europe. The British are chipper because after sliding for years, their economy appears to be on the mend. Even the West Germans are optimistic: While their country's economy is in the doldrums, they remain confident that the "locomotive of Europe" will soon pick up steam.... In the next few years, the economies of Britain and Italy might surpass the size of France's.

This continual skepticism about France—and its flip side, the fleeting enthusiasm for one or another of its neighbors—is not just the privilege of journalists. Financial correspondents and economic columnists have echoed liberal economic thinkers and much academic work, as well as international institutions like the IMF, the OECD, and the European Commission. They consistently urge France to implement structural reforms, especially to reduce the weight of the state, its army of civil servants, its "interventions" and tax impositions and over-regulation—all to prevent its collapse. In France itself, a vast intellectual movement constantly blames a *mal français* (French sickness)—the title of a best-seller by Alain Peyrefitte, the former Gaullist minister, that appeared in 1976. The doom-predicting authors come and go, but the ideas stay the same, feeding the clichés about France beyond its borders. The French do not work enough. They do not have enough confidence, in themselves or in others, in institutions, in the market. They refuse to carry out the adaptations necessary for globalization. They are too attached to their "acquired" advantages. They do not have an economic "sensibility." They do not have the spirit of entrepreneurs (though this word comes from French). They refuse order. The labor unions have too much influence—and at the same time, not enough. And so on.

And yet in 2013 France still ranks as the world's fifth-largest economy (ahead of the United Kingdom) and the eurozone's second-largest economy (ahead of Italy). The resistance of the French economy to the Great Depression was remarkable and distinctive. For several decades, this economic resilience, despite seemingly inappropriate institutions, has defied the analyses of most of the economics establishment.

This book adopts a historical perspective to explain this puzzle. It proposes to follow, step by step, four decades of the economic environment, and the state of the knowledge applied to it, the public policies employed in France since the first oil shock (in 1973). French history offers a remarkable prism for tracing the great evolutions and revolutions in economic situations and ideas up to now. Basically, it illustrates that the standard levers of economic policy are not very effective in determining economic outcomes. This book demonstrates the essential factors that explain both why France has not fallen and why it has been incapable of taming unemployment. In these four decades France has not enjoyed a period of euphoria that might have made it the model to follow. Certainly employment and workers' activity rates have never been particularly low in relation to the average in the other countries of old Europe. Most of these have experienced an economic resurgence, along with (at least temporarily) a level of unemployment close to that at the start of the 1970s. Since the crisis born in 2008, France has been distinctive for its durably mediocre performance on the employment front, despite the obsession with full employment that has animated all of its governments, on the right and on the left.

Relying on many international comparisons, my own reading of recent economic history shows that it is impossible to pinpoint a single cause. France does not suffer from a specific and crippling illness. In reality, its maladies are rather banal. Modern capitalism everywhere results in instability in the labor market and in chaotic growth, except that the French respond with a form of blindness that is repeated in each decade. The economic policies they have put in place might have been useful for employment, social cohesion, and growth. But most of the governments in power—whatever their political colors, obsessed as they were with the rapid return to full employment—were not able to grasp the current changes in world capitalism, its opportunities, and its dangers. In turn, this generated economic errors or delayed adaptations. It is the persistence of these habits and the difficulty of thinking beyond the immediate horizon that together comprise the history of job and growth policies. France has stumbled after the opportunities of a capitalism that has been undergoing significant evolution for four decades.

The industrialized world has experienced major economic upheavals: petroleum shocks and counter-shocks, stagflation, then "the end" of inflation, the "new economy," the flux and reflux of mass unemployment, the deep transformation of modes of production and of working, globalization, the financial crisis, and the Great Recession. The turn of the 1970s marked the entry into a phase of transition between two industrial revolutions, between Fordist modes of production and a knowledge economy propelled by the technologies of information and communication. This transition has translated into a learning period for all economic agents, as well as important changes in how firms, institutions, and subsidiary activities are organized. Learning has been necessary to extract new productivity gains, that is to say, to try to produce more goods or services with the same quantities of labor and capital. In fact, the crisis of the 1970s and

1980s was above all a crisis of productivity. Deepened by the oil shocks, this crisis was at first thought to be temporary, precisely because it was linked to the disequilibria generated by these shocks.

The policy of the government of Jacques Chirac in France from 1974 to 1976 did not depart from this vision. On the one hand, France launched into the energy economy, and on the other, it organized national solidarity in the face of rising unemployment. But during this time, the decline of traditional industries and mining, perceptible since the mid-1960s, accelerated. And gradually, unemployment affected all social categories. Conservative governments have chosen to stigmatize some of these categories of the population, focusing primarily on immigrants, ever since the Chirac government of 1974. Chirac clearly proclaimed his populist vision: "There should be no employment problem in France. We have a million people out of work and 1.8 million immigrants."[2] Several contemporary economists supported this assessment. In their eyes, the immigrant, who had been a source of wealth a few years previously, had become the cause of the impoverishment of natives; this reinforced the rampant discrimination in businesses and framed the debate in an obsessive Malthusian logic. From his arrival as the head of the government in 1976, prime minister Raymond Barre fingered a second social group: young people. They were judged unsuitable for the requirements of firms—and thus their difficulties in entering the labor market were worsened. Young people were no longer considered an opportunity for growth, for innovation, for creation in a company, but as a risk, and even more so if they had immigrant origins.

Simultaneously, most of the so-called industrialized countries dropped their wait-and-see position by following more or less the same clutch of policies that had been haltingly and gradually put together: struggling against inflation; structural reforms of the markets for goods and services and of the labor market; a policy of industrial redeployment; and stimulating innovation. In all the major economies, the mutations in capitalism had the effect of profoundly modifying work requirements. They destabilized professional status and doomed whole sections of the workforce to difficulties in entering the job market, or precariousness once they got there. From this point of view, there is no French exception.

From the early 1980s to the first half of the 1990s, the best economic results were obtained by the countries that knew how to be the first to catch the train of the new industrial revolution or to best manage the transition phase from one revolution to the other. And during the following decade, those that enjoyed the most solid economic growth, usually accompanied by a sharp drop in unemployment, were those that had fully entered into the "new economy." This term appeared around the end of the twentieth century to refer to U.S. recovery in productivity growth and the visible results of the technological progress propelled by information and communication technologies and by globalization.

Such progress happens in the sectors that directly produce these technologies, and sectors that use them, and producers of goods that incorporate them. In fact, it was not solely the great champions of information and communication technologies like the United States that came through the transition phase. By breaking its industrial and social models, the United Kingdom learned very early how to wager on the financial sector and business services. More recently, Germany has imposed itself as the key supplier of industrial equipment to emerging countries and of computer software for companies.

France has not remained totally outside this dynamic. Investments in information technologies and organizational changes have been realized. And public policies have accompanied this process, notably through an educational effort to create a workforce that is adapted to the knowledge economy and through significant deregulation of the labor market. But the process has never been totally set in motion. Though it was one of the first countries in terms of expenditure on research and development at the start of the 1990s, we shall see that France suspended its effort just when most of its partners were accelerating theirs. It did not see the train of the new economy until it had left the station. France found itself even more poorly armed in the first decade of the new millennium; yet its economy was able to absorb the shock of the Great Recession.

Before analyzing modern French economic history, a first chapter presents the sources and the various consequences (especially for employment) of four decades of ruptures in all market economies. The subsequent chapters follow a chronological order but do not necessarily stick to political changes in France. Chapter 2 covers the period between the first oil shock and the new monetary policy implemented by the U.S. Federal Reserve; it overlaps Giscard d'Estaing's presidency, which was marked by misdiagnosis of the economic crisis and consequently inadequate policies. Chapter 3 analyzes in depth the years 1981–1986. It shows how the Left, headed by Mitterrand, the first socialist president of the Fifth Republic, shifted from the goal of state control of the economy to social liberalism, including deregulation of financial markets and massive investment in secondary education. The years 1986–1993, which were marked by progressive growth recovery and then a recession, are presented in chapter 4. The victory of the conservatives in 1986 was just a parenthesis. Fascinated by the Thatcher revolution and captured by clienteles, their policy fractured French society. The wish for a pacifying policy explains both Mitterrand's reelection in 1988 and the lack of ambitious policy in his center-left government. Chapter 5 covers the key period of 1993–2002, during which the perception of the "new economy" arose only in the very last year of the century. Rather than entering into the knowledge economy, efforts conducted by governments of both the Left and the Right were focused on low-paying jobs, in the hope of adaptation to a stagnant economy. The next chapter studies why the legislature of 2002–2007 resulted in the disintegration of French labor and industrial policy. The Great Recession of 2008 was a surprise for French leaders (and economists). Chapter 7 proposes an analysis of the European crisis and the multifaceted policy deployed by two presidents, Sarkozy and Hollande (up to 2014). The last chapter provides a necessarily incomplete portrait of the French economy after four decades of mass unemployment and an accumulation of diverse (and divergent) policies. My conclusion challenges some of the common clichés about France.

NOTES

1. Steven Greenhouse, "In France, Economic Malaise," *New York Times*, July 29, 1987.
2. Interview in *Le Monde*, February 19, 1976.

CHAPTER ONE

Four Decades of an Industrial Revolution

In both common perception and from the perspective of much modern economic history,[1] a historic shift stands out in the industrialized world: three decades (1945–1973) were marked in the major market economies by strong growth and full employment, and followed by decades when crises and booms alternated, before they all crashed into the Great Recession in 2008. In France, the first period has been nicknamed *les trente glorieuses* (the Glorious Thirty), after a book published by Jean Fourastié in 1979. On top of economic prosperity came a modernization of the country's economic, social, and cultural structures. The second period, by contrast, some French scholars characterize as "piteous," because France proved incapable of curbing mass unemployment. Such a demarcation, whether implicitly or explicitly, makes the first oil crisis of 1973 the watershed of the economic turn from glorious to piteous. However, I will argue that this watershed had much more to do with the new industrial revolution, this time organized around information and communication technologies, which began in the 1970s. It is this revolution that forms the background for the four recent decades that this book covers.

A quick overview of the year 1970 will contextualize this chronology. Performance of the European economies remained good—even excellent. The fifteen countries that would form the European Union enjoyed annual growth close to 5%. Employment figures also seemed very good. The Federal Republic of Germany announced an unemployment rate of only 0.5%; Great Britain had 2.2%, and France 2.3%.

However, a deeper analysis shows that France, like several European economies, was experiencing the first disequilibria. Unemployment was slowly rising. In 1965, it had been 1.5% in France and 1.2% in Great Britain. The rise accelerated throughout 1970. In France, the number of job seekers increased by a quarter between January 1, 1970, and January 1, 1971; and the situation deteriorated even more the following year. Almost 600,000 French workers were unemployed. Jobs decreased in construction and in public works; young people and women were the most affected in other sectors. The British economy was the sick lady of Europe. Economic growth there was erratic, and the pound sterling was regularly devalued. Inflation soared starting in mid-1970, and a year later it exceeded 10%.

Meanwhile, across the Atlantic, the United States was apparently stuck in a situation that contrasted with other developed nations. The world's principal economy was carrying out a major war in Vietnam, with half a million men engaged on the ground. After a very remarkable 1969, the unemployment rate in 1970 rose back to 4.9%. This was still lower than in 1964, that is, before the massive American commitment to the war in Indochina. But the main reason for the unhealthy economy was that several years before the oil crises, the economy was in stagflation—a mixture of inflation and the absence of growth. Annual growth of GDP was only 0.2%, yet the rise in consumer prices reached 5.7% during that year. In fact, inflation accelerated after the second half of the 1960s and would not return to low levels until the end of the century. In 1970, the dollar fell sharply against the deutschmark. In August 1971, president Richard Nixon decided to suspend the convertibility of the dollar into gold, signaling the crumbling of a system that had been in effect since the 1944 Bretton Woods Conference. He also established a 10% tax on imported products, underscoring the loss of competitiveness of the American economy.

THE FIRST PRODUCTIVITY SLOWDOWN

Nevertheless, Western business, especially American business, was quickly developing automation in both the industrial and administrative spheres, meaning the use of automatic machines that required limited human intervention (robots and calculating machines). In reaction, the USSR made the automation of industry an essential axis of its 9th Plan (1971–1975).[2]

But despite these technological advances, American growth had been faltering for several years. Fundamentally, the motor of economic growth and competitiveness—gains in the hourly productivity of work—was crumbling (figure 1). From an annual pace of 3% at the start of the 1960s, the gains gradually diminished, without any particular break during the oil shocks. A trough below 1.5% was reached during the 1980s. It was only after the mid-1990s that hourly productivity in the United States would recover an average growth higher than 2%.

The United States was not the only country touched by the productivity slowdown. Angus Maddison's breakdown of growth

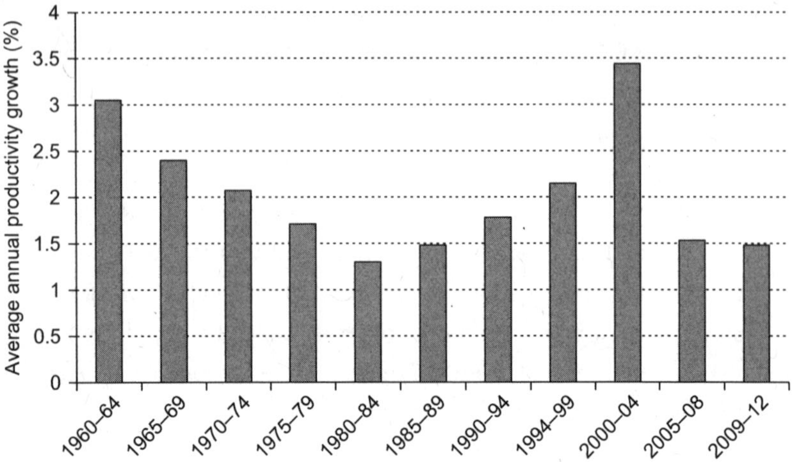

Figure 1. Productivity growth in the U.S. business sector (excluding agriculture), 1960–2012. Author's calculation using Bureau of Labor Statistics productivity series (January 16, 2014).

over two sub–periods, 1950–1973 and 1973–1992, clearly shows the cost of the reconfiguration phase.[3] The factors he took into account in economic growth arose from: 1) the evolution of the number of hours worked (the volume of labor); 2) the accumulation of capital; 3) the effect of foreign trade; 4) economies of scale in productivity; 5) improvement in the quality of the labor force (level of training); and 6) a residual component. These factors were combined to achieve total productivity growth, and this figure was interpreted as the visible contribution of technological progress in the wider sense.

The slowing of growth between the two periods (i.e. after 1973) is common to the United States, France, Germany, and Japan. The effect of foreign trade is systematically minor. The most striking thing is that the accumulation of capital remains rapid, accounting for more than 3 percentage points of the growth from 1973 to 1992 in all four countries. But this accumulation was accompanied by a drop in the productivity of capital. From 1973 to 1992, the technological transition was ensured by the renewal of capital, but this had not yet been translated into gains in efficiency. In fact, the apparent contribution of technological progress to growth fell between 1 and 2 percentage points between the 1950s and 1960s and the following two decades. Again, it was only in the mid-1990s that several countries began to recover sustained productivity growth.

INFORMATION AND COMMUNICATION TECHNOLOGIES

What does this abrupt break in the growth of productivity in the second half of the 1960s signify? I think it signals the transition from one industrial revolution to another, specifically from a Fordist regime to the "new economy" (or "knowledge economy") that was induced by the spread of information and communication technologies (ICTs), of which industrial automation was the prelude. The United States would henceforth be the cradle of successive technological waves, from computers to smartphones via the Internet. These technologies were, foremost, responses to demand from American firms, which possessed a breeding ground of personnel who were better educated than in most of the major industrialized countries (including France), employees who had the capacities to adapt and to be mobile.[4] These new technologies (and the organizational styles that would be associated with them) favored the most qualified in the workforce; on the American model, ICTs would require flexibility in both the nature of work and in the structure of employment. American predominance would therefore have major consequences for the characteristics of the industrial revolution that we will examine more closely in the chapters that follow.

The ICTs are not neutral technologies. Like electricity, for example, they belong to the category of general purpose technologies (GPTs), which are characterized by three properties[5] that explain their preponderant role in the growth and evolution of economic structures:

1. The performance of these technologies enjoys rapid progress that may extend over several decades. This progression is accompanied by a collapse in *hedonic prices*: from one year to the next, a more advanced version of the technology is available at a cost similar to that of the previous version. In the case of ITCs, the progression is dual. First, the basic components see their operating power, their storage capacity, and their miniaturization all advance in an exponential manner. On top of that, waves of innovation overlap each other: computers, for example, go from low-speed Internet to high-speed, then to the current mobility and immateriality of "the cloud."
2. GPT use spreads across the whole economy. And this use intensifies. For example, from 1992 to 2007, the proportion of Internet users within the OECD went from 2% to 66%. Moreover, this process is worldwide, extending over the last decade to countries with very low average incomes.
3. These technologies improve the processes of innovation. ITCs are widely utilized in all realms of creation. All scientific domains benefit from it, ranging from simulation in aeronautics to human-genome sequencing

in biology. In addition to their calculating power, ITCs facilitate exchanges among actors engaged in various kinds of innovation.

By cutting through a mass of research in different fields of economics and management, we may penetrate into the "black box" of this industrial revolution and inspect the various mechanisms at work, and their consequences, over four decades of the "new economy" that was to last until the eve of the financial crisis of 2008. The key point is that the process generated by a GPT is long. It is only after a phase of reconfiguring the methods of production, of adaptation by institutions and workers, that we observe the productive benefits of this technology. This period would last two decades in the case of electricity.[6] It would be of the same order of magnitude for the first wave of ICT.

What are the consequences of this protracted productivity leap?

INFLATION—THEN DEFLATIONARY EFFECTS

The collapse over several decades of productivity gains induced tensions in both prices and employment. The mechanism is simple, formalized since the start of the 1970s in the notion of NAIRU: the non-accelerating inflation rate of unemployment. Gains in productivity allow firms to respond to employees' salary demands without having to increase the prices of goods. But when these gains diminish, firms (in order to conserve their profit margins) finance salary increases by raising prices, thus creating inflation. This inflation itself modifies the employees' expectations: in turn they demand wage hikes, which stimulates demand, hence monetary creation. To avoid increasing prices too much, firms then cut jobs, which reduces their overall salary costs. At the macroeconomic level, this translates into a rise in unemployment; in turn, the fear of losing one's job associated with the rise in under-employment, and the competition for jobs, both work to limit wage demands. We then arrive at a new equilibrium characterized by both higher inflation and higher unemployment.

Thus, technological transition carries with it a risk of inflation. The oil shocks catalyzed this. In an exogenous manner, they increased costs for businesses, and they deeply affected agents' expectations about inflation. This led to a sharp rise in inflation—well beyond the impact of oil prices alone—in Europe as well as in North America, in the second half of the 1970s. As we shall see in the rest of this book, the policies adopted in most countries to break this vicious wage–price cycle would enable them to achieve lower levels of inflation starting in the second half of the 1980s.

Then, starting in the 1990s, the rising power of the new economy took over. On the one hand, North American and many European economies recovered a total productivity growth based on long-term factors. On the other hand, ICT products, either by themselves (for example, computers) or as incorporated into other products (automobiles) or into services (communication), represented a significant proportion of consumption. But thanks to rapid technological progress, the prices[7] of the latter declined quickly, with a major deflationary effect. This mechanism is still at work today, leading to low underlying inflation.[8] Thus, despite major budget deficits in 2009 in all the OECD countries, no inflationary pressure has emerged. Inflation stabilized below 2% in the eurozone in 2013, while Japan was trying to extricate itself from protracted deflation.

REVAMPED WORKPLACES AND LABOR RELATIONS

The return of sustained growth in productivity (which initiated a virtuous circle) came about through a reshaping of the organization of work within firms. American and then European companies developed innovative ("high-performance") work practices that gradually took the place of Taylorist modes. These practices enabled extracting productivity gains from the use of information technologies, generating a new and flexible style of production. Thus, even a country that did not produce ICTs could gain in performance by means of industries that made use of these technologies.

We may observe recurrent adoption of certain key and complementary work practices: work in autonomous teams, rotation of tasks, approaches to quality control and to just-in-time workflows.[9] These approaches comprise a set of procedures implemented to achieve high quality standards. The procedures might be formalized—in order to obtain an ISO (International Organization for Standardization) certification, for example, in Europe—or they might evolve slowly, continually improving the production process. The spread of innovative work practices was rapid in the 1990s. The growth in the number of ISO-certified firms was remarkable, with a quintupling in most OECD and emerging countries in five years. Organizational changes also affected the frontiers of enterprise. Just-in-time production allowed a segmentation of wealth creation through increased use of subcontracting. The complementarity between technology and work organization involved all sectors, in industry as well as services. For example, ICTs enabled optimizing flows—of products, clients, and employees—in major corporations.

The accelerated modernization of the retail and wholesale trade in North America, associated with the takeoff of the big-box distributor Wal-Mart, would contribute around half a point annually to American growth in the second half of the 1990s.[10]

Beyond the technical complementarity between technologies and innovative practices, ICTs increase the exchange of data and the effectiveness of the innovation process. The consequent acceleration of innovation then pushes the ensemble of businesses in all sectors, even those that are not very ICT-intensive, to engage in just-in-time production.

In parallel, the search for flexibility requires both an intensification of work and an enlarged pool of precarious workers, either temps or on short-term contracts; firms have found young people who are just leaving the educational system to be a breeding ground for short-term hires. Moreover, the pace of business creation and destruction adds to the instability of jobs. Even if large enterprises try to maintain an internal work market[11] by retraining their existing personnel, the process of organizational—and especially technological—innovation is associated with high employee turnover.[12] In the European countries,[13] the proportion of the working population that from one year to the next has either changed occupation, found a job elsewhere, or become unemployed has typically increased from 15% to 30%. This pattern specific to flexible production has been everywhere accentuated by the restrictive policies of the "rigid" labor market; the rationale of these policies is precisely that the right to work should not be an obstacle to the processes of innovation and wealth creation.

Flexible production also has a direct impact on the activity and influence of trade unions. The flexibility of schedules, the reduction in work breaks, the direct transmission of instructions among employees, and project teamwork all tend to eliminate periods when employees can find each other within the company and thus organize collectively. The development of multitasking and task rotation also tend to reduce the pertinence of classification by detailed occupation, making it difficult to mobilize collectively around a common identity. The intensive use of on-site subcontracting[14] and of fixed-term or temporary contracts fragments the personnel within the same workplace, adding an additional obstacle to the emergence of a union counterweight to management. Moreover, the unions that were powerful in the 1960s were built on a working-class identity. The acceleration of tertiarization of the economy and the rise in education have likewise reduced the pool of union recruits.

In fact, after a phase of relative stability during the 1970s, the de-unionization movement became massive in the 1980s in most of the OECD countries (table 1). This erosion is particularly clear in the English-speaking countries where unions were initially strongly implanted (Australia, Great Britain, New Zealand, and Ireland). Countries where collective bargaining continues to play a structuring role (as in the Netherlands and Germany) have not escaped this process. This is also the case in France, which has nevertheless tried to strengthen the scope of its unions. With an already weak level at the start of the 1970s, since 1990 France has had the lowest share of unionized workers within the OECD—below even the United States.

In short, only countries where the unions institutionally guarantee the main social benefits to their affiliates, notably regarding unemployment insurance, have seen stability or progress in the unionization rate over thirty years. In fact, the emergence of large-scale unemployment in the 1970s provoked waves of unionization in order for individual workers to be able to

TABLE I

Unionization rates, in percent, among employees in the private and public sectors within the OECD, 1970–2010

A. Countries where unions guarantee benefits to their members

Year	Belgium	Denmark	Finland	Norway	Sweden
1970	42.1	60.3	51.3	56.8	67.7
1980	54.1	78.6	69.4	58.3	78.0
1990	53.9	75.3	72.5	58.5	79.4
2000	49.5	74.2	75.0	54.4	79.1
2010	50,6	68.5	70.0	54.8	68.2

B. G7 countries

Year	Canada	France	Germany	Italy	Japan	UK	US
1970	31.0	21.7	32.0	37.0	35.1	43.0	27.4
1980	35.3	18.3	34.9	49.6	31.1	49.7	22.1
1990	35.8	10.0	31.2	38.8	25.4	38.2	15.5
2000	30.2	8.0	24.6	34.8	21.5	30.2	12.9
2010	27.4	7.8	18.6	35.5	18.3	26.4	11.4

SOURCE: OECD trade unions database (http://stats.oecd.org), May 15, 2014.

benefit from the associated collective benefits. This was the case in all the Scandinavian countries.

In 2001, Belgium had a unionization rate of more than 50%, comparable to Norway. Let us linger over the Belgian case and the lessons we may take from it. Non-union workers are insured against the risk of unemployment by a government body, the Caisse Auxiliaire. For those in the unions, their organizations take part in the management of the risk as recognized bodies for paying unemployment benefits. The jobs bureau, the Office national de l'emploi (ONEM), determines entitlements, but the request must be introduced via these bodies. The union payment offices help workers fill out forms and then pass them on to the ONEM. They serve as permanent intermediary with the ONEM and make sure that it respects the rights of the unemployed. On the salary level, Belgium has kept a strong indexing of wages to prices, and has a minimum wage that is among the highest in the OECD.

Thus, Belgium challenges the view that one might call "post-culturalist,"[15] which sees de-unionization as a phenomenon linked to a low degree of cooperation in the economy and to state regulation of wages. Moreover, Belgians are culturally and socially much closer to the French or the Germans than to the Scandinavians. This is corroborated by the World Values Survey studies that are widely used in culturalist research.

Although in Belgium and the Scandinavian countries, maintaining the influence of the unions does not seem to have been an obstacle to business reorganization, elsewhere, the decline of unions may well have been an accelerator of this reorganization. The retreat of a union allows firms to replace general salary increases with incentive tools that complement multitask organization.[16] Similarly, it usually requires a reorganization that modifies job contents and may at least temporarily cause deterioration in working conditions, or even displace the boundaries of the firm.

FINANCIALIZATION AND GLOBALIZATION

The decline of trade unions is also linked to capitalist movements. On the one hand, liberalization and deregulation of major monopolies, and corporate mergers and acquisitions, shrink union bastions, or dilute them. On the other hand, these trends are facilitated by the weakening of the unions in their midst. However, the move to privatization originates from clear ideological choices in many English-speaking countries, or in Europe from the principles of free competition. It is also imposed by a "pragmatism" in the economic context that was inherited from the technological transition phase. In many countries, and especially in the United Kingdom and France, privatization offered an important source of revenue for the government, allowing it to smooth out the budgetary consequences of the atrophy of growth, and even to develop plans for investing in the knowledge economy. Privatization and deregulation—for example in air transportation—also fostered, through competition, a drop in prices, which helped counter inflation (accentuated by the negative impact on the salaries of employees in these enterprises). In telecommunications, putting operators into competition with each other not only reduces prices but also fosters the spread of innovations; thus, without the deregulation of this sector, the development of high-speed Internet in France would have been slow and limited to a fringe of consumers and companies. Thus, the new economy has also been facilitated by the deregulation of certain public services.

On the other hand, the trend toward capitalist reconfigurations of private businesses (where mergers and acquisitions are a classic phenomenon)[17] thrives during the assertion of a GPT. Rapid technological progress induces accelerated depreciation of existing capital. Hobijn and Jovanovic show that the global collapse of stock prices in the United States after the start of 1973 (several months *before* the first oil crisis) was due to the awareness among actors of the emergence of the information technology revolution.[18] The advent of the first microprocessor, produced by Intel in 1971, made palpable a "law" enunciated by Gordon Moore, the director of this firm, a few months earlier:

the speed of the processors doubles every 18 months. Seen in detail, it was not the companies most exposed to soaring oil prices whose value declined, but those most closely tied to "old" capital.

In parallel, new actors entered the new growth markets. Taking into account the cost of entering such markets—the costs of acquiring a reputation, of adapting capital, of reorganization—meant that acquiring or merging with these new actors (the first movers) became the privileged route for firms wishing to invest in these markets. Many Internet startups were bought or merged in the 1990s, before becoming predators themselves. This movement has enabled extracting exceptional levels of profitability during phases of synergy—which, however, are by nature short-lived.

The massive capitalist reconfigurations in the last two decades of the twentieth century also required vast financial engineering. Therefore, it was long the basis of the growth of the major international business banks and the investment departments of the generalist banks. In addition, the ICTs facilitated sophistication in finance. Thus, in the 2000s, these banks were able to find a driver for growth, this time without any actual link to the real economy, in securitization[19] (for example of subprime loans), before they collapsed at the start of the financial crisis of 2008. Despite this crisis, the financial industry carries major weight in most of the developed economies.

The interactions between globalization (the internationalization of trade, at least) and the new economy are more complex. The reinforcement of competition among countries of the global North and between countries of the global North and South, as facilitated by multilateral, bilateral, or regional free-trade agreements, tends to accentuate the process of externalization and to stimulate innovation and corporate internal reorganization. Firms develop defensive strategies of innovation that permit maintaining their competitiveness without resorting to either relocating or abandoning a market.[20] The targeted search for production of certain components in low-wage countries may be part of this attempt to maintain competitiveness and national jobs; for example, the exporting power of Germany partly lies in localization of the low-value-added segment of production in the countries of Eastern Europe.[21] Overall, one may interpret the relative weakness in the preponderance of trade in the OECD countries with low-wage countries as a result of these defensive strategies.

This internationalization is also a catalyst for innovation in ICTs. In effect, trading goods and services from one country to another presupposes intensive recourse to ICTs—and guarantees that the new technologies will have vast potential markets. In return, progress in these technologies facilitates commerce and the relocation of activities, notably in digitalized services (finance, call/customer service centers, data processing, etc.). In fact, the movement to transfer activities has not yet stabilized. The new forms of competition in quality and in time that have been made possible by information technologies require the proximity of firms to markets.[22] Responsiveness to the chaotic evolution of demand and just-in-time production makes it costly to be overly distant from suppliers. The quest for cheap labor also becomes more difficult, since the growth of emerging countries is accompanied by internal salary inflation.

RISING INEQUALITIES AND EROSION OF LABOR *VIS-À-VIS* CAPITAL

All these transformations have had impacts on workers.[23] In addition to reducing job security, they have abetted rising inequality.

International competition, de-unionization, and technological and organizational changes are the principal factors explaining the spectacular rise in inequality, both in salaries and in jobs, starting at the end of the 1990s. A considerable literature tries to differentiate and weigh these various factors. The multiple interactions explain why these studies lead to disparate findings. These factors probably tend to mutually reinforce each other.

However, most studies agree that technological and organizational changes are the driving motor of inequality. In fact, any new technological wave that has a tendency to make experience obsolete creates a bias in favor of the most qualified workers and those with high adaptability.[24] Thus, it reduces the relative demand for the less qualified—particularly when they are "seniors"[25]—and increases the wage heterogeneity within groups that are qualified.

In the United States, the rise in wage inequality was at first very pronounced in the lower half of the salary (and income) scale, with even a slipping of real salary at the lower end of the spectrum, accelerated by the stagnation of the national minimum wage.[26] Inequality did stabilize in the lower half of the salary distribution during the 1990s. This time it was the inequality in the upper half of the scale that was accentuated,[27] suggesting that the post-computing technological wave disadvantaged groups with average levels of qualification. Meanwhile, the financialization of the economy propelled remunerations in the world of finance to levels comparable to those observed before the Second World War. A rocketing of financial bonuses (at least until the crisis of 2008) occurred everywhere, including France.[28]

In continental Europe the evolution of salary inequality has been less marked. But rising unemployment and falling job security have particularly affected the least qualified, dragging down their average income. In France this phenomenon was clear among those starting their careers, even before the Great Recession. According to the French Labor Force Survey,[29] one to four years after the end of initial training, the unemployment rate among graduates of higher education in 2007 was only 9%, but it was 37% for young people with a basic technical school certificate.

Thus, the less educated have been the first victims of mass unemployment arising from macroeconomic disequilibria and restructurings; and then of the drop in relative demand for them (the ICTs require qualified workers); and then of de-unionization, job insecurity, and finally the intensification of work linked to new organizations. To counter these mechanisms, both individuals and governments have increased their efforts at education to increase the level of qualification of those generations entering the labor market. Increasing the number of qualified workers has probably curtailed rising unemployment. But it has also contributed to accelerating the emergence of the new economy. Having access to increasingly qualified workers, firms have been able to demand greater versatility to make their investments in ICTs pay off, augmenting the demand for these technologies as well as the associated innovation effort.

However, the increasing level of qualification of the workforce has not been sufficient to avoid distorting the global division of value added in favor of capital and the most highly paid, signifying a worldwide weakening of the bargaining power of individuals and most collectives. According to EU KLEMS (November 2009), labor's share of value added in the market economy slid from 73% in 1970 to 68% in 2007 within the EU 15.[30] In the United States, over the same period, the division among workers has been most distorted; the highest-paid 10% have captured most of the gains, to the detriment of the other 90%. These distortions have become a major source of capitalism's instability.

THE SECOND PRODUCTIVITY SLOWDOWN

In parallel, one of the essential motors of economic growth—growth in the productivity of work—has run out of steam again, both in the countries of the G7 (apart from Japan) and in the Scandinavian countries (figure 2). According to the OECD productivity database, as an average over the years from 2008 to 2012, the hourly productivity of work stagnated, or even dropped, in the major European countries as well as in Scandinavia, though it was dynamic at the beginning of the century. The contrast is striking in comparison to the preceding recession, in the first half of the 1990s, when productivity sharply increased. North America has not escaped this slowdown; productivity gains are slowly falling to their levels before the "new economy."

Yet, except for France and the United Kingdom, these countries are all putting historically unprecedented efforts into research and development. As in the 1970s and 1980s, technological progress no longer seems to translate into economic growth. Intense academic research is currently focused on analyzing this phenomenon, which seems consistent with a Kondratiev wave—that is, an industrial revolution reaching its maturity. In the OECD countries, the use of ICTs is now nearly universal. Likewise, the expansion of innovative work organizations seems saturated. Since the start of the 2000s, the process of work intensification has shown a clear-cut pause, at least in Europe.[31]

In several countries (including France and the United States), the slowdown of productivity gains preceded the Great Recession by several years. Alongside the financial excesses and the inability of European institutions to deal with the crisis (considered in chapter 7), this slowdown suggests an interpretation of today's deep crisis. On the one hand, faced with declining

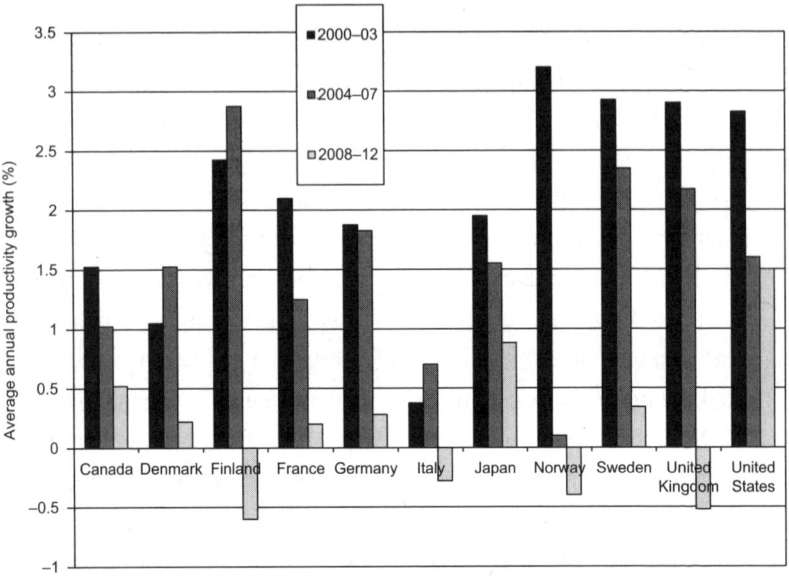

Figure 2. Productivity growth in the G7 and Scandinavian countries, 2000–2012. Source: OECD productivity database (January 16, 2014).

prospects in the productive sphere, investors and companies are engaged in a search for growth drivers through financial tools—effectively looking for virtual growth. On the other hand, the productivity slowdown feeds doubts regarding the long-term capacity of nations to pay back public debts, as well as regarding the durability of social protection. The crisis in sovereign debts might derive not from overspending but from potential economic growth being hampered by the long fading of productivity gains.

The present period is comparable to the situation in the 1970s, and not only with regard to changing productivity. On top of that, the current political disarray of a Europe stuck in a long recession, of a Japan undergoing deflation, and of a United States faced with a "fiscal cliff"—all are reminiscent of the disarray that prevailed four decades ago.

A POLITICAL SCHEMA COMMON TO THE LAST QUARTER OF THE TWENTIETH CENTURY

In the first half of the 1970s, the developed economies found themselves faced with several major challenges: falling growth, stalled productivity gains, and mass unemployment. In reaction, we find a common political schematic path derived from both domestic experiments and observation of neighbors' policies. The first phase of this schema dates from the end of the 1970s: to halt inflation, by modifying (via monetary policy) the expectations of economic agents (though this would accelerate the rise in unemployment) and by eliminating the economic mechanism of indexing salaries (despite the deepening of inequality). The second phase was much more heterogeneous: to cure sluggish growth and mass unemployment by taking the medicine of liberalism or by extending benefits and non-market jobs, while massively building up a better education system. The third phase was to reduce the transition period from one revolution to the next by fostering a return to growth drawn from productivity gains, and again by supporting innovation and education, and finally by reforming the markets for products and for labor.

The fourth phase required a belief in the ability of the monetary authorities to contain crises, as well as in the self-regulation of economic and financial systems, to be "attested" by weak macroeconomic volatility. By eliminating the risk of crisis, this Great Moderation would permit more deregulation and render the dependence of nation-states on the exigencies of the markets less painful. This phase would be smashed with the Great Recession.

Not all countries advanced along this schematic path at the same speed. Some (like France) seem never to have fully gone through the transition phase, which left them with appreciable margins of potential growth, at least until the world crisis of 2008. Others (like the United States) clearly passed through the transition, accompanied by massive investments in knowledge. But it is probably the United Kingdom that most precociously accomplished its industrial transition.

The United Kingdom was one of the first countries to fall into stagflation, even before the first oil crisis. It was also one of the first to extricate itself, back in the 1980s. The renewal of the British economy was largely the result of the economic policy conducted by the Conservative governments of Margaret Thatcher. They were able to exploit important advantages inherited from their Labour predecessors: modern public services, effective welfare protection, a discovery of North Sea oil amid the second petroleum crisis, and significant and rationalized participation by the state in the competitive economy. In appearance, Thatcher's conservative revolution was an abandonment of *any* industrial policy: it included privatization, the elimination of subsidies to enterprises, and the absence of support for small or medium-size businesses. However, what is essential about this revolution can be read precisely as an industrial policy: the development of the City of London, and more generally of financial services to the commercial sector. This choice would prove astute. The financial industry is one of the first sectors to be thrown into upheaval by information and communication technologies, since it is one of the principal users of these technologies. Contrary to received opinion, information technologies have a tendency to accentuate the agglomeration of activities based on knowledge, rather than breaking them up.[32]

By halting investments in public services, the British government could finance a massive lowering of taxes for the wealthiest. The marginal income tax rate dropped from 80% to 40%. Thus, citizens with more than three times the median income had their taxes cut in half. On the one hand, this reduction enabled those in the highest income brackets to dispose of liquidities by shifting them into the financial system; on the other hand, tax cuts drastically contracted the socio-fiscal burden on the best-paid employees in the financial sector. The financial industry and its commercial services thus possessed the technological conditions, the domestic market, and the socio-fiscal environment—all of which were optimized for its development.

At the cost of growing social inequality, of abandoning public services, of a collapse of the manufacturing industry and a consequent strong (but transitory) spurt in unemployment, and finally of vulnerability to the financial cycle, Great Britain was one of the first countries to recover gains in productivity, from the early 1980s, by surfing on the opportunities offered by information technology. This "Thatcher miracle"[33] illustrates that an ultra-liberal policy of massively cutting the fiscal contribution of those in the highest income brackets is not an economic end in itself. To succeed across the Channel and in the wider world (at least in terms of growth), it had to be at the service of a specific policy of innovation.

THE FRENCH BLIND DECADES

How can we understand why France never really exited from the crisis of the 1970s before entering that of 2008? Why was it unable to escape four decades of mass unemployment but able to maintain its economic status? This book's step-by-step review of the policies applied in France since 1970 will suggest answers to these questions.

The decades of blindness that would afflict France cannot be explained by a total absence of relevant analyses of the contemporary world. Certainly in this chapter I have been examining the major economic changes since the 1970s after the fact. And of course, in the 1970s and 1980s an understanding of economic mechanisms was still very partial. But back in 1967, the French prime minister, Georges Pompidou (who would be president of the republic from 1969 to 1974), and his secretary of state for employment, Jacques Chirac (who would be either prime minister or president for sixteen years between 1974 and 2007), were in possession of a report by the planning commissioner, François-Xavier Ortoli, called *Rapport sur les conséquences sociales de l'évolution des structures de l'économie* (Report on the Social Consequences of the Changing Structures of the Economy).[34] This report acknowledged the end of the postwar period of expansion: "In recent months these fears [by union organizations] have been reinforced by certain events: the moderate but continued rise in unemployment, the acceleration of company mergers, the difficulty experienced by some young people in finding a job after leaving school, and of certain managers in redeploying themselves" (p. 1). Farther along, we read: "These observations should not mask what is essential: a profound transformation in the labor market is underway. In order to proceed without serious social problems, this requires the creation of a first-rate arrangement that is exactly adapted to this new situation, an 'active jobs policy.' There is a rigorous link between the application of such a policy and the lucid acceptance of the social phenomena that always accompany progress" (p. 3).

The report anticipated transformations in the economy and the labor market. "In a progressing economy, greater job mobility is inevitable and necessary" (p. 3). "Technological evolution, exactly where the demand is noticeably increasing, transforms the structure of employment by appealing to a labor force with different and higher qualifications.... We will shift from one type of economy to another, ... from a highly protected market to an open market, to which we have to make a rapid series of structural adaptations" (p. 6). In admiring the results and institutions of the Scandinavian countries, the recommendations of the Ortoli report even referred to the principal components of what thirty years later would be called "flexicurity."

Alas, this awareness of profound changes would be obfuscated by blindness among the political actors. Worse still, errors of analysis would be at the root of political mistakes whose consequences became structural. They also delayed appropriate reforms, though some major reforms concerning education and labor regulations were finally implemented. And France today still retains some major assets (an educated workforce, high productivity, an efficient health system, and so on—see chapter 8).

Errors have been made by all French governments, despite a great variety of political configurations. From 1974 to 1981, president Valéry Giscard d'Estaing, of the pro-European center-Right, was flanked by a Gaullist prime minister, Jacques Chirac (from 1974 to 1976) and then by a centrist economist, Raymond Bare. Then came Socialist president François Mitterrand, from 1981 to 1995. He had seven prime ministers. Pierre Mauroy was at the head of a Socialist-Communist majority from 1981 to 1983, then reduced to Socialists alone; Laurent Fabius was the bearer of liberal social democracy from 1984 to 1986; from 1986 to 1988, a new Jacques Chirac became the apostle of Thatcherite reforms; Michel

Rocard extended the presidential majority of the Socialists to a portion of the center-Right until 1991; Edith Cresson and Pierre Bérégovoy adopted a management-style socialism; this was swept away in 1993 by the return of a wide coalition of Gaullists and Liberals directed by Edouard Balladur. Then, for the twelve years from 1995 to 2007, President Chirac had four prime ministers. The first was his right-hand man, Alain Juppé, until 1997. Then, for the five years of a leftist legislature, Lionel Jospin led a "plural majority" of Socialists, Communists, Greens, a nationalist Left and Social-Liberals. Then came (2002 to 2005) a pro-European centrist, Jean-Pierre Raffarin, who had a single party that assembled all the components of the Republican Right; and finally, from 2005 to 2007, the flamboyant liberal Gaullist, Dominique de Villepin. Nicolas Sarkozy, a one-term "hyper-president" (2007 to 2012) and an admirer of George W. Bush, relegated prime minister François Fillon to a secondary role. And finally, since 2012, the return of an (overly) "normal" president, François Hollande, has meant firstly a government, directed by Jean-Marc Ayrault, that mixed Socialists, the center-Left, and the Greens, followed in 2014 by a government without the Greens and directed by Manuel Valls.

NOTES

1. Paul Bairoch, *Economics and World History: Myths and Paradoxes* (Chicago: University of Chicago Press, 1995).

2. On automation and its harmful effects on productivity in the USSR, see Vladimir Peysakhovich, *Economics of Automation in the Soviet Machine-Building Industry* (Falls Church: Delphic, 1987).

3. Angus Maddison, *Monitoring the World Economy,* 1820–1992 (Paris: OECD, 1995).

4. For a theoretical approach to the link between human and technological endowments, see Daron Acemoglu, "Why Do New Tech-

nologies Complement Skills? Directed Technical Change and Wage Inequality," *Quarterly Journal of Economics* 113 (1998): 1055–89.

5. Boyan Jovanovic and Peter L. Rousseau, "General Purpose Technologies," in *Handbook of Economic Growth* (vol. 1), ed. Philippe Aghion and Steven Durlauf (Amsterdam : Elsevier/North Holland, 2005), 1181–1224.

6. Paul A. David, "Computer and Dynamo: The Modern Productivity Paradox in a Not-Too-Distant Mirror," in *Technology and Productivity: The Challenge for Economic Policy* (Paris: OECD, 1991), 315–47.

7. Prices are measured by the hedonic price method. This method takes into account the quality of the goods. Thus, a computer selling at the same nominal price as the year before, but which includes a more powerful microprocessor than the preceding one, would be considered by statisticians as actually selling at a lower price. In computing hardware, the drop in hedonic price is between 20% and 30% per year.

8. The underlying inflation expresses the profound evolution in production costs and the confrontation between supply and demand, once seasonal and conjunctural/transitory effects are removed.

9. The heart of the just-in-time principle is that production is triggered by orders, to which there must be a quick response. The desirable consequences are greater responsiveness and smaller inventories.

10. Bart van Ark, Robert Inklaar, and Robert McGuckin, "'Changing Gear' Productivity, ICT and Services: Europe and the United States," Research Memorandum No. 60 (Groningen: Groningen Growth and Development Centre, 2002), www.eco.rug.nl/ggdc/homeggdc.html.

11. Luc Behaghel, Eve Caroli, and Emmanuelle Walkowiak, 2012, "Information and Communication Technologies and Skill Upgrading: The Role of Internal vs. External Labour Markets," *Oxford Economic Papers* 64, no. 3 (2012): 490–517.

12. Philippe Askenazy and Eva Moreno Galbis, "The Impact of Technological and Organizational Changes on Labor Flows: Evidence on French Establishments," *LABOUR* 21, no. 2 (2007): 265–301.

13. Directorate-General for Employment, Social Affairs and Equal Opportunities of the European Commission, *Employment in Europe 2009* (Luxemburg: Office for Official Publications of the European Communities, 2009).

14. Subcontracting firms intervene directly on the premises of the firm that is placing the orders.

15. See e.g. Philippe Aghion, Yann Algan, and Pierre Cahuc, "Civil Society and the State: The Interplay between Cooperation and Minimum Wage Regulation," *Journal of the European Economic Association* 9, no. 1 (2011): 3–42.

16. Assar Lindbeck and Dennis J. Snower, "Centralized Bargaining and Reorganized Work: Are They Compatible?" *European Economic Review* 45, no. 10 (2001): 1851–75.

17. Michael Gort, "An Economic Disturbance Theory of Mergers," *Quarterly Journal of Economics* 94 (1969): 624–42.

18. Bart Hobijn and Boyan Jovanovic, "The IT Revolution and the Stock Market: Evidence," *American Economic Review* 91 (2001): 1203–20.

19. Securitization is a financial technique that transforms assets for which there is no veritable market into asset values that are easily negotiable.

20. Adrian Wood, *North-South Trade, Employment and Inequality* (Oxford: Oxford University Press, 1994).

21. Lionel Fontagné and Guillaume Gaulier, *Performances à l'exportation de la France et de l'Allemagne,* Conseil d'analyse économique report no. 81 (Paris: La documentation française, 2009).

22. The typical example is that of clothing, where the European leader Zara located most of its production in the Iberian peninsula and rapidly flooded the European markets. Bruno Amable, Philippe Askenazy, Daniel Cohen, Andrea Goldstein, and David O'Connor, "Internet: The Elusive Quest for a Frictionless Economy," in *The ICT Revolution*, eds. Daniel Cohen, Pietro Garibaldi, and Stefano Scarpetta (Oxford: Oxford University Press, 2004), 141–231.

23. See for a review, Richard B. Freeman, "Globalization and Inequality", in *The Oxford Handbook of Economic Inequality*, eds. Wiemer Salverda, Brian Nolan, and Timothy M. Smeeding (Oxford: Oxford University Press, 2009), chapter 23.

24. Philippe Aghion, Peter Howitt, and Giovanni Violante, "General Purpose Technology and Wage Inequality," *Journal of Economic Growth* 7, no. 4 (December 2002): 315–45.

25. Patrick Aubert, Eve Caroli, and Muriel Roger, 2006, "New Technologies, Organisation and Age: Firm-Level Evidence," *Economic Journal* 116 (2006): 73–93. In addition, workers who have had long careers in difficult occupations suffer from health problems that limit

their capacity to keep up the pace demanded by the new production systems.

26. David H. Autor, Lawrence F. Katz, and Melissa S. Kearney, "Trends in U.S. Wage Inequality: Revising the Revisionists," *Review of Economics and Statistics* 90 (2008): 300–23.

27. We have observed an explosion in income among the highest 1% (Thomas Piketty and Emmanuel Saez, "Income Inequality in the United States, 1913–1998," *Quarterly Journal of Economics* 118 (2003): 1–39), and this has also been found in France since the start of the century (C. Landais, "Les hauts revenus en France (1998–2006): Une explosion des inégalités?" Mimeo, Paris School of Economics, 2007). It is hard to invoke a technological explanation for this movement, which is instead a mechanism for capturing rents.

28. Olivier Godechot, "Is Finance Responsible for the Rise in Wage Inequality in France?" *Socio-Economic Review* 10, no. 3 (2012): 447–70.

29. The full microdata files are available on the INSEE website (www.insee.fr).

30. For a summary overview of the methodology and construction of the EU KLEMS database, see Mary O'Mahony and Marcel P. Timmer, "Output, Input and Productivity Measures at the Industry Level: the EU KLEMS Database," *Economic Journal* 119, no. 538 (2009), pp. F374–F403.

31. See the *Fifth European Working Conditions Survey—Overview Report* (Dublin: Eurofound, 2012).

32. This was already the case with the telephone, which accelerated urban growth and the supply of services.

33. Richard G. Layard and Stephen Nickell, "The Thatcher Miracle?" *American Economic Review* 79, no. 3 (1989): 215–19.

34. Unpublished report, April 1967. I thank Jacques Freyssinet for providing a complete copy of this text.

CHAPTER TWO

1974–1981

The Creation of Mass Unemployment

The seven-year term (1974–1981) of president Giscard d'Estaing saw unemployment settle in for the long haul at the top of the agenda of French political preoccupations and social fears. Henceforth, the obsession with full employment would not disappear from the public scene; it would eventually come to characterize the French theme in the symphony of industrialized countries. The policies applied during this period not only illustrate a distinct failure to fully understand the problems of the day, but also contributed to aggravating the situation for a long time to come. Successive governments would bequeath to those that followed them a framework of analysis and action that was unsuitable for accomplishing economic transition effectively. Even today, France remains partially hidebound by the reading of the labor market that became prevalent in this period. Most importantly, the policies initiated then were self-fulfilling; they constructed a contaminated labor market just when the mutations of capitalism were already destabilizing it. Stigmatization of youth and migrants, taxes on labor, and inefficient labor policies were enlarged under Giscard's presidency.

NASCENT DISEQUILIBRIA

At the end of WWII, France had adopted multi-year economic planning. While the pursuit of economic growth did not cause worry at the beginning of 1974, the state of the labor market was already a concern of the Sixth Plan, developed in 1971, well before the oil crisis. Figures on unsatisfied demand for jobs showed that the number of job seekers had been rising since 1962. But disequilibria appeared to be inevitable, due to the arrival on the labor market of baby boomers (from 100,000 to 200,000 additional entries per year, compared to the end of the 1960s) and to an increase in the number of working women. However, these imbalances were considered transitory and absorbable by the strong economic growth foreseen under the plan.

The other difficulty affecting the labor market was the modernization of the French economy. Launched as soon as the war was over and accelerated by the process of European integration, it required mobile workers in an initial context of recurrent shortfalls in manpower. Thus, a qualitative and geographic adjustment of manpower became necessary. Further development of the Agence nationale pour l'emploi (National Employment Agency), created in 1967, was a priority. It was assigned a higher budget and objective targets. The goal was not so much to fight unemployment as to ensure a better functioning of the labor market. In parallel, the Fond national de l'emploi (National Employment Fund) continued its support for professional retraining and for individuals' geographic mobility.

Despite this support, and despite various measures designed to deal with unemployment of a frictional kind, the social partners (unions and employers' organizations) and the state entered into a major formative compromise in 1972. Thus, the "inter-professional" (i.e. covering all industries) agreement of March 1972 created a "guarantee of resource redundancy" reserved for workers over 60 who were to be dismissed (though the legal age for retirement was then 65). For the labor unions, this was a step toward the requirement for full retirement at age 60. For the employers, it was a godsend, a way of getting rid of aged employees. And for the government, there would be that many fewer people unemployed. In fact, it was the first plan for preretirement and most especially an arrangement whose logic would long be the organizing principle of policies toward seniors in the workforce.

LIMITED KNOWLEDGE

The second worry was inflation. Inflationary tensions emerged in the second half of 1972. Macroeconomic arbitration between inflation and unemployment became more difficult. The political concentration on this arbitration betrayed the limited theoretical knowledge of the microeconomic foundations of the job market. Labor economics was in its infancy; the standard academic journal, the *Journal of Labor Economics,* would not start publishing until 1983. Thus, the reigning approaches were principally accounting or macroeconomic. The two essential tools were the Phillips curve and the non-accelerating inflation rate of unemployment (NAIRU).

In the 1950s, the Phillips curve (on which was founded the question of inflation versus unemployment) shed light on a decreasing relation between the level of inflation and the level of unemployment. The less unemployment there is, the more salary demands increase, and the greater the inflationary tensions. Conversely, fighting inflation by restraining growth destroys jobs. The work of Milton Friedman also fed into the economic analysis: monetary policy can only have short-term effects, because the level of unemployment is determined by structural factors (inadequate training of workers, friction in the labor market, etc.).

The notion of the NAIRU, developed in the mid-1970s, synthesizes both arguments. As I stressed in the first chapter, a simple formalization of this concept shows that unemployment is effectively tied to a structural factor: growth in labor productivity. In effect, it is productivity gains that permit a business to absorb rising labor costs and maintain employment. A lack of productivity gains will be translated into higher unemployment to keep inflation constant.

The concept of the NAIRU thus allows us to perceive the major source of a rise in unemployment or inflation: a breakdown in productivity gains at work. However, this phenomenon (already perceptible in the mid-1970s) was not understood until the 1980s, especially in France. Instead, in 1974, attention was focused on the first oil shock generated by the embargo of oil-producing countries during the Yom Kippur War. Between the months of October 1973 and January 1974, the price of a barrel of crude called Arab Light quadrupled, rising from $2.30 to $9.00; in France this meant a rise in gasoline prices of over 10%.

THE HESITANT STARTS OF THE GISCARD PRESIDENCY

In the context of the growing crisis, coupled with concern in French society, France elected (in a close race against François

Mitterrand) a "young" president, Valéry Giscard d'Estaing, who had been the minister of economy and finance until his election. He was supported by the Independent Republicans, a center-right formation that was liberal and pro-European, and the Gaullist Party, led by Jacques Chirac. The new president had a majority on the right in the National Assembly after the legislative elections of 1972.

The setting of economic policy was shared with his prime minister, Jacques Chirac, flanked by Jean-Pierre Fourcade (a former member of Giscard d'Estaing's finance office). Of the economic experts, the key player was Edmond Malinvaud, who in 1974 went from directing forecasts at the Ministry of the Economy to directing the INSEE (Institut national de la statistique et des études économiques: National Institute for Statistics and Economic Studies). At the time, his work on French growth was considered authoritative on both theoretical and empirical-analysis levels. French economic thinking remained principally within the logic of planning and the search for major equilibria.

Stop-and-Go

Under this government, the French economy ran at full steam, showing a growth of more than 6% in 1973.[1] The forecasts were optimistic. The OECD was counting on an annual growth rate of 3.25% for the second half of 1974, and a soft landing at 2.5% for the first half of 1975. Fundamentally, the economic elites seemed convinced that postwar growth could only continue. Malinvaud wrote, in a book published in 1973, "Everything considered, the extraordinary development that France and many other countries have experienced since the last world war should not slow perceptibly for several years."[2]

Inflation went into double digits in all the major industrialized countries, except for Germany. In the face of this inflation, in line with the stabilization plan of 1963 constructed by Giscard when he was minister of finance, Jean-Pierre Fourcade in June 1974 launched a policy to contain it. This included a hike in the interest rate, credit restrictions, an increase in income tax on top revenues, and a business tax. But by the autumn this policy had proved itself totally unsuitable. It tended to deepen an economic recession that was clinched by increasing failures of small and medium-size firms but also by difficulties at major corporations like the automobile firm Citroën. In effect, the worldwide economic slowdown, notably in international trade, had been seriously underestimated—as had the resilience of the French economy, which had enjoyed particularly regular growth for thirty years. France plunged into the deepest recession since the Liberation in 1944. Industrial production fell 12%—the same as in the United States and Japan—returning to its 1972 level. In total, the GDP contracted by 0.25% in the second half of 1974 and by 5% in the first half of 1975. Despite a marked recourse to short-time work, this collapse was translated into a spurt in job demand at the end of each month. These went (from September 1974 to September 1975) from 534,000 to 946,000. Young people were particularly affected; their unemployment rate reached 8%.

These difficulties were compounded by a campaign of small shops against the hypermarkets, and unrest in agriculture, which reinforced the arguments of those who, like Jacques Chirac, were partisans of a stimulus policy. In fact, the prime minister was in phase with the current majority view among macroeconomists, for whom the mechanisms at work were temporary. For them, the oil shock had merely accentuated the end of an economic cycle. This analysis would persist throughout the Chirac government, even if we find some hesitation in the work of the INSEE. Thus, in January 1976, François Eymard-Duvernay, then at the labor department of the statistical institute, wrote: "The year 1975 undoubtedly marks the low point of the cycle that began that began in 1968.... Most of the current crisis did not originate in the way the labor market works."[3]

The idea that the crisis was not structural justified a concentration on short-term policies. At the macroeconomic level, the government marked a turning point by financing a contra-cyclic stimulus.[4] Retaining the current European (Maastricht) definition, the budget balance shifted from +0.3% of the GDP in 1974 to –2.7% in 1975. A rapid return to a "normal situation" would require slowing down employment dismissal processes to avoid a social crisis that would handicap the recovery. The government on the right thus imposed a requirement for prior administrative authorization on any collective or individual layoffs, and increased provisions for short-time work under the control of the Labor Inspection Department.

In parallel—since the crisis was not expected to last—the state embarked on expensive commitments. The *allocation speciale d'attente* (special allowance for waiting [for the recovery]) in October 1974 was the most spectacular, and the most emblematic of the dominant vision of a short transition. Those laid off due to the economy would benefit for a year from 90% of their last salary. Investments by firms were supported by the state's picking up 10% of the cost of equipment orders placed before the end of 1975, in the form of a reduction in the VAT tax collected.[5] In addition, social transfers were supposed to stimulate consumption (extending social security to the unsalaried; hikes in the old-age minimum and in family allocations). Thus, to compensate for choosing to act in June 1974 (out of phase from the immediate conjuncture) and to stimulate its economy as fast as possible, France decided (though this was unusual within the OECD at the time) to resort to a net accentuation of social transfers. In total, these transfers increased by almost 3% of GDP between 1974 and 1977, displacing France from a median position within the OECD to a position among countries where the burden of transfers was more significant.

Another stimulant for consumption was a sharp compression in the salary scale, which was propelled by a rapid rise in the minimum wage. According to OECD data, the minimum wage—the *salaire minimum interprofessionnel de croissance,* covering most salaried workers—grew in real terms by 8.4% in 1974, and by 6.6% in 1975, and then by 4.7% in 1976. Despite the reduction in overtime hours offered by firms, from April 1974 to April 1976 the weekly salary of production employees grew by 6.6%, and that of nonsupervisory employees by 7.5%, while managers benefited over two years from only a modest rise of 1.3%. Finally, 15,000 public-service jobs were created in the postal and telecommunications department.

This short-term policy was not without effects. A growth rate over 5% persisted into 1976, but also inflation close to 10%. And two aspects of economic policy had eluded the rationale of the short-term response: energy and immigration.

Energy Independence

The surge in the price of oil had underlined France's high energy dependence, which was over 75% in the midst of the oil crisis. The objective of the Chirac government, which would be adopted by most successive governments, was to recover independence in this domain. The government's slogan was, "In France we don't have oil, but we have ideas." Coal mines were artificially revived through government support, which would bequeath to subsequent governments the problem of closing them and reconverting the sites. But the heart of the energy policy was the development of alternative energy sources, coupled with energy savings. The nuclear energy industry, constructed since the end of World War II, was obviously privileged. The public corporation Electricité de France was its driving force. As of 1974, it was authorized to begin work on six nuclear reactors of 900 MW each, and the following year on seven supplementary installations. The authorizations for 1976 and 1977 initiated construction of plants with a total power of 24,000 MW, representing in four years the construction of more than a third of the power of French nuclear installations today.

In parallel, the Agence pour les économies d'énergie (Agency for Energy Savings) was created. It fostered research on technologies for saving energy. Thrifty investments would benefit from subsidies or tax incentives: *chassez le gaspi* (get rid of waste) was a priority.

Immigration Policy: A Structuring Decision[6]

At the same time that France was trying to reduce its energy dependence on the Arab world, it was building a new immigration policy with respect to it.

From the beginning of the crisis, many European countries began to revise their immigration policies. Thus, in November 1973, West Germany decided to ban the hiring of foreigners from outside Common Market countries, Switzerland, Austria, and the United States; certain *Länder* (states) even forbade foreigners from settling in cities that were already more than 12% foreign.

Though in 1973 France had only 1.8 million foreign workers (compared to 2.4 million in West Germany), it did not escape this defensive reaction. With the heritage of decolonization conflicts, in particular the Algerian War and the repatriation of French citizens from Algeria, both social context and national policy were already harsh on this subject.[7] The racist violence in the southwest of France peaked in 1973, principally with regard to "Arabs." To protect its nationals, Algeria suspended any emigration to France.

The economic downturn gave support to the idea that France could no longer allow itself to welcome new immigrants, since it was the countries of origin of the "Arabs" that were thought to be causing the crisis the French were suffering. In fact, immigration at the time came largely from European countries: Portuguese, Spanish, and Italians outnumbered North Africans.

The new government's policy would ride this sentiment and thereby deeply infuse French society with this conception of the immigrant and his responsibility for the economic and social situation.[8] To increase "efficiency," the Chirac government included a secretary of state in the labor ministry in charge of immigrant workers. André Postel-Vinay, who held the post, resigned after a few days because he refused to apply an anti-immigrant policy. He was replaced by Paul Dijoud.[9] As of July 1974, the government set as goals: (1) suspending any new contracts introducing foreign manpower; and (2) stopping families from coming over to join the breadwinner. This policy bore "fruit." While Algerian immigration was still almost nil, the entry of immigrant workers (from outside the European Community) shrank by 70% between 1974 and 1975, to 16,000 official entries.

Beyond these actions, policy discourse wandered.[10] In a speech broadcast on July 29, 1975, the president of the republic stressed that "there are some tasks that in France should now be performed by the French." Simplistic arithmetic, coupled with hugely inflated immigration figures, prevailed. Michel Durafour, minister of labor, said: "Why hide it? The job situation in France has an absurd aspect. There are a million unemployed, but at the same time, there are two million immigrant workers."[11] Jacques Chirac agreed: "A country in which there are 900,000 unemployed, but where there are more than two million immigrant workers, is not a country in which the job problem is insoluble."[12]

Studies by experts and intellectuals supported this argument. The interministerial commission set up by the government offered a scenario based on the FIFI macroeconomic model,[13] according to which a *sustained* drop of 250,000 in the number of immigrants in France would translate into 80,000 more jobs for nationals.[14] The same view was held by some politicians and legal experts. For example, Catherine Wihtol de Wenden (who would later become a defender of open immigration) announced that "the complementarity that economically 'justified' recourse to immigrant workers is ceding to an increasingly accentuated competition between national manpower and foreign manpower for a limited number of jobs."[15] More insidiously, it was the children of immigrants who were accused: "It seems that the current tendencies, characterized by family immigration and the insertion of the 'second generation,' move in the direction of an aggravation of the economic situation of employment."[16] Neither of these assertions was supported by solid theoretical or empirical evidence.

This work by experts, coupled with declarations from the highest leaders in government, was grist for the mill of anti-immigrant popular discourse. It became anchored in public opinion and offered fertile ground for the growth of the extreme Right in the late 1970s, as well as polluting French public debate. To preserve their electoral interests, both Right and Left felt obliged to preserve a discourse that was hostile to and condemnatory of immigrants and their French-born children.

THE DELETERIOUS POLICY OF RAYMOND BARRE

In the second half of 1975, growth again became positive, as part of a strong dynamic: 7% annually on average. But with more than a million unemployed, plus a budget deficit of more than 2.5% of GDP, and double-digit inflation in 1975, the policy of Jacques Chirac seemed a resounding failure. Internal dissent in the center-right majority opened the way to a new head of government, who would be more in phase with the president.

Minister of foreign trade Raymond Barre acceded at the end of August 1976 to the post of prime minister, which he combined with the economy portfolio (although with a minister delegated to it, Robert Boulin), before leaving that to the duo of Renée Monory and Maurice Papon,[17] the former on the economy and the latter on the budget. Thus, Raymond Barre now had all the levers to direct France's economic policy. Known for his university textbooks, he was presented by the president of the republic as "the best economist in France" and thus able to straighten up the country.

Raymond Barre was not just a professor. He was the archetype of the academic engaged in the application of economic policy. This economics PhD had become the principal secretary of the minister of industry (1959–1962). In 1962, Barre reassumed his chair at the Paris Institute of Political Science (Institut d'études politiques, or "Sciences Po"). There he directed an office of research on economic activity that had important ties with French economic administrations. Thus, he participated in the training of future "*énarques*"—the elite of the French technocracy—at the ENA (École nationale de l'administration). In 1967, de Gaulle named him to the Commission of the European Communities, of which he became vice president. As the commissioner responsible for economic and financial affairs, he developed a plan for European monetary stability that aimed to strengthen the coordination of economic policies and to institute mutual monetary support. This plan gave rise in 1970 to the creation by the European central banks of just such a mechanism. In fact, Raymond Barre was obsessed with monetary stability. On his departure from Brussels in 1973, he was charged with elaborating a reform project to better articulate secondary and higher education in France; this project had no result, but the mission would make him sensitive to the fate of young people.

As minister, Barre provided himself with a bureau of experts. He kept Chirac's social advisor, Raymond Soubie (who would make a fortune in consulting on human resources, before becoming social affairs advisor to President Sarkozy in 2007).

While Paul Dijoud was committed to immigrant workers, assuring continuity of policy on the issue, elsewhere the first Barre government displayed a strong desire for recovery. On the one hand, because the forecasts of the 7th Plan suggested an average annual growth during 1976–1980 of between 5% and 6.6%, this was primarily a matter of restoring macroeconomic equilibrium; on the other hand, the struggle against unemployment included a variety of microeconomic interventions.

Isolated Austerity and an Explosion in Social Taxes

For the new government, reducing inflation and eliminating the budget deficit were complementary priorities. It used many levers to achieve them. Breaking with policy that had been in place since May 1968, the gains in purchasing power of the minimum hourly wage would be cut in half (see table 2). Public service saw its real earnings stagnate, which was also part of stabilizing public expenditure. For Barre, "the government rejects an authoritarian control of revenues and especially of salaries [in the private sector]."[18] In April 1978 he moved from a process of "social openness" to a "conventional" policy,[19] widened to include improvements in career tracks for workers, reform and adaptation of unemployment benefits, and control of working time. But this strategy would result in very few agreements between unions and employers' organizations.

Nevertheless, public spending was affected by the social transfers introduced by the Chirac government, producing a rise in unemployment and the costs of associated social benefits, on top of the cost of Barre's plans for employment and industrial policy, notably in energy. The government therefore had to pursue a policy of raising taxes on businesses as well as on individuals. However, the VAT on most goods and services was lowered from 20% to 17.6% to slow down rising prices.

Public accounts, which had a deficit of 2.7% of GDP in 1975 (according to the current Maastricht criteria), returned to equilibrium in 1980. France's deficit compared to GDP was thus brought back in 1980 to its 1973 level. But this strict policy was isolated within the European Community. Germany sustained its growth with a moderate and deliberate deficit that expressed

TABLE 2

Limited gains in purchasing power (%), 1975–1980

	1975	1976	1977	1978	1979	1980
SMIC (hourly minimum wage)	6.6	4.7	2.9	3.3	1.7	1.8
Wages in the public services	5.0	1.6	0.5	1.2	−0.9	−0.4

SOURCE: OECD study, France (Paris: OECD, 1976, 1977, 1978, 1979, 1980, 1981, 1982, 1983)

its preference for unemployment reduction. Overall, France appeared as a "good student"[20] within the OECD; its political system enabled promoting clear majorities for periods of at least five years (the presidential term), and it was praised for its capacity to escape the electoral constraints that impelled resorting to deficits. Balancing the budget allowed France in 1979 to join a European Monetary System dominated by the deutschmark. In 1980, France had the lowest deficit of the major countries of the OECD (figure 3).

But this policy also had significant economic costs. On the one hand, it handicapped both consumption and employment. On the other, it dramatically accentuated the weight of social security contributions in France, especially on labor, from 13.0% of GDP in 1971 to 17.3% in 1980, according to INSEE national accounts. In fact, contrary to the usual understanding, it was not in the 1980s, under governments of the Left, that the cost of social taxes exploded and placed France at one of the highest levels in the OECD; rather, this occurred under the seven-year mandate of Giscard. The increase in social contributions explains a good third of the bump observed in the share of value added at the turn of the 1980s.

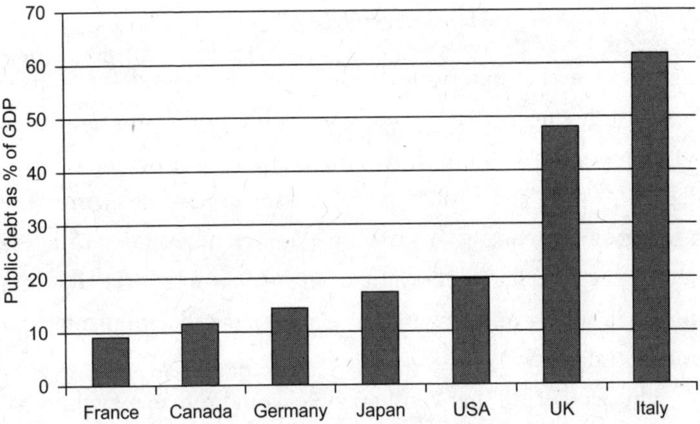

Figure 3. Public debts in 1980. Source: Nouriel Roubini and Jeremy Sachs, "Political and Economic Determinants of Budget Deficits in the Industrial Democracies," *European Economic Review* 33 (1989): 903–38.

While it reached its goal of re-establishing public finances, Raymond Barre's policy of austerity was a failure with respect to the fight against inflation. It did fall below 10% in 1977, but the second oil crisis annihilated this progress; by 1980, inflation was back to its 1974 level.

Moreover, the restrained economy could not reach the objectives set in the 7th Plan. Though the most pessimistic scenario held growth to 5% on average over 1976–1980, in fact growth was irregular over the whole period and reached only 3.5% on average.

But strong growth was the necessary condition for the labor market's absorbing the demographic shock of the baby boomers and the increasing presence of women in the workforce since the start of the decade. Young people, particularly young women, were joining a queue that grew longer from year to year. The unemployment rate among students coming out of the education system skyrocketed.

The Stigmatization of Youth

Faced with this deteriorating situation, Raymond Barre proposed a diagnosis that rested principally on the stigmatization of young people: "France, like all comparable societies, should face up to the job problems that relate to several factors: the aspiration to work by a growing number of women, which is legitimate; the flight of youth from manual jobs; and the mismatch in supply and demand for employment, due to insufficient initial training."[21]

The accusation that young people would refuse manual work was unfounded. For example, in the fall of 1977, the young men registered with the Agence nationale pour l'emploi were more numerous than the older unemployed seeking jobs in industry.[22] Nevertheless, by taking a central position in the prime minister's line of argument, this blaming of youth would further anchor stereotypes among employers—and in society as a whole.

On the other hand, the inadequacy of initial training was a well-established point, even if the young were better trained than they had been in preceding generations. In the 1970s, people started worrying about "educational inflation";[23] however, France had not yet launched a policy of educational democratization as advanced as in many industrialized countries. Thus, only 32.6% of young people leaving the education system in 1976 held a *baccalauréat* (high school diploma), as compared to 33.4% in 1973; the proportion of those holding a BA or higher degree was also shrinking, from 9.4% to 9.2%.

Despite the absence of comparative data in this domain, studies done at the time bearing on young people in the 1970s permit us to grasp French educational backwardness in relation to other countries of the European Community, apart from Italy. The gap is wide in relation to Germany as regards secondary education. France was very far from having reabsorbed its massive flow of underqualified young people; 41% of those aged 15 between 1972 and 1981 would not achieve a high school diploma, compared to 16% of Germans and 36% of Britons.

In access to higher education, too, France lagged behind its European partners, again except for Italy (table 3): in France less than 20% (among those who reached age 20 between 1972 and 1981) succeeded in earning a degree, as opposed to almost 30% of young Britons or Danes. The gap even widened under the Barre governments.

If Raymond Barre was aware of his education deficit, he did not reach the conclusion that the new industrial revolution required workers able to adapt to it and that this ability required more general education. On the contrary, the prime minister intended to lead a "revalorization of manual labor." On top of this, the government would try to free up manual jobs by reversing migratory flows and resorting to early retirement (see the following section). This policy choice was doubly mistaken. On the one hand, young people were being trained for industrial jobs while European deindustrialization was proceeding inexorably—as Barre's contemporaries well understood[24]—which would worsen the mismatch between training and the needs of companies. And on the other hand, the democratization of general education, notably at the university level, was left lying fallow.

Jeopardizing Youth Employment

Since the evolution of the educational system could only be gradual, while the difficulties of entering the job market were

TABLE 3

Percentage of persons reaching age 20 between 1972 and 1976, and between 1977 and 1981, holding a college degree in 2002

	France	Germany	UK	Italy	Denmark	Ireland	Belgium	Netherlands
Age 20 between 1972 and 1976	18.8	22.9	27.1	9.4	28.3	17.3	23.4	22.9
Age 20 between 1977 and 1981	19.5	24.3	29.6	11.1	30.5	21.8	25.6	24.7

SOURCE: Eurostat Labour force survey results 2002 (Luxembourg: Office for Official Publications of the European Communities, 2003).

exploding, Raymond Barre would introduce job agreements principally oriented to the young. Most of the OECD countries at the time were enacting specific policies to employ this age cohort. These relied essentially on consolidation of ways of entering the workforce that had been prevalent before the first oil crisis. For example, the United States subsidized summer jobs for disadvantaged youth; West Germany helped businesses ensure a minimum reserve of apprenticeship.

Barre's strategy was fundamentally different. It overthrew the existing mechanisms for getting young people into employment, substituting the massive creation of internships and subsidized fixed-term contracts. The new priority given to inserting and training of young people in workplaces as they left the school system would become a fiasco, jeopardizing their prospects.

The prime minister sketched his strategy quickly, based on exemptions from social taxes, but it was implemented only in the second half of 1977, after seven months of discussions that mobilized French economic expertise. This lag of almost a year fostered a wait-and-see posture among employers, resulting in a crumbling of job offers.[25] The rate that job demands were satisfied each month fell by between 11% and 16% (per OECD or INSEE data, respectively) in June 1977, on the eve of the first Employment Pact, to below the level reached during the worst of the recession in 1975. And the duration of unemployment was increasing. In parallel, job security fell rapidly: employers resorted to short-term contracts to be able to hire later under contracts aided by the government.[26] Young people and women were particularly affected. In 18 months, signups at the Agence nationale pour l'emploi following the end of a fixed-term contract (apart from temps) increased by a factor of 4.4 for young women and 4.0 for young men.

Instead of struggling against this exceptional jump in the precariousness of access to employment for young people, the Employment Pact of 1977–1978 simply institutionalized it. Eventually, the end of a fixed-term contract or a company training program would become the prime cause of unemployment among young people still in school. Several significant provisions were introduced simultaneously: being hired as a trainee with exemption from payroll taxes; internship training centers; contracts for on-the-job training; and practical internships in companies. These provisions were very generous for employers: they directly opened the way to exemption from all employer contributions for one or two years—that is, to the government's assuming the responsibility for paying all these trainees.

The first pact was addressed to a mass of 550,000 young people, at a cost of 4 billion francs, or 0.2% of GDP. The second pact (1978–1979) was less generous: the range of qualifying firms (or the level of exemption) was reduced. Despite the extension of these provisions to women who were heads of households, the number of beneficiaries fell by half—and as a corollary, so did the cost. The third pact (1979–1980) was again larger: its cost exceeded 3 billion francs. The campaign of 1980–1981 was of the same order.

Were the pacts effective for employment? Why were their scopes so variable? Did they help bring young people into the workforce? We should first note that a micro-econometric evaluation of the pacts is methodologically impossible. The various provisions were massive, simultaneous, and addressed to the same groups. Moreover, we do not have even a vague subject or control group.[27] Nevertheless, we can make a good sketch of the impact of the plans. The variation in their scope testifies to uncertain navigation, linked to the perverse effects of their provisions. There was great "success" for the first pact, measured by the amount of practical training offered by companies. More than 140,000 young people, ages 16 to 25, were involved. The sectors on offer were those in expansion, with high workforce instability, or with needs for unskilled labor. The primary user was retail trade (21,000 trainees), in particular the supermarkets. However, the government soon realized that traineeships tended to replace paid jobs; the Forecasting Office (Direction de la prévision) of the Economy Ministry estimated the rate of substitution at between 30% and 40%, or about 50,000 jobs lost by the young. The second plan tried immediately to correct this bias. The range of eligible firms was restricted; the positions offered had to be in manual labor; and the administration of the Department of Labor performed strict verification before certifying traineeships. The result was a collapse of the number of trainees, which fell to only 20,000. This figure was considered too small to be a measure of effectiveness; the third plan started up again with 55,000 beneficiaries. In banks and insurance companies, the number of "Barre trainees" was only 3,900 with the first plan, and only 4 with the second, but rose to 700 with the third.

The largest scheme—tax exemptions for hiring young people less than a year out of school—did indeed benefit new entrants, but only to the detriment of those who were already working. Employers performed a rational fiscal and social optimization: they replaced young people who were just past a year out of school with newly graduated young people recruited into initial training schemes. Under the pacts, the training periods (like the exemptions) merely shifted young people's difficulties by a year.

On the other hand, there does not seem to have been a substitution effect between young people and employees over 25; on the

TABLE 4

Reduction of unemployment (in thousands) thanks to job pacts, as estimated by the Ministry of Finance in 1979

	Q41977	Q11978	Q21978	Q31978	Q41978	Q11979
24 or younger	73	104	75	26	33	35
25 or older	28	39	29	10	13	14

SOURCES: Direction de la prévision, "Evolution du chômage depuis 1997" (Evolution of Unemployment since 1977) (1979) and "Effets des pactes nationals pour l'emploi" (Effects of the National Employment Pact), D 79–4-141 DFM G (1979).

contrary, the subsidies to companies under all the Barre measures might have worked in favor of preserving jobs for the over-25s.

Similarly, apprenticeships do seem to have stimulated labor, especially during the third plan, which ensured total exemption from social contributions for both the employer and the wage-earner; the take-up of apprenticeships was between 40,000 and 60,000 greater than those observed in years preceding the new plan.

At the macroeconomic level, the rise in youth unemployment paused just after the first plan, but overall (from September 1977 to September 1978), the youth unemployment rate rose 10 percentage points.

In 1979, the work of the forecasting department recorded the relative failure of the pacts. Modeling industry employment in the absence of the pacts,[28] an internal document suggested that their effects on youth unemployment, as well as on that of those over the age of 25, were weak—if not *very* weak (table 4). And if we omit trainees, these estimates are consistent with net job *destruction*: employees being replaced by cheap interns.

If the plans' impact on employment was weak, nevertheless, long-term effects linked to an improvement in the human

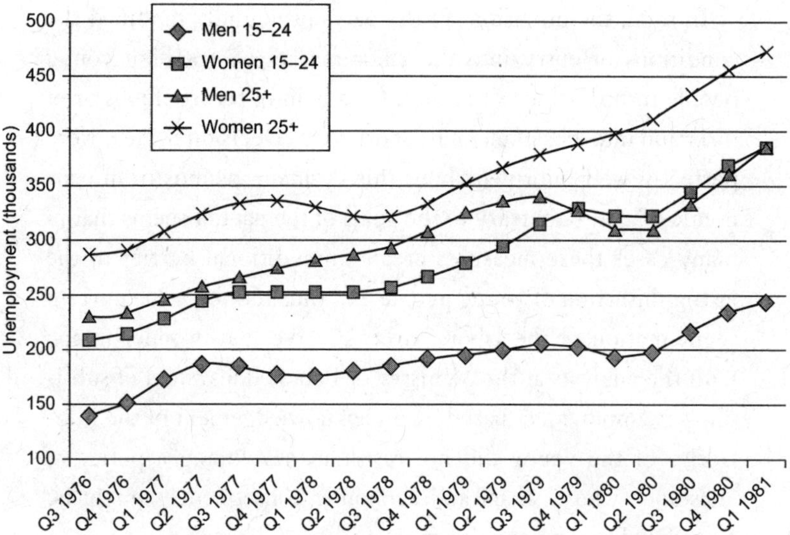

Figure 4. Rising unemployment in metropolitan France under the Barre governments, by age and gender. Source: DARES-INSEE unemployment series, based on International Labor Organization concept.

capital (skills, experience, etc.) of beneficiaries could be observed. The data from studies of what became of the beneficiaries suggest that the most intensive on-the-job training programs did offer better insertion into the workforce. After practical traineeship, half of the young people found themselves unemployed, and the other half were largely in fixed-term contracts; while 85% of those exiting on-the-job training contracts remained with the company that had recruited them. But the training offered was poor. Once again, it is impossible to determine whether this was an effect of the program itself, or of trainee selection. In any case, if there was an effect, it must have been small, since it cannot be discerned in job statistics by age cohort (figure 4).

In total, the provisions of the pacts profoundly modified the conditions of entry into the labor market by trapping young people in precarious situations, for a gain in terms of jobs or of insertion into jobs likely to be short-term. Decision makers were perfectly well informed about this by many memos from economic offices. "Contrary to the goals of the pact, it seems that in many cases these measures create an additional barrier to the lasting insertion of young people and thus reinforce the current segmentation of the labor market."[29] "We may wonder (along with the analysts at the Ministry of Labor) if a system of subsidies for employment based on an acknowledgement of the inferiority of the young did not result in developing a policy of assistance whose social and economic consequences might be prejudicial to the young themselves."[30]

In the first quarter of 1981, after three job pacts, metropolitan France counted 1.5 million unemployed (in the International Labour Organization sense), including 380,000 women under 25 and 270,000 men under 25 (figure 4). The portion of the young among the unemployed had remained stable—between 40% and 43%—during the whole Barre period.

Recourse to a Facilitated Fixed-Term Contract and Industries Dependent on Subsidies

The last piece in the transformation of the labor market into a market segmented between protected employees and precarious ones saw Barre trying to liberalize the use by firms of the fixed-term contract. In the absence of a legislative framework, the Court of Appeals had gradually framed strictly the recourse by firms to fixed-term contracts.[31] The law of January 3, 1979, swept away this jurisprudence. For the first time, it inserted into the work code provisions specific to fixed-term contracts: employers could now establish fixed-term contracts with no limitation on duration; they could also renew them without limit.

The law thus permitted the use of such contracts to provide permanent jobs. But salaried workers employed under these conditions were in fact excluded from the application of the legal and customary provisions usually applying to permanent employees—thus they offered firms a kind of flexibility.

With the added effects of the job pacts, the proportion of fixed-term contracts in employment (apart from temps and apart from interns) would double in three years. In April 1980, 27% of industrial and commercial establishments with more than ten employees were using workers under fixed-term contracts (apart from temporary agency staff), and these employees represented 3% of the workforce; back in April 1977 (date of the first ACEMO [Activité et les conditions d'emploi de la main-d'oeuvre] survey), only 12% of these establishments had declared that they used this type of contract, and the employees concerned represented only 1.4% of the whole workforce. Women were particularly affected by this new insecurity. At the end of the legislature, a new avenue was opened, presented during the electoral campaign as a solution to female unemployment: over the opposition of the feminist movement, which rejected the notion of cut-rate jobs for women, a law in December 1980 established part-time jobs in the public sector, and a law in January 1981 organized their use in the private sector.

Women were also hit hard by industrial restructuring. While the textile industry, with its intensive use of female workers, was left to its decline, the Barre governments would inject massive public funds into heavy industry to maintain permanent jobs. Steel-making alone would draw three times the credit that was allocated to job pacts. The state put the major firms into an agglomeration through partial nationalization. After a "steel plan" worth 7 billion francs of investment began in 1977, the state in 1978 took over their debts (at a cost of 22 billion francs) in return for a majority share in the capital of Usinor and Sacilor. The creditors became shareholders at about 30%, the state at 15% directly, plus 30% via the Caisse des dépôts et consignations (Deposits and Consignments Fund) and 10% via the Crédit national. These rescues were accompanied by plans to eliminate positions staggered over time, after 1981, of which a good third were retirees starting at age 50. Thus did the state artificially maintain employment. According to national accounting, in full-time equivalent, salaried employment in automobiles and metallurgy contracted by only 45,000 between 1973 and 1980 (a third of the contraction in clothing and textiles), while the labor share in value added reached 90% in these sectors; but between 1980 and 1987, employment there contracted by 225,000 positions.

A Plethora of Job Measures

Apart from the specific programs for young people, the Barre governments multiplied measures to deal with the rising unemployment. The existing policy of supervising restructuring was augmented by the creation of a special fund for "industrial adaptation."

In line with the desire to place young people in manual jobs, the state tried to vacate posts occupied by immigrants and seniors. The first pact instituted a guaranteed revenue of 70% of last salary for workers over the age of 60 who quit between mid-July 1977 and the end of March 1979. By the beginning of 1981, the effective average age of retirement had fallen to 60.5 years.

Elsewhere, Barre pursued the policy of closing France to immigration. Legalization of immigrants was halted, and the reuniting of families made even more difficult. The government even tried to reverse the migratory flows. Incentives to return to native countries, set up in May 1977, were slow to take off; beneficiaries numbered only 5,000 by the last day of 1977. The flow of accepted applications had accelerated by 1978; but of these 18,000, 60% were for Spaniards or Portuguese. This plan does not seem to have stimulated the outflow of migrants, which remained stable around at 70,000 to 75,000 per year.[32]

While firmly rejecting dividing up labor,[33] Barre favored a shortening of the workweek. The maximum duration of the working week was lowered from 50 to 48 hours. Sector agreements went farther, for example in construction, which proposed a 5-day week and a schedule of 45 hours. The average workweek continued to shorten: from 43.3 hours in 1973 to 42 hours in 1975, then 41.4 in 1977, and 40.6 in 1979.

In tandem, the *allocation speciale d'attente,* which had become too costly and was thought to be a disincentive, was abolished. Aid to the unemployed who created firms was set up, benefiting 14,000 persons, largely qualified men, in 1980. Thanks to subsidies, companies would hire 3,000 long-term unemployed over age 45. The last job pact instituted a bonus for hiring the first salaried employee in artisanal firms.

Beyond the young people, the failure of the whole employment policy did not escape the attention of people at the time. Memos from several economic offices tried to alert the government; these memos are now available to researchers in open archives. In 1980, the forecasting office launched Operation Variants to try to take a bearing on these policies, proposing a medium-term scenario and alternative paths. The conclusions were unequivocal. "The pacts have caused a perturbation in the seasonal cycle but have had no lasting effect on the underlying growth of youth unemployment.... The pacts have not perceptibly increased the offer of salaried jobs."[34] The ineffectiveness of such tools was not confined to France. "An overview of the measures taken in the United Kingdom sheds light on the inherent difficulties [in specific programs undertaken to aid the target groups—the young, the long-term unemployed]: on the one hand, the granting of subsidies to firms is probably without effect, and on the other hand, while the extensive efforts of job placement services might prove effective, they remain costly and certainly incompatible with the relative smallness of their numbers."[35] But what was most worrying was the rise in job demand starting in 1977, attributed to "new modes of personnel management" in companies, that is to say the rise in short-term and temporary agency personnel, and the fate of young workers. The Forecasting Office concluded at the start of 1981 that "the development of forms of precarious employment, including the pacts, can only maintain a high level of unemployment, and it would be useful to reflect on the means of avoiding what might end up entraining a generalization of recurrent unemployment. The problem is all the more urgent in that this would represent a definitive transfer of wage costs to the public, with firms periodically substituting unemployment compensation for salaries."[36]

The seven-year term of Valery Giscard d'Estaing heavily modified the fundamentals of the French economy in terms of the functioning of both the microeconomics and the macroeconomics of the labor market. More than just high levels of unemployment, he left a legacy of a series of problems that he himself constructed: stigmatization of immigrants and young people, casualization of employment and especially of entryways into the job market, and a hike in obligatory deductions, in particular those linked to work. Clearly, today's major economic and social evils are the results of policies initiated by Jacques Chirac and especially by Raymond Barre.

By thus distorting the labor market, this policy also carried the germs of a structural weakening of workers *vis-à-vis* employers. Ironically, the experts (called *les technos*) in the ministers' cabinets who implemented this policy would find themselves leaders of French capitalism in the following decades—ranging from Michel Pébereau (who would become de facto boss of French capitalism as CEO of BNP Paribas, the biggest French bank), to Thierry Desmarets who would take the reins of the petroleum giant Total, the highest-valued company on the French stock market.

NOTES

1. Chapters 2 and 3 exploit notes and data from the Direction de la prévision of the French Ministry of Finance. They are archived at the Centre des archives économiques et financières (Savigny-le-Temple).

2. Jean-Jacques Carré, Paul Dubois, and Edmond Malinvaud, *Abrégé sur la croissance française* (Paris: Le Seuil, 1973), 263.

3. François Eymard-Duvernay, "L'emploi au cours du VIe plan," *Economie et Statistique* 74 (January 1976): 29–50.

4. A stimulus is contra-cyclic when it opposes a descending economic cycle and tries to attenuate the cycle. In contrast, stimulating in a context of sharp economic growth is called a pro-cyclic strategy: it increases the amplitude of the economic cycle.

5. This measure would improve the accounts of firms but had little effect on investment; in fact, many firms profited from the boon to place orders to be delivered only in 1977 or 1978.

6. On the long-term history of immigration policies in France, see Patrick Weil's *How to Be French: Nationality in the Making since* 1789 (Duke

University Press, 2008) and *La République et sa diversité: Immigration, intégration, discrimination* (Seuil/La République des idées, 2005).

7. The hateful editorial in the major right-wing regional daily *Le Méridional-La France* on 26 September 1973 (a few days before the Yom Kippur War), after the murder of a streetcar worker from Marseille by an unbalanced immigrant, speaks for itself.

Of course they will tell us the assassin is crazy, since isn't an explanation necessary to satisfy those who refuse to admit that racism is Arab before it is European? And that in the end there is European racism, but only because for too long all the abuses of the Arab world have been tolerated ... for vulgar reasons of oil. Insanity is not an excuse. This assassin (even if he is crazy)—the public authorities are even more seriously guilty of having let him onto our territory. We have had enough. Enough Algerian thieves, enough Algerian burglars, enough Algerian braggarts, enough Algerian troublemakers, enough Algerian syphilitics, enough Algerian rapists, enough Algerian pimps, enough Algerian madmen, enough Algerian killers. We have had enough of this savage immigration that brings to our country a whole rabble from across the Mediterranean and their mixing with (for their misery—and they know it and are with us when we denounce the evil) honest and brave workers who have come to earn their living and that of their family ... because independence has brought them nothing but misery, contrary to what they were led to expect. Yesterday it was an unfortunate Marseille bus driver who was the victim of the wicked beast that M. Boumediene has sent us in the guise of Cooperation. So, another worker—after the taxi drivers, shopkeepers, defenseless old people, and young girls or women—attacked when coming home alone. How long will this go on? What are they waiting for to do something about it, we ask again? Will those in high places understand too late that this risks ending very badly? And will they let these leftist criminals—what else should they be called?—maintain hatred of Whites among Arab immigrants ... to make use of them and obtain what they want most: a racist attack! That's their dream! For then France might finally be made an outcast from civilized nations.

8. Y. Gastaut, "Français et immigrés à l'épreuve de la crise (1973–1995)," *Vingtième Siècle* 84 (2004): 107–18.

9. Dijoud was one of the French figures questioned about their responsibility in the genocide in Rwanda in 1994.

10. Marius Apostolo, "Une politique à la mesure de la crise," *Droit Social* 5 (May 1976): 34–38.

11. *France-Soir,* February 10, 1976.

12. TV broadcast, "L'Evènement," February 19, 1976, quoted by Apostolo.

13. FIFI was the mathematical model of the French economy that was dominant then. It was specially conceived for the planning by researchers at CEPREMAP (at that time: Centre pour la recherche en économie mathématique appliquée à la plannification). The interested reader may refer to the special issue of the *Revue économique,* vol. 24, no. 6 (November 1973), available at www.jstor.org.

14. Henry Bussery, "Incidence sur l'économie française d'une réduction durable de la main-d'œuvre immigrée," *Economie et Statistique* 76 (March 1976): 37–46. One senses the embarrassment of the author, who stresses at length the methodological weaknesses of the exercise.

15. Catherine Wihtol de Wenden, "Les étrangers et le marché de l'emploi," *Droit Social* 5 (May 1976): 29.

16. Ibid., 30.

17. In 1998, Papon was sentenced for complicity in crimes against humanity for acts committed when he was general secretary of the Gironde Prefecture between 1942 and 1944 under the German occupation.

18. Interview with Raymond Barre in *La Croix,* November 17, 1978.

19. A "conventional" policy aims to inscribe in the labor law the agreements signed by unions and employers' organizations.

20. Nuriel Roubini and Jeremy Sachs, "Political and Economic Determinants of Budget Deficits in the Industrial Democracies," *European Economic Review* 33 (1989): 903–38.

21. Policy speech to the National Assembly, October 6, 1978.

22. Pierre Mormiche, "Les jeunes sur le marché du travail à la rentrée 1977," *Economie et Statistique* 98 (1978): 11–25.

23. Pierre Bourdieu, "Classement, déclassement, reclassement," *Actes de la recherche en sciences sociales* 24, no. 24 (1978): 2–22.

24. See for example Alexis Jacquemin, "Le phénomène de désindustrialisation et la Communauté Européenne," *Revue économique* 30, no. 6 (1979): 985–99.

25. *OECD Economic Surveys: France* 1977, www.oecd-ilibrary.org/economics/oecd-economic-surveys-france-1977_eco_surveys-fra-1977-en.

26. Only after 1982 do labor-force surveys permit a distinction between fixed-term and open-ended contracts. On the other hand, Agence nationale pour l'emploi statistics detail the causes of unemployment. Thus, in September 1977, without including temporary agency staff, the ends of short contracts represent almost 50% of job losses (58%, including temps)—twice as many as in 1976.

27. Studies following up on the future of the beneficiaries of the provisions cannot be related to other sources, notably the French Labor Survey before its redesign in 1983. Already incapable of distinguishing between fixed-term and open-ended contracts, this survey was also affected by significant biases; thus, the job figures it produced do not agree with employer sources, suggesting that many more trainees reported having jobs.

28. For the specialist reader, this is not a microeconomic assessment of the provisions but an estimate based on a macro-industry model of the French economy. Macro-industry identification is pertinent since the pacts (especially the first one) represented the first large-scale application of employment measures.

29. Direction de la prévision, *Les pactes pour l'emploi des jeunes,* 80.BD4.113 (1980).

30. Direction de la prévision, *Les politiques de l'emploi en France: Passé, présent, avenir,* 80.BD4.24 (1980).

31. G. Poulain, "La loi du 3 janvier 1979 relative au contrat à durée déterminé," *Droit Social,* March 1979, 67–79.

32. André Lebon, "L'aide au retour des travailleurs étrangers," *Economie et Statistique* 113 (1979): 37–46.

33. "One might try to resolve the [problem] by adopting a Malthusian attitude consisting of dividing the workload among a greater number of parties. This attitude would in time entail a limitation on income and a slowing of growth" (general policy speech, October 6, 1976).

34. Direction de la prévision, *La montée du chômage et les pactes nationaux pour l'emploi des jeunes*, 81.BD4.127.21 (March 1981).

35. Direction de la prévision, *L'administration et le marché de l'emploi*, 81.BD4.04.01 (January 1981).

36. Direction de la prévision, note BD4.81.05.28 (1981).

CHAPTER THREE

1981–1986

The Socialists Try

At the start of 1981 a tight election race opened in France. The outgoing Giscard–Barre team stressed its successes—the stabilization of public finance, the relative solidity of the franc—and proposed to pursue its employment policy by opening two new paths: part-time work and a reduction of working time in industries that benefited from gains in productivity due to electronic technologies. On the other side, the Common Program of the Left (Socialists, Communists, radical leftists) proposed a massive stimulus package, an increase in minimum social benefits, and job-sharing of working hours.

The victory of the Socialist candidate François Mitterrand in the presidential election (which was answered by a crash on the Paris stock market), and then the massive victory of the Left in the legislative elections, seemed to portend a desire to make a break with the Barre years. This new legislature would indeed be marked by major reorientations—overall, the Socialists would strengthen the rights and protections of workers—but at the same time the Left would (in some ways) convert to economic liberalism. Socialists initiated a modernization of the French economy, which included the restructuring of large manufacturers and investments in education. This modernization contrasts with dramatic failures in macroeconomic policy. In reality, the new majority did not possess (any more than the old one had) the theoretical keys to understand the macroeconomic environment created by the new policies of the U.S. Federal Reserve ("the Fed").

The debate in France in 1981 was not about which foreign model should be followed. The major industrialized countries were all experiencing great difficulties. Sweden had an unemployment rate of merely about 2%, but at the price of an obese state, a significant budget deficit, and a balance of payments in marked deficit, which would result in a massive devaluation in 1981. The United States was experiencing a rapid rise in unemployment, with 1.5 million more unemployed in one year. The situation was even worse in the United Kingdom of Margaret Thatcher, which, with almost 750,000 more people out of work in a year, reached 2.4 million unemployed. Germany, too, saw unemployment creep up for several months, against the background of a national debt whose service charges (annual repayments) reached 8% of GDP (including nearly 3% in interest alone).

Because of the strong interaction between the French and German economies, West Germany was still a country much emulated by France. Until the recent deterioration, the Federal Republic of Germany had managed not only to keep inflation well below 10%, but also to avoid a surge in unemployment. In 1980, the number of unemployed fell to its 1974 level, and the number of young people without work was only 225,000—a third of the rate in France. Despite a relatively lax budgetary policy, the low relative inflation allowed the deutschmark to assert itself and to increase steadily in value. The results were interpreted by the French economic administrations as a corollary of the very sophisticated policy of the Bundesbank. In reality, French analysts could not see the heart of the mechanics that had been at work in Germany since 1973.

RULES AND DISCRETION

Yet, for several years monetary macroeconomics had been adopting innovative tools for interpreting the mechanisms of inflation and the role of monetary authorities. These theoretical tools were forged by young American scholars of the Chicago school, including Robert Lucas, who would win the Nobel Prize in economics in 1995; Thomas Sargent, winner in 2011; Robert Barro; and the 2004 Nobel winners, Finn Kydland and Edward Prescott. Back then, however, their theories were not yet being applied when Paul Volker arrived in 1979 as the head of the Fed.

After the second oil crisis, inflation exceeded 10% in the United States. The American economy was in full stagflation: a mixture of weak growth and strong inflation. Volker hesitated to initiate a restrictive policy. The economists at the Fed stressed that in order to break inflation the economy would have to be plunged into a deep depression for several years.

The proponents of the new theories had a much less alarming view, based on the "Lucas critique" of the then-dominant models. The keystone of their reasoning was that, contrary to the claims of the Keynesian approach, economic agents form rational expectations,[1] especially about how prices are evolving. And agents' expectations are self-realizing: if workers anticipate a rise in prices, they will demand a raise in salaries—which businesses will accept, because they too anticipate price rises—so these ultimately will take place. But the monetary authority can break this mechanism by applying a restrictive policy. Economic agents, particularly businesses, are aware of this. Thus, expectations are rational. When they think it likely that the central bank will apply a restrictive policy, they will expect low inflation; if the central banks are lax, they will anticipate a rapid rise in prices. To break inflation effectively, a central bank has to credibly display the desire to break it. But until then the Fed had conducted a discretionary policy: either it announced no policy at all, or it announced restrictions and then ultimately—faced with economic slowdown—relaxed them. The prescription of the new theories was simple: announce a regulation, and then stick to it whatever the economic change, to gain credibility and ultimately to modify expectations.[2] This was the path that Volker chose. He announced the Fed's desire to contain inflation, then abruptly raised the interest rate and tightened all lines of credit. Lo and behold, agents did not modify their inflation expectations. They thought that again the Fed would not respect this rule. Inflation exceeded 13% in 1980 and unemployment soared. Yet Volker did not modify his policy; and this therapy made inflation fall to around 10%. At the end of 1981, the United States (which had just elected Ronald Reagan) suffered the worst recession since the 1930s. It seemed to be accepted that a "maniac" who was ready to torpedo the American economy to fight against inflation was now at the head of the Fed—and the Fed had become credible. Taking the new situation into account, agents rationally expected a drop in inflation. Inflation fell to 6% in 1982, and then to less than 4% in 1983.

Inflation was vanquished—and this despite the policies of President Reagan: lower taxes, a huge increase in military expenditures, and an abysmal budget deficit. The federal government could conduct an expansionist budgetary policy at the very moment when the independent Fed was holding onto monetary policy and making itself the guarantor of a mastery of inflationary tensions. As of the middle of 1983, the economy had recovered significantly. Industries in high technology and research were stimulated by military expenditure, while Americans fully spent the taxes that the Treasury was no longer collecting.

This action by the American monetary authorities when faced with inflation had given birth to a new paradigm, and the world would convert to it in the following decades—up to the Great Recession. The creation of a Central European Bank, independent and responsible for dealing with inflation, would be one of the illustrations of this new paradigm.

Obviously, in 1981, French analysts (like those of the OECD) did not know about this American experiment. However, the Bundesbank had done the same thing in 1974. A central and independent bank, it had applied a restrictive policy since 1973. At the start of 1974, during salary negotiations, the unions and employers' organizations did not take seriously its stated desire to pursue this path in the context of the oil crisis. The negotiations resulted in a nominal hike in salaries of 13% on average. Haunted by the memory of the terrible inflation between the two world wars, the Bundesbank staunchly maintained its line of conduct. Strangled and incapable of following salary inflation, German companies were obliged to massively cut positions. Unemployment tripled in the Federal Republic in a year. In the end, inflation barely reached 7% in 1974. And in 1975, wage negotiations ratified the moderate anticipations of inflation—rightly so, because inflation then fluctuated between 3% and 6%, despite the budget deficits incurred to maintain activity and to stabilize unemployment.

1981–1982: AN UNEXPECTED INTERNATIONAL ENVIRONMENT

With a healthy budget, bequeathed by the restrictive policy of Raymond Barre, the new Socialist government led by prime minister Pierre Mauroy enjoyed significant budgetary margins. These would be used to stimulate consumption, to hire in the public sector, and to nationalize the major banking establishments and various industrial conglomerates. Although some Communist ministers entered into the governing coalition, the Socialist group was already in a majority in the National Assembly. Thus, president François Mitterrand and prime minister Pierre Mauroy could put ministers from the center-left in control of economic policy.

Jacques Delors, former advisor to the Gaullist Chaban-Delmas, became minister of economy and finance; Pierre Dreyfus, former chairman of the Renault automobile firm, minister of industry; Laurent Fabius, junior minister of the budget; and Michel Rocard, minister of state—together, they would pilot the new policy. This crew of ministers, who were mainly social-democratic (or even social-liberal), would implement the promises of Mitterrand. Expectations of the evolution of the international conjuncture argued for a recovery in France. In effect, at the beginning of 1981, most institutions—national and international, from the OECD to the French Observatory of Economic Conjunctures (a bureau that had just been created by Raymond Barre)—were forecasting a sustained worldwide recovery starting in 1982. The same analysis prevailed in French economic offices, notably the INSEE (National Institute for Statistics and Economic Studies, still led by Edmond Malinvaud). It was hypothesized that Volker's monetary policy, which had made the United States plunge, would soon reach its culmination, reviving the American economy while reducing the attractiveness of the dollar. Thus it was thought, quite logically, that European currencies (including the franc) were going to appreciate, which would curtail an energy bill drawn up in dollars—and therefore reduce imported inflation.[3] France could then register a rise in exports, a fall in the value of imports, and reduced inflationary tendencies.

These optimistic parameters gave a margin of maneuver to a recovery policy that would surf on worldwide growth. Moreover, from the beginning of 1981, the Barre government had started to relax its discipline, in part for electoral reasons, by increasing subsidies to farmers and reducing health insurance contributions (by one percentage point). Some in Mauroy's administration thought that a recovery was both realistic and necessary, to avoid the scenario of unemployment at 2.5 million on the horizon in 1985.[4]

Beyond the desire among the new political majority for a break with the past, such a stimulus seemed pertinent in the international environment that they could discern. In the first place, it assumed a redistributive character. Social benefits were increased spectacularly. The housing allowance grew in two phases, by 25% in July 1981, and by 20% in December; the old-age minimum went up 50% over a year and a half; family allowances increased by 25% in July 1981 and again by 25% (for families with at least two children) in February 1982. In total, in real terms, welfare benefits received by households increased by 5% in 1981, and by around 7% in 1982. The minimum wage was also raised, by around 5% in real terms, in 1981 and again in 1982.

Job creation in the public sector was huge. Between 1981 and 1983, 130,000 jobs were added in government departments, and

30,000 in hospitals, not including regional and community administrations.

In addition, the policy of nationalization and its rationale were clearly enunciated in a general policy speech given by the prime minister to the National Assembly on July 8, 1981:

> No new policy is possible without effective control of credit.... Therefore, it is suitable, as an extension of the laws of 1936 and 1945, to nationalize the banking sector.
>
> Thus the government will acquire the means to implement a renovated credit policy that is oriented to the improvement of the services rendered to its users and to the economy.
>
> Equality of access by all (especially small and medium-sized firms) to financing in both the short term and the long term will be sought. Banking establishments will become more concerned with the general interest in the distribution of credit, and will add this long-neglected criterion to those they already use to decide on making loans.

NATIONALIZATION AND MODERATE PUBLIC DEFICITS

The nationalization of thirty-six banks and two financial companies was begun in February 1982. Thus 95% of national deposits became controlled by the state, on top of the control of monetary policy by the Bank of France. Now the government could stimulate credit, notably via subsidized loans to businesses.

Nationalization also involved five major industrial groups: the Compagnie Générale d'Electricité, Pechiney-Ugine-Kuhlmann, Rhône-Poulenc, Saint-Gobain-Pont-à-Mousson, and Thomson-Brandt. In the same speech mentioned earlier, Pierre Mauroy claimed: "Through nationalization the state is ensuring its mastery of the industrial hubs that appear to us to require a dynamic policy of investment and employment."

The budget deficit went from 0.1% of GDP in 1980 to 2.2% in 1981, then to 2.8% in 1982—thus returning to its 1975 level. But while the opposition parties saw it as unsustainable, this level of deficit was totally absorbable by a French economy that was only slightly indebted. It is astonishing to reflect that this period has stayed in French popular opinion—and beyond—as an era of deficit, though its actual level was below the 3% criterion in the European Maastricht Treaty which was ratified a decade later and which would become the keystone of Europe's budgetary discipline.

In fact, faced with increasing expenditure, the Socialist-Communist majority had to find new resources. It significantly increased the taxes on the highest incomes and instituted a tax on major fortunes, which would affect 1% of French fiscal households. The plan to finance social security in the fall of 1981 went in the same direction, in line with countering the effects of the revival: the reestablishment of the percentage point of salary contributions for health insurance that had been eliminated by Raymond Barre, and a hike in employer contributions for high salaries.

FRANCE ISOLATED

Although the budget deficit was not in itself a problem, the global economic forecasts for 1982 that were issued in 1981 and maintained until the very beginning of 1982 proved to be completely wrong. All the institutes, and experts in all the departments, were grievously mistaken.[5] Their basic hypothesis—that Volker would relax his monetary policy—was not borne out. The restrictive American policies were maintained. Moreover, the French stimulus policy was isolated in Europe. In contrast to

Barre's management, most of the other countries had already over-utilized budget deficits. The withdrawal of the state was pursued in the United Kingdom. Germany did not intend to go any farther in its support of the economy. Italy was stifled by a large annual deficit, averaging 9% of GDP since 1975. The Netherlands had to straighten out public finances that had been floundering despite the oil manna—and so on. The number of those out of work in the United States shot up from 8 million in the first quarter of 1981 to almost 12 million in the last of 1982. High American interest rates supported the dollar; instead of depreciating, the dollar continued to appreciate, weighing down France's energy bill and feeding price tensions. The growth of world trade was 6% less than forecast. The GDP of the OECD contracted by 0.5%, though it had been expected to grow by 2%. In short, the predictions were false right down the line.

The initial bet by the majority Left on a global economic recovery that would have lifted French economic policy was null and void. And its very scaffolding was collapsing. Out of sync with its European partners under Barre, French macroeconomic policy was again set by Mauroy, but now heading in the opposite direction.

France (and to a lesser extent the other European countries that were not engaged in an expansionary policy) was destabilized by the Fed's credibility strategy.[6] Moreover, the patent lack of investment in non-financial enterprises in France (whose average annual volume from 1977 to 1980 had remained at the level of 1973)—which was a result of the restrictive policy of the Barre governments—caused a strong but untargeted rise in French demand, which necessitated resorting to exports. At the same time, monetary creation induced inflation, undermining the competitiveness of French products.

In an unexpected international context, the result of these combined mechanisms was deterioration in the French balance of trade and a need for major devaluations of the franc, which occurred starting in the autumn of 1981. In tandem, unemployment continued to rise, though more slowly. The Socialist recovery was more prudent in budget terms than Chirac's of 1975, but it ran up against the absence of such a policy among economic partners.

1982–1986: FROM "RIGOR" TO "COMPETITIVE DISINFLATION"

From mid-1982, the failure of the Socialist policy was apparent. The devaluation of the franc in June 1982 was accompanied by a government-ordered price freeze, despite the VAT's normal rate being raised by a point, to 18.6%. Salaries were also frozen (apart from the minimum wage and already-agreed salary raises) until the end of October 1982. Unemployment contributions were increased in the fall. Among the Socialists, two ideological positions confronted each other. They relied on a common diagnosis: that the Left had underestimated France's dependence on the international economy, and that if it wanted to remain open to the outside, it would have to adopt the new liberal precepts current in English-speaking countries. Meanwhile, the leader of the sovereignty wing of the Socialist Party, Jean-Pierre Chevènement, argued for a closing of the French economy and an exit from the European Monetary System, which would permit developing an autonomous policy. In contrast, Jacques Delors and Laurent Fabius wished for a clear social-liberal turn, fostering a market economy tinged with redistribution.

Nevertheless, the disputatious "couple" of Volker and Reagan in the United States would prove that the Socialist interpretation was partly false. Equipped with a guarantee of non-inflation from the Fed, Reagan could develop a "Keynesian recovery"—very marked politically in favor of the highest income brackets and military expenditure—and more particularly targeted to increase demand in American economic sectors. But this disconnect between the Fed and the White House was not visible at the end of 1982 (while the American economic situation continued to deteriorate); it would only be apparent in the second half of 1983.

The French government was alone in steering the economy of France, since the Bank of France would not be independent until 1994. The state, therefore, had to either gain credibility or make France autonomous. At the start of 1983, François Mitterrand decided to back the views of Pierre Mauroy, meaning that the Delors–Fabius position was validated. This was a "turn to rigor" (*tournant de la rigueur*)—with priority given to the battle against inflation. The exercise was all the more difficult in that the French government was Socialist (and Communist), whereas Great Britain (where the central bank was not independent) had a Conservative government with credible hostility to salary inflation.

In March 1983, the franc was devalued by 8% in relation to the mark. Behind this, a new Mauroy government came in, again with Communist ministers in the coalition. Delors was at the head of a vast Ministry of the Economy, keeping as advisors Philippe Lagayette (future head of French activities of J. P. Morgan) and Pascal Lamy (future director-general of the World Trade Organization). Laurent Fabius inherited the key Ministry of Industry and Research, armed with an office of *technos* directed by Louis Schweitzer, inspector of finance (son of the managing director of the IMF from 1963 to 1973; future CEO of Renault). In March 1983 expenditure in the public sector was reduced and income taxes increased. Salaries in the public sector—including in companies owned by the state—were deindexed: they would now evolve in line with the inflation announced by the government at the beginning of the year, systematically below what actually occurred. Thus, the salaries of state employees would diminish in real terms.

The Communists were in an untenable position and quit the governing coalition. Laurent Fabius was named prime minister. His government from 1984 to 1986 no longer included Communist ministers. He maintained the strategy initiated in 1983. Minister of social affairs in the preceding government, Pierre Bérégovoy inherited the large Ministry of the Economy, Finance and Industry, keeping as his private secretary Jean-Charles Naouri (who in the 1990s would take control of a leading food retail chain, Casino). Soon the strategy would be called "competitive disinflation." Yet the Fabius government rejected a dramatic change in the social contributions paid by employers, instead favoring a higher VAT. Presented in the twenty-first century in France as an innovation, and then key to the Danish policy in the 1990s, the idea of a "social VAT" was advanced by French business leaders at the start of 1983.[7] Analysis concluded at the time that the social VAT was equivalent to a devaluation that was favorable to competitiveness, but that it would be translated into a price rise that would neutralize it over time.[8] Neutral in long-term competitiveness, the social VAT was incompatible with the policy of disinflation. Moreover, ministerial economic experts had previously expressed very strong reservations about it. In particular, the Ministry of the Economy had taken a clear position about the difficulties that management would have with it, after a report in 1982 from a working group piloted by a young *énarque*, Henri de Castries (future CEO of AXA, the largest European insurance group).[9]

The result of both rigor and deindexing was quite satisfactory with regard to inflation: the rise in the consumer price index slipped below 8% in 1984 and declined to less than 3% (the level of France's principal European partners) in 1986. The oil counter-shock in early 1986 definitively ratified the new anticipations with regard to inflation among economic actors, an inflation that would indeed remain weak or moderate.

In parallel, European restrictive policies that were accentuated with the arrival in power of the Christian-Democrat Helmut Kohl in Germany led to modest growth in France: 1.2% in 1983, 1.5% in 1984, and 1.7% in 1985—as compared to 2.4% in 1982. Yet, despite the rigor, the French budget remained in deficit. And this rate of growth was incapable of offering enough jobs for the natural rise in the active population.

WORK, EMPLOYMENT, INDUSTRY: POLICIES BOTH AMBITIOUS AND CONSERVATIVE

In addition to the major shifts in macroeconomic policy, the legislature's sectorial policies on work and employment would go through successive swerves. In 1981, the Mauroy government inherited a situation in which, due to the series of plans of Raymond Barre, entire sections of the industrial tissue were bleeding. The nationalization of major corporations and their support through subsidized credits would initially amplify this policy. For example, the state directly aided Usinor-Sacilor, with the approval of the European Commission. Even coal mining was revived, through the hiring of 20,000 miners. On the other hand, the supposed priority given to the development of small and medium-sized firms was not made concrete, notably with respect to the promise of easier access to public markets—an idea that would come back in the debates during the presidential elections of 2007 and 2012, now rehabilitated under the term "Small Business Act" (referring to the law passed in the United States in 1953). Only aid to the unemployed who started businesses was significantly strengthened. In parallel, fearing that suppression of the provisions of the Barre plan would have a negative effect on employment in the short term, the government extended them, content to tinker, and leaving young workers in their precarious work-insertion trajectories.

This conservatism broke with the Socialists' cultural policy; and in fact it was also an industrial policy. Media deregulation permitted free radio stations—but also the birth of Canal Plus, a private pay-TV channel that was supposed to support audiovisual production in 1984. These new media were to permit France to have a powerful cultural and audiovisual industry around a myriad of new actors; France could remain the prime producer of films in Europe.

Modernization also occurred through the transformation of industrial relations. This relied on two principles developed in a report by Jean Auroux in 1981 for the president of the republic and the prime minister: "Citizens is what workers should be, and also in their place of business; workers should become actors for change in companies."[10] The laws passed successively from August to December 1982 created rights and responsibilities for actors in the business world that still appear natural today in France. The discretionary disciplinary power of the CEO was finally circumscribed. Industrial relations were to be based on internal regulation. Discrimination was banned: "no salaried employee may be sanctioned or fired due to his political opinions, his union activities, or his religious convictions."[11] Employees could express themselves about their working conditions without risking sanction; they benefited from a new right to retire in cases of grave and imminent danger. An annual obligation to negotiate within the company over salaries and the duration and organization of work was established—but this only went into effect if an agreement was reached.

Since 1975, state support for mature manufacturing sectors (like steel) had taken the shape of a slowing in the destruction of jobs and the maintenance of salaries in major industries, but at the price of distorting the balance sheets of these firms. The share of remunerations and social contributions (according to 1982's national accounts) thus reached 82% in metallurgy, 84% in manufacturing equipment, and 92% in the automobile industry. With the turn to rigor, this artificial policy was abandoned, leading to an abrupt adjustment. These three sectors lost 240,000 jobs in four years.

The deindexing of salaries and the manna of the oil countershock made capital share in the value added in 1986 rise to its level before the crisis.

THE LIBERAL TURN OF THE SOCIALIST LEFT

But the Fabius government went beyond deindexing and the restructuring of industries. It took a veritable liberal turn, particularly in the financial domain. The transformation of the City of London served as a stimulus. Deregulation simplified banking activities and digitalized them, eliminating the supervision of credit. Disintermediation[12] and deregulation of capital flows were expected to enable a significant entry of foreign capital. There only remained the supervision of the products of household savings. On the one hand, this policy meant greater selectivity and responsiveness in the banking sector and thus acceleration in the destruction of businesses (but also the creation of them).[13] On the other hand, the stock exchange was bullish, and the capital of the listed firms was diversifying. The owners of French companies were internationalizing, marking the start of a movement that would lead to half of the capital of the companies on the CAC 40 (the benchmark French stock market index, quoting the forty most significant values) being held by non-residents today. The market conditions were assembled to proceed to the massive privatization that would be effected by subsequent governments. Meanwhile, France acquired an agency to manage its public debt. This very liquid debt was offered to worldwide investors, enabling a lowering of the rates paid by France. This strategy explains why today non-residents hold two-thirds of the French debt.

At the time, Paris dreamed of becoming one of the principal financial centers of Europe; but it was London that already held this enviable position. Despite the desire to follow this model, Paris could never rival its homologue across the Channel, which benefited fully from the effects of agglomeration in the finance industry.

STIMULATING EDUCATION

Fabius, the "youngest prime minister France has ever had" (as François Mitterrand referred to him), did not just set a liberal course. He also took action, starting with his general policy speech in July 1984 to the National Assembly, on France's educational backwardness and the constant mutations of work:

> An insufficient level of education and training, even more among women than among men, has in the course of the last fifteen years put a brake on our economic evolution. In Japan, more than 90% of the current age cohort successfully completes secondary studies, as compared to less than 35% in France. As evidenced by hundreds of thousands of skilled jobs that might be created between now and 1990 in electronics, but which could not find competent candidates, there is too often a divorce between the content of training and the needs of business and industry. Yet competence and professional qualification are the true resources of our country. Let us remember that the young people who now reach working age will still be active in 2020. How many times between now and then will they have to change jobs and even careers! So they have to be prepared for these changes.

The minister of education set a goal of 80% for an age cohort for the *baccalauréat.* The educational curriculum also adapted, with a plan for "computing for everybody" and the appearance of the first computers in schools; meanwhile the revolution in personal computing was getting underway. In tandem, research was stimulated. Expenditure on research and development (R&D) rose to 2.2% of GDP in 1986—the same level as in Britain, but still far from the 2.7% in Germany, Japan, and the United States. In three years, the personnel in public and private R&D swelled to a total of 15,000 workers.

The proportion of educated young people 16 to 25 did certainly grow, but slowly: from 31% in March 1984 to 33% in March 1986.[14] We may add the 1% of young people in new on-the-job training programs. But alongside this voluntarist policy, it was the social treatment of youth unemployment that occupied the foreground, especially with the creation of TUCs—*travaux d'utilité collective.* TUCs were training programs at half time for a maximum of six months in public services like hospitals or public institutions, which were reimbursed at a little under half the minimum wage. Two hundred thousand youth were enrolled in TUCs in March 1986. In fact this new program made it even more precarious for young people to enter the work market. At the same time, internships—even reformed—did not decline. The 22nd proposal of the 110 in candidate Mitterrand's platform—that open-ended contracts would again become the standard—was being violated by the state itself. Even if TUCs are considered as actual jobs, only 290,000 young people were at work nine months after leaving school, compared to 630,000 in 1973.

With the TUCs, the Socialists, too, ratified the notion that work could be paid at well below the minimum wage. Fundamentally, it was the idea of reducing inequality by compressing salary hierarchies that was abandoned. Henceforth, the buying power of the hourly minimum wage, like that of the median wage, would not progress—not until 1997.

ABANDONING THE 35-HOUR WEEK

Another policy was abandoned in 1983: the RTT, or *réduction du temps de travail* (reduction of working time). The initial project of the legislature had been a gradual shift to 35 hours per week for full-time (with hours beyond that being counted as overtime). The RTT was not in itself a novelty. Since the first oil crisis, working time had been declining regularly, with the disappearance of overtime hours, through sectorial agreements supported by governments on the right. The duo of President Giscard and Prime Minister Barre had wished to accompany industrial automation with a reduction in working time.

Nor was the RTT a French peculiarity. The German unions had negotiated it. In the Netherlands, the RTT would be at the heart of the Wassenaar Agreement signed in 1982 under pressure from the new coalition government of Christian-Democrats and Liberals. Lower salaries to boost competitiveness, and disinflation, were exchanged for a shorter workweek, which in many industries went from 38 to 36 hours a week for full-time.

In France, adopting the logic of the Popular Front (which had mandated a 40-hour workweek in 1936), the initial project of the majority was both to create jobs through the sharing of work and to offer a new social victory through a massive reduction in work time. Against hostile management, the Mauroy government proceeded with an edict in January 1982. In February, the legal workweek (beyond which any additional hours worked were considered overtime) went from 40 to 39 hours. A fifth week of paid vacation became generalized. The law was rapidly effective. An ACEMO study showed that the working time of reference for wage workers and salaried employees went from 40.3 hours in January 1982 to 39.3 hours in October.[15] Most businesses proceeded to total salary compensation—that is, the monthly wages were unchanged despite the shorter working time.

The most optimistic assessment advanced at the time by the Ministry of Labor suggested a gain of 70,000 jobs. But on the contrary, recent microeconomic studies conclude that jobs were destroyed—perhaps as many as 100,000.[16] Even using sophisticated methods, the estimate is very tentative due to the generalization of the reduction and the multiplicity of contemporaneous economic measures affecting the employees directly governed by the 39-hour week, as well as those who were not (part-time workers, and employees in companies that already had a collective working time of 39 hours or less).

The principal effect of the 39-hour week and the fifth week of paid vacation, visible in macroeconomic data series, seems to be

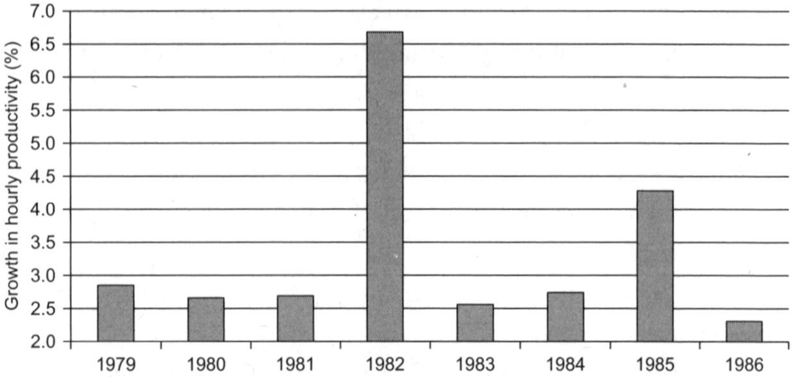

Figure 5. Annual growth in hourly productivity in France, 1979–1986. Reduced working time was accompanied by an equivalent increase in the hourly productivity of work. Source: National Accounts, INSEE (base 2000).

an exceptional hike in work productivity in 1982 (figure 5).[17] Overall, with such a rise in productivity, the impact of the policy on employment or competitiveness was probably negligible.

The sustained rigor of the liberal political turn signaled a pause in the reduction in working time. Henceforth, since employers and unions were incapable of reaching significant agreements, the average full-time working week would not drop any further—not until 1997.

SHRINKING THE WORKFORCE

While the RTT did not have an impact on unemployment, policies to reduce the size of the workforce did. Even if the Mauroy government, when it came to power, did effect some large-scale regularizations of the immigrant workers who were already present in France (130,000 in August 1981), the curtailing of immigration (as per the 81st campaign promise by Mitterrand "to fix the annual number of foreign workers admitted into France") was a protracted process.

The most powerful measure for workforce reduction was early retirement. Already initiated during preceding legislatures, the number of early retirees rose rapidly. At the start of 1984, almost 700,000 persons benefited from many measures, notably a general convention of social protection of steelmaking that instituted the possibility of retiring at age 50 for employees in this restructuring sector; contracts for resigning under early retirement "solidarity" schemes enabled firms to "replace" an employee over 55 years old with a new hire—which came as a godsend.

On the other hand, given that in 1981 the average age of retirement was already 60.5 (far below the legal limit of 65), and taking into account the mass of early retirees,[18] the voluntary retirement at age 60 that started in 1983 (which guaranteed full retirement at 70% of final salary after 37.5 years of contributions) would have only a slight impact on the size of the workforce.

In total, the ensemble of jobs policy measures did prevent an overly rapid rise in unemployment. Unemployment rate stabilized at 6.9% in the last quarter of 1981 to the end of 1982. The rise tapered off. There would have been up to half a million unemployed at the start of 1984 without the new measures of employment policy. But this was just a tapering off, and the effects were in large part transitory (early retirees would in any case have retired on a pension). Given its cost, the key measure—early resignations—was revoked in January 1984. Thus, in metropolitan France, the number of unemployed (in the ILO sense) went from 1.7 million in the last quarter of 1982 to 2.2 million in the first quarter of 1986 (on the eve of the legislative elections)—including more than 800,000 young people (for them, an unemployment rate of more than 20%). The Phillips curve for the relation between inflation and unemployment moved inexorably to the right.

• • •

While the active working population had been reduced, by a policy sustained by all French governments since the emergence of mass unemployment, the economy was consistently incapable of creating a higher volume of employment. According to the national accounts (based on 2000), France offered 21.6 million jobs in 1973 and 21.9 million in 1986. Jobs outside the public sector actually *declined*, due to the crumbling of the manufacturing industries, which had lost 2 million jobs in thirteen years.

A DISAPPOINTING ASSESSMENT, BUT NEW WORKERS' RIGHTS

Misdirected from the start by the totally erroneous diagnostics from economic experts, the majority Left had not been able to do better than Giscard's seven-year mandate on the employment and unemployment fronts, although they had partially adopted the recipes promoted by Chirac and Barre. On the macroeconomic plane, the economic balance sheet of the Socialist legislature appeared quite mixed. Growth was sluggish but positive, able to avoid in 1982 the recession observed in the United States, Germany, the United Kingdom, and Italy. Inflation was in check (as in most of the major industrialized countries). The insertion of young workers was heavily hampered by chronic job insecurity, most affecting the least qualified; but a new educational effort was launched. A redeployment of the productive fabric was underway.

Public debt (in the Maastricht sense) grew from 21% of GDP in 1980 to 31% in 1986, which was still quite moderate (by way of comparison, it reached 90% of GDP at the end of 2012, compared to 68% in 2008). In 1986 the state held major shares in banking and industry, sectors that it was able to restructure, thereby opening the way to the godsend of future privatizations in a France converted to financial liberalism (without any true policy debate). In total, the net state debt at the time in France was the lowest of major industrialized countries.[19]

However, the heritage of the Left was notable on the social plane. The years 1981–1983 bequeathed an improvement in welfare benefits, and concomitantly higher public expenditures and contributions. In total, welfare benefits and other social transfers, which had stabilized after the strong hike of 2% of GDP under the first Chirac government, grew again by 3% of GDP from 1980 to 1985 to reach 22%, a level that would be maintained until the Great Recession (it was 23% of GDP in 2008). Within the business world, the Auroux laws of 1982 profoundly modernized social and industrial relations.

On the policy plane, the Left found itself transformed by the exercise of power. Henceforth, in the Socialist Party, "good management" became a leitmotiv: each expense would have to find its financing, and any ambitious policy would have to be microeconomically neutral for the sake of commercial competitiveness.

NOTES

1. See for example Thomas J. Sargent and Neil Wallace, "Rational Expectations and the Theory of Economic Policy," *Journal of Monetary Economics* 2 (1976): 169–84.

2. Finn E. Kydland and Edward C. Prescott, "Rules Rather Than Discretion: The Inconsistency of Optimal Plans," *Journal of Political Economy* 85 (1977): 473–92.

3. Higher prices for products imported into France, notably energy, induced additional inflation in France: this was "imported inflation."

4. In a short note dated March 18, 1981 (assigned no reference number in the archive), a few weeks before the presidential election, the Direction de la prévision sketched "a first diagnosis of the job policies that could be envisaged": "1. Job creation necessarily requires revival of business[,] revival of housing[,] creation of public or para-public jobs[, and] use of new energy sources .... 2. Growth that is richer in employment ... would almost necessarily mean a reform of the division of social security contributions .... 3. A lowering of the duration of working time." It is striking to find in this memo a series of key ideas for the French governments of the following three decades.

5. Alain Fonteneau, "Les erreurs de prévisions économiques pour 1982," *Observations et Diagnostics Economiques, Revue de l'OFCE* 4 (June 1983): 81–97.

6. Jean-Paul Fitoussi and Edmund S. Phelps, "Politique économique aux États-Unis et croissance du chômage en Europe," *Revue de l'OFCE* 18 (January 1987): 123–47.

7. See for example the editorial by Claude Douillard, president of the fiscal commission of the CNPF (the main organization of employers), "Moins de chômage et d'inflation?", *Le Monde*, May 26, 1983.

8. Henri Sterdyniak and Pierre Villa, "Faut-il substituer de la TVA aux cotisations sociales des employeurs?" *Revue de l'OFCE* 6, (1984): 93–101.

9. Henri de Castries, *Les possibilités et les conséquences d'un changement d'assiette des cotisations patronales de Sécurité sociale,* Inspection Générale des Finances, February 1982.

10. *Les droits des travailleurs,* report to the president of the republic and the prime minister (September 1981).

11. Law no. 82–689 of August 4, 1982 ("Law Auroux"). Laws passed in the next decades extended the antidiscrimination to genetic background, ethnicity, sexual preferences, name, physical characteristics, gender, age, and family status.

12. Banking disintermediation is the dismantling of the privilege conferred on credit establishments solely to receive deposits and transform them into credits.

13. Marianne Bertrand, Antoinette Schoar, and David Thesmar, "Banking Deregulation and Industry Structure: Evidence from the 1985 Banking Act," *Journal of Finance* 62, no. 2 (2007), 597–628.

14. Nicole Coëffic, "Les jeunes à la sortie de l'école: poids du chômage et risques de déclassement," *Economie et statistique* 193, no. 1 (1986).

15. "Activité et les Conditions d'Emploi de la Main-d'Oeuvre," a study run by the French Ministry of Labor.

16. Bruno Crépon and Francis Kramarz, "Employed 40 Hours or Not-Employed 39: Lessons from the 1982 Mandatory Reduction of the Workweek," *Journal of Political Economy* 110, no. 6 (2002), 1355–89.

17. These *ex post* facts are consistent with the monographs that the state had ordered from the Centre for Scientific Management in the Ecole des Mines to check its macroeconomic models. See the memo from the Forecasting Office, "Réduction de la durée du travail: un essai de synthèse entre l'approche macroéconomique et l'observation des entreprises," September 9, 1981.

18. To which could be added the many existing possibilities for retirement at age 60: manual workers who had contributed for 41 years; working women who were heads of households with three children and had contributed for 30 years; women who had paid in for 37.5 years; military veterans; deportees; those unfit for work; etc.

19. The net debt at the end of 1985 represented 17% of the French GDP, compared to 22% in Germany, 26% in Japan, 27% in the United States, 31% in Canada, 47% in the United Kingdom, and 96% in Italy. Nuriel Roubini and Jeremy Sachs, "Political and Economic Determinants of Budget Deficits in the Industrial Democracies," *European Economic Review* 33 (1989): 903–38.

CHAPTER FOUR

1986–1993

From Hard to Soft Economic Liberalism

The failure of the Socialist government to control French capitalism, followed by the turn to rigor, would liberate the field for new ideas. Economic liberalism would flood into this vacuum. It triumphed with the re-election of Margaret Thatcher in Great Britain, and of Ronald Reagan in the United States, and the victory of the liberal–conservative coalition of Helmut Kohl in Germany. The liberal wave that struck France occurred in two phases. During the first one, a Right converted to hard liberalism came to power; the second wave confirmed the Left's abandonment of the economy to the market(s). This double wave coincided with a worldwide recovery marked by a return of sustained growth that was extinguished at the start of the last decade of the century. But unfortunately this favorable environment was not used to build a long-term growth strategy for France—in stark contrast to the concurrent diplomatic French activism in favor of reinforcing the European Union and initiating full integration of the new Europe following the fall of the Berlin Wall.

Let us begin with the parenthesis of the first *cohabitation*—a term that refers to the coexistence of a president and a National Assembly of opposite political persuasions—under the Fifth French Republic. The Republican Right was opposed in 1986's legislative elections by the seriousness and modernity embodied on the left that year by Laurent Fabius, and it was also facing the rise of the extreme-right National Front. The Republican Right coalition—especially the RPR (Rassemblement pour la République, part-heir of Gaullism)—swept the legislative elections with a program of drastic change: a shift to economic liberalism that adopted the ideas of those French bosses who were fascinated by the Conservative revolution in Great Britain. This shift was associated with drastic anti-immigration.

Despite this defeat in the National Assembly, President Mitterrand did not resign, and he still had two years to prepare for the next presidential election. The slim majority obtained by the Right coalition carried to Matignon Palace (the prime minister's residence) a new Jacques Chirac. He was no longer the man of 1974 who had favored increasing social benefits. New times, new fashions.

EURO-SCLEROSIS AND HYSTERESIS

However, on a strictly economic level, the British "model" was not particularly flourishing in 1986. The United Kingdom had the worst unemployment rate of the major industrialized countries. As in other European countries, unemployment had not stopped growing—though in the United States since 1983 it had begun to decline sharply. Whether a European country executed a liberal purge, or cut budgets severely, or developed subsidized job programs, they all seemed to be experiencing the same malady, which at the time was dubbed "Euro-sclerosis."

For several years, a microeconomics of labor had been emerging on both sides of the Atlantic, pioneered by a new generation of economists. It deeply challenged the view that the labor market was similar to a product market. In fact, labor is characterized by very particular mechanisms. Two American economists, Shapiro and Stiglitz (who would receive the Nobel Prize in 2001), introduced in 1984 the "shirker" or "efficiency wages" model. Firms cannot perfectly observe the effort of everyone, so they offer higher salaries to ensure the investment of all employees, and to retain those who are truly invested in their work. This tends to push salaries to a level that creates involuntary unemployment. The organization of work technologies can thus influence structural (or non-inflationary) unemployment.

Cypriot-Briton Christopher Pissarides (recipient of the Nobel Prize in 2010) theorized unemployment as the result of flows of job destruction and creation. The key element lay in the encounters—the "matching"—between employers and employees, in which case the level of unemployment would depend on many parameters of how the matching (or mismatching) worked out. Better matching would enable reducing equilibrium unemployment; this would require policies like an effective employment bureau but also a government's being able to apply sanctions to the unemployed who refuse appropriate job offers or who do not actively search for a job. Both aesthetically pleasing and flexible, this model has since become dominant in the formalization of the labor market, inasmuch as it enables (under certain conditions) generating empirical graphs like the Phillips and Beveridge curves.

But to explain Euro-sclerosis, the "insider-outsider" approach has proved the better candidate. Developed by a Swedish economist, Lindbeck, and an American, Snower, but also by the British duo of Layard and Nickell, it relies on the fact that bargaining within companies—whether over salaries or over jobs—is carried out either by representatives of the company's employees or by permanent union and managerial staff. In both cases, those who negotiate are already within the company—they are *insiders.* They do not take into account the interests of *outsiders*—those who are outside the company, that is to say the unemployed (or temporary workers). Through their bargaining power (threat of a strike, for example), insiders obtain conditions superior to what the market should give; this causes or prolongs the exclusion of outsiders. This mechanism can then generate "hysteresis," a concept popularized by two economists in their thirties: American Lawrence Summers—future secretary of the treasury under Clinton and then director of the National Economic Council under Obama—and Frenchman Olivier Blanchard, a professor at MIT and chief economist at the IMF since 2008.[1]

The idea of hysteresis is borrowed from physics and postulates that an unfavorable macroeconomic shock or a bad policy can have durable and quasi-irreversible effects. Even if the economy takes off again or if the policy is corrected, insiders are going to try to reap the gains of the new situation, to the detriment of a return to work by outsiders. This is what seems to have happened in Great Britain. Despite the weakening of trade unions and despite very high unemployment, firms continued to offer increasing salaries.[2] The extreme weakness of unions in the United States, and correlatively the preponderance of individual negotiations between employee and employer, was thought to produce a much more "pure and perfect" functioning of the labor market—and hence salary adjustments working in favor of employment. However, the drop in unemployment in the United States correlated with an erosion of workers' real salaries.

If the hysteresis model of salary inflation also fit the United Kingdom case, then ought it not to result in a drop in unemployment in France, like the one observed in the United States? In fact, the deindexing of wages launched by Fabius marked the end of a model of negotiation that had prevailed since the turn to rigor. Yet unemployment did not recede in France.

A better model would have to take into account the various institutional environments. Hysteresis presents many variations that offer alternative explanatory frameworks. Thus, if policy mistakes are not rapidly corrected, with a sluggish work market and only moderate creation and destruction of firms, then a long-term unemployment situation arises: those out of work for a long time lose human capital, which makes them unemployable—unless they are willing to take a sharp pay cut. This mechanism seems relevant in the European case, especially for France. In fact, European countries commonly have a very high level of long-term unemployment (12 months or more). The contrast with figures for the United States in 1986 was impressive (table 5). Thus, prescriptions to bring European unemployment back to the American level seemed clear: on the one hand, the government should help those excluded from the labor market (with financial aid, and help in returning to employment), and on the other, it should reduce the power of the insiders.

Through the multinational character of research on the labor market, the hysteresis and insider-outsider theories enjoyed rapid dissemination within OECD countries' economic departments. They would lead to specific policy efforts to reach the excluded. But starting in 1987, the unemployment rate dimin-

TABLE 5

Unemployment rate and the proportion of long-term unemployed in the major industrialized countries in 1983 and 1986 (all figures in percent)

	1983		1986	
	Unemployment	*Share of long-term*	*Unemployment*	*Share of long-term*
France	7.1	41	9.1	47
West Germany	8.2	42	8.8	48
Italy	7.4	58	8.9	67
UK	10.8	47	11.2	48
Japan	2.7	13	2.8	17
US	9.6	13	7.0	9

SOURCES: OECD StatExtracts, unemployment by duration statistics, and harmonized unemployment rate (except for Germany); ILO LABORSTA, unemployment rate (Labour Force Survey) for Germany.

ished sharply in the United Kingdom, then in Germany, and then in 1988, in France and in most European countries. Hysteresis seemed to be vanquished. In reality, it would come back in force after 1991, with surging unemployment right across Europe.

LIBERAL AGITATION

Arriving in power as prime minister with a slim majority and with the presidential election approaching, Jacques Chirac had only two years to carry out the liberal swerve of the French Right. This neo-liberalism adopted the Thatcher recipe. In fact, France presented similarities with the Great Britain of 1979, notably a heavy involvement of the state in the productive sphere. Even the world economic environment was favorable: the oil counter-shock mechanically propelled a growth boom of about 1% per year over two years, a boom that was sorely needed; world trade resumed sustained growth. Moreover, the restructurings of nationalized firms had been largely executed by the previous Fabius government, which left companies more competitive overall.

Chirac's key ministers in the economic and social domains were: Edouard Balladur at Finance, with Jean-Claude Trichet (future president of the European Central Bank) as permanent secretary and Christian Noyer (future governor of the Bank of France) as advisor; the very liberal Alain Madelin at Industry; and Alain Juppé at Budget, flanked by a brilliant secretary, Daniel Bouton (who would direct the second-largest French bank, the Société Générale, from 1997 to 2008). The Gaullist strand was confined to Philippe Seguin as minister of labor. The cabinet's agenda was overloaded: massive privatizations, deregulation, tax cuts, reshaping the jobs policy, and electoral reform.

The program was essentially carried out through *ordonnances*, or edicts. An edict is an executive statute passed by the Council of Ministers in an area normally reserved for laws passed by the legislature. The government first introduces a bill before authorizing itself to use *ordonnances* to implement its program; an *ordonnance* must be signed by the president of the republic. But the interpretation of the French constitution was (and still is) controversial. Must the president sign, or can he or she refuse? Under *cohabitation*, Socialist President Mitterrand took a middle path: he refused to sign three of the eleven *ordonnances*, invoking the higher principles of legality and national independence.[3]

The privatizations were executed in pursuit of a quadruple objective: to reduce the role of the state in the economy, to find the money to finance tax cuts, to develop popular shareholding, and to obtain an economic plebiscite in favor of reforms. The privatization program was particularly ambitious. Spearheading this task, first as undersecretary in charge of privatizations and then as advisor to Balladur, was Jean-Marie Messier, future CEO of Vivendi (which would buy Universal Studios before he drove his multinational to the brink of bankruptcy).

The first company concerned, in 1986, was a flagship of industry, Saint-Gobain, a multinational dating back to the seventeenth century. The movement accelerated in 1987 with massive privatizations in finance—including Paribas, Suez, Société Générale, and Mutuelle Générale Française—but also in the media—the advertising agency Havas, and the most viewed television channel in Europe, TF1. All together, the privatized companies employed almost half a million employees, or 2% of all the jobs in France. The popular success was undeniable: in a context of stock market euphoria, millions of French people bought shares; receipts from these privatizations approached 2% of GDP.

But this initial policy success soon turned into a fiasco. On the one hand, the stock market crash of the autumn of 1987 transformed what had seemed a good deal for individual investors into a nightmare. On the other hand, the constitution of "core kernels" of prime stockholders seemed to favor those closest to power[4]—as did the 1986 law on the press, which helped concentrate multimedia groups that were friendly to the government.[5]

In public opinion, this merely reinforced the sentiment that the Chirac government was actually animated by a desire for social revenge, a comeuppance for the Socialists, symbolized by the suppression of taxes on major fortunes and a fiscal amnesty on the flight of capital abroad (to tax havens), in contrast with the absence of any nudge upward of the minimum wage.

Inspired by the CNPF (the principal body of French employers), a series of "Seguin Laws" (named for the minister of labor) marked a new turning point in jobs policy. The objective was to correct the "rigidities" of the labor market, which were accused of discouraging hiring. The edict of August 1986 on "differentiated work" facilitated the use by firms of part-time workers, fixed-term contracts, and temps. On top of that, the requirement for administrative authorization of any firings (which had been created by Jacques Chirac himself in 1975) was abolished. (In fact it had been merely a formality.) The possibilities of modulating work schedules without reducing working hours were enlarged.

The Seguin Law of July 1987 consecrated apprenticeship as a path to professional training. Previously reserved for those holding a CAP (Certificat d'aptitude professionnelle, the lowest vocational diploma), apprentices could now aspire to all levels of vocational skills. The state would assume responsibility for the social security contributions of all apprentices. This had been offered to companies with less than ten employees since 1971; the scheme was now extended to all companies. While this law resulted in the emergence of vocationalism at the upper secondary school level, it was not until the 1990s that the extension boosted apprenticeship significantly.

Although the idea of a social VAT (see the preceding chapter) was not defensible at a time when inflation had just been tamed, the social insurance contributions paid by employers were lightened via two measures. Officially speaking, the goal was to sustain certain depressed regions and to make inexperienced youth whose marginal productivity was too low more employable. The exemption of firms from social security payments in return for hiring young people was reinstated and made more attractive. Companies pounced on the arrangement. In the last eight months of 1986, 400,000 young people were hired. The windfall effect was so great that as of 1987, the exemption was limited to work-study contracts. The other measure was the creation of "enterprise zones" (on the model of what had been done in the United Kingdom) in devastated areas like the former shipyards of Dunkirk, Toulon, and La Ciotat, which introduced ten-year exemptions from the social security contributions normally paid by employers.

Meanwhile, social treatment to palliate unemployment was stepped up, with a maze of provisions (a multiplicity of work placements and local initiative plans), mixed with training measures and alternating with contracts for the reintegration of the long-term unemployed. Public works projects (*travaux d'utilité collective,* TUC) were maintained. In total, over one year the number of beneficiaries of the jobs policy increased by half a million. Of course, the early retirement schemes were partially dismantled, but the "dispensation from searching for work" for those over 57 grew proportionately: recipients could get their unemployment allowance or, if they reached the end of that, a "specific allocation of solidarity," without having to prove they were actively seeking work.

This policy was not without effect on the employment of young people. The number of jobless youth, which had already shrunk by 130,000 between the third quarter of 1984 and the second quarter of 1986 under the effect of the public works projects, fell another 110,000, bringing the youth unemployment rate below 18% in the first quarter of 1988, on the eve of the presidential elections. But the precariousness of the road back to employment for youth remained, and most of the assistance measures actually contributed to it. Moreover, the situation of unemployed youth contrasted with those over 25: in two years they went from 1.4 million to 1.6 million. Overall, the government could not get unemployment to decline.

Job creation remained insufficient. After years of stagnation, salaried employment grew cautiously between the second quarter of 1986 and the first quarter of 1988, by 350,000 positions. The restructuring phase of the manufacturing industry initiated under Laurent Fabius slowed down. Employment increased in most of the service sectors. In the wake of the educational democratization plan, personnel working in education increased. The revival of worldwide tourism benefited the hotel and restaurant sectors. Above all, business services gained almost 200,000 positions, boosted by the spurt in temporary jobs and in computing services. In fact, the use of information technologies began to extend beyond industry, into pharmacy, metallurgy, automobiles, chemistry, and so on.

THE LACK OF AN INDUSTRIAL GOAL

However, unlike Thatcherite liberalism, which was accompanied by the construction of a powerful financial industry, the Chirac government, though claiming to be inspired by British principles, did not have a clear plan for production. The fragility of French manufacturing industry was being accentuated, while the new industrialized countries of Asia, the so-called "dragons," were assuming a growing place in world trade. French exports grew very little, producing a significant foreign trade deficit. Despite energy expenditures' being reduced by more than half (120 billion francs) between 1985 and 1987, the trade deficit, weighed down by consumer goods, widened by almost 40 billion francs.

At the same time, the growth of hourly work productivity slipped. Still at 2.3% in 1986, its annual rate dropped to 0.9% in 1987, below that of 1.2% in 1975, in the midst of the recession (and then, too, under Chirac). In fact, this was the lowest level since the Liberation in 1945. In consumer goods industries, it fell over two consecutive years (–0.4% in 1986, –2.4% in 1987). Nor did the gap in research and development efforts as compared to the foremost three world economies decrease even slightly.

On the public finance level, the income from privatizations and the moderate return of growth did not suffice to restore a balanced budget. Reductions in taxes and employer contributions eroded the budget. According to the current (so-called Maastricht) criteria, the budget deficit exceeded 3% of GDP in 1986. The rigor of Barre no longer figured on the agenda of a liberal Right that did not balk at a deficit—as long as it enabled the transformation of economic and social structures. A few years after the Left, it was now the ideological guideposts of the Right that were in turn profoundly and lastingly changed.

Agitation was extended to education with the "Devaquet Law," which tried to make universities independent of the state, especially in how they selected students, provoking demonstrations that were aggravated by the president of the republic, and ending with the abandonment of the project. The immigration policy of interior minister Charles Pasqua (symbolized by his loading charter planes to expel immigrants from Mali) shocked public opinion, although it also boosted the government's zero-immigration policy. The tragic events in New Caledonia would ultimately reveal Jacques Chirac as the candidate of the hard Right.[6]

THE ECONOMIC IMMOBILITY OF ROCARD

In the 1988 presidential ballot, the newly centrist discourse of François Mitterrand assured him a comfortable reelection. The legislative elections that followed gave only a relative majority to the Socialist Party in the National Assembly, but they seemed to call for a quieter political program. Michel Rocard, who for ten years had cultivated his image as the pivot of the center-left, became prime minister and enrolled several ministers from the center-right, while Pierre Bérégovoy, returning to Finance, incarnated rigor. This was "openness": in effect, an openness of the Left to Barre's economic policy.

The economic prospects were good. On the international level, the 1987 crash had been left behind, and American monetary policy had avoided an extension of the crisis to the real economy. Both the ebb of unemployment and the advance of world trade continued. On the domestic level, firms had recovered significant margins of maneuver, thanks to salary austerity, and were finally reaping dividends from their efforts at research and development.

This upturn translated into growth that exceeded 4% at an annual pace in 1988 and 1989. From the second quarter of 1988 to the first quarter of 1991 (on the eve of the firing of Rocard), France created 850,000 jobs. The majority were in the private sector, notably in business and personal services. The decline in manufacturing employment was halted, stabilizing at around 4 million; it even rose, if one included the temporary workers in industry, who were categorized in company accounts as business services. Consequently, unemployment ebbed. In metropolitan France, the rate went from 8.9% to 8% between the second quarter of 1988 and the first quarter of 1991. But the new government continued to foster stagnation in the buying power of salaried workers, especially those at the low end of the scale.

While economic policy did break with the preceding seven-year mandate, it also appeared totally consistent with the Barrist policy of the 1970s. Privatizations were frozen. A plan to modernize school and university buildings (Université 2000), including construction of 3.5 million square meters of new premises, was raised in priority. Still, this expansion would prove insufficient, as long as the effort to democratize school and university education was being pursued at the same time. The creation of a vocational baccalaureate in 1985 produced its first graduates. But it is the old general "*bac*" that principally explains why the total number of those earning the exam-based diploma went from 250,000 in 1985 to 300,000 in 1988, then to 400,000 in 1991. The acceleration was spectacular. In only six years, 150,000 additional *bacs* were being awarded every year, as compared to the seventeen years from 1968 to 1985, when only 80,000 had been awarded each year. Now almost half a generation was holding a *bac* diploma. But, paradoxically, this revolution was not accompanied by any significant reform of structures or teaching methods.

The jobs policy of the exiting majority was also maintained overall. The restrictions on immigration remained. "France cannot receive all the misery of the world," declared the prime minister, adding "but we should do our part to remedy it." Exemptions for social security contributions were prolonged for the hiring of young people or the long-term unemployed; they were even strengthened in 1991 with the "exo-youth" program, reserved for the underqualified. But these programs were being merely tinkered with and rationalized. The TUCs (public works) and PILs (local initiatives) were merged into a single measure, called the *contrat emplois solidarité* (CES). Now the effect of specific measures aimed at young people had reached saturation. At the start of 1990, the youth unemployment rate started to rise again. This rise in the ratio of the number of unemployed youth to the number of active youth was due not to a rise in the numerator (which continued to decline) but to a drop in the proportion of young people participating in the work market. Educational democratization was playing a key role by reducing the number of potential workers under 25—they were staying in the education system longer.

Again, continuity is found in the policy on working hours. A reduction in the workweek (which had been halted during the turn to rigor) was not reactivated. France found itself running counter to many European countries, Germany especially. In fact, the technological environment was favorable to a reduction: firms on the other side of the Rhine were combining the modernization and productivity gains that resulted from information technology with a reduction in the length of the working week. Even if overall this movement does not seem to have been translated into significant job creation,[7] for workers it indeed represented social progress.

THE REVENU MINIMUM D'INSERTION

Despite the ebbing of unemployment, the proportion of long-term unemployed remained worrying, because it represented an increasing number of those out of work so long that they were no longer entitled to benefits. A significant proportion found themselves without resources, because they did not qualify for the multiple social security nets designed for target groups like the handicapped and single-parent families. In 1988, those without resources were estimated at about 300,000 persons.

It was to respond to this social emergency that the Rocard government mounted its principal social measure, the Revenu minimum d'insertion (RMI), passed almost unanimously by the

Assembly. In the United Kingdom since 1948, everybody except those working at least one-third time had been entitled to benefits. In Germany, the federal law on social aid of 1962 had established subsistence aid guaranteed to any resident who did not have sufficient resources to attain a minimal socio-cultural standard of living. This principle was now adopted in France, whose minimum-income allocation varied according to the composition of the household and the number of dependent persons. The RMI was a differential allocation (meaning subsidiary to other sources of revenue or allocations; for example, it diminished if the person was already receiving housing benefits, in proportion to this other aid). The monthly amount of the RMI allocation per recipient was fixed in December 1988 at 2,000 francs (about 470 euros at 2013 rates) for a single person in metropolitan France, that is to say, about the same level as the German allocation. However, it was reserved for those over 25. Below that age, the state was counting on family solidarity to cover young people. The amount was revised each year as a function of the price index. Until it was replaced by the Revenu de solidarité active (RSA) in 2009, the indexing of the RMI to prices alone would imply its gradual decline in relation to wages. However, this arrangement would undergo a series of modifications favorable to persons leaving unemployment. In particular, in the event of resuming paid work, the RMI might be paid concurrently for a while with the income from paid activity or remunerated training. Again, those under 25 remained excluded (with rare exceptions) from the RMI/RSA, making France (with Spain and Luxembourg) one of the rare countries in the OECD not to provide any social security net for young people.

The RMI also included an "insertion" provision. The minimum revenue was a tool for struggling against "exclusion" (especially of unemployed people no longer eligible for insurance), consistent with anti-hysteresis prescriptions. Beneficiaries were supposed to be monitored. But the breadth of poverty in France (and hence the number of potential beneficiaries) had been seriously underestimated. Upon its introduction, almost a million people claimed RMI benefits. Faced with this massive demand, the new measures of insertion would never be implemented, conveying the idea that "insertion" had been simply assistance. A tax on fortunes was reestablished to pay for the scheme; it was now called a "solidarity tax" on the wealthy. But it was insufficient, given the number of RMI recipients.

Meanwhile, the world economic environment was becoming much more uncertain. The effect on the European economies of the sudden German reunification was difficult to measure. (It still is!) On the one hand, it was part of an enormous revival in Germany, with huge transfers to the East; it favored the exports of its European partners, and hence their economic activities. On the other hand, through monetary parity, it required tougher interest rates to avoid a resurgence of inflation, a tension that hampered the internal growth of Germany's partners.

The American economy, in continuous growth since the end of 1982, experienced a classic end to an economic cycle and entered into recession at the start of 1991. At the same moment, Western countries were bearing the cost of their involvement in the first Persian Gulf War and the consequently rising price of oil.

"ENRICHMENT" OF GROWTH

French growth slowed. Though it was still at a good level (2.6%) in 1990, from the beginning of 1991, France entered into a phase of sluggish growth, amounting to between 1% and 2% in 1991 and 1992. This proved insufficient to counter unemployment, which resumed its advance in the first quarter of 1991.

Meanwhile, the Socialist government was suffering from its internal dissensions as much as from the political and financial scandals that marked this period. François Mitterrand would try to recover politically by appointing Edith Cresson as the first female prime minister. But she brought no social project of any scope, confining herself to advocating rigor. Very unpopular, she was replaced after less than a year by Pierre Bérégovoy.

Despite this instability, Dominique Strauss-Kahn was summoned to Industry in the Cresson government and was confirmed. A professor of economics, then junior commissioner for planning, elected deputy in 1986, then becoming president of the National Assembly's Finance Committee, he possessed strong credibility. The same was true of Martine Aubry (daughter of Jacques Delors), who became minister for labor and employment. A former director-general of labor—the highest administrator in the labor ministry—from 1984 to 1987 under both Socialist and Right governments, at the time she was junior director of Pechiney, the French aluminum giant.

Business leaders of course warmly welcomed the arrival of these two, Strauss-Kahn and Aubry. On the work and industry side, moreover, certain positions of the French government were close to those of industrial lobbies. The most striking concerned the use of asbestos. France would continue to advocate its "controlled use." Thus, it would firmly oppose Germany on the banning of asbestos at the European level. Armed with scientific evidence, a coalition of Germany, the Netherlands, Italy, and Denmark were in favor of a total ban and obtained a draft directive to this effect from the Office of Industrial Affairs of the European Commission. But France, at the time the principal

European user of asbestos (four times as much as Germany or Great Britain), blocked the directive. Disputing the idea that the harmfulness of asbestos had been demonstrated in "controlled use," the French authorities organized stalling maneuvers, calling on the World Health Organization for an evaluation of risks tied to asbestos, without which France said no decision to ban it was warranted. Though it managed to block the European process, France could not prevent Germany or Italy from prohibiting asbestos on their territories in 1993. It would take four more years and an "asbestos scandal" for France to finally ban this substance that was responsible for tens of thousands of national deaths.

Likewise, the jobs policy and the struggle against unemployment did not encounter hostility from employers. Despite Rocard's establishment of the Contribution sociale généralisée (CSG)[8] to finance social protection, the budgetary situation of social security was fragile. The branch of social security charged with paying unemployment compensation was profoundly affected by the rising unemployment, and so contributions from both employees and employers were increased. Above all, the various allocations were merged into a single sliding-scale allocation. The allocations of former workers with low salaries when they were in unemployment were significantly lowered when they went beyond nine months out of work. But the construction of a single regime had the result of spectacularly increasing the aid to those out of work for a long time, and of former workers with high salaries; for example, after fifteen months of unemployment, a manager whose monthly reference salary was 26,000 francs (about 5,000 Euros at 2013 rates) received an allocation of 10,000 francs—compared to slightly more than 2,000 francs under the previous measures. The advantage was such that it resulted in a drop in the resumption of work among the most qualified.[9] France is still distinguished today by the generosity of its system of compensation for former high-wage earners.

Another anti-redistributive policy put into place by Aubry in 1992 was a tax reduction for jobs involving working at home (childcare, housekeeping, gardening). Taxpayers benefited from a tax reduction on income equal to half of their salaries and contributions. This measure did have true success. Such home-based jobs abruptly shot up by more than 100,000. It is impossible to know whether this was due to actual job creation or to a reduction in undeclared work. Whatever the case, this measure was costly, and the most comfortable households in France profited from it the most. As of 2013 this measure was still in place.

Fundamentally, this policy edifice was based on a new view of what a jobs policy was for. Since the state had given up influencing economic growth, which was not expected ever to return for any length of time to its levels during the *trente glorieuses* (thirty years of prosperity), the government had to "enrich growth": to reach the same level of growth, just create more jobs.

One of the most promising avenues was the development of part-time work. European countries that had been able to profit in terms of employment from the economic dynamism of the second half of the 1980s were places like the Netherlands, where part-time work—especially by women—had developed considerably. While only a quarter of French women were working part-time in 1992, 45% of British women were, and more than 60% in the Netherlands. Two non-exclusive interpretations vie with each other to explain such differences: a significant slide to jobs that have to be stimulated by making them "solvent," and the differences between countries that arise mainly from cultural factors. The former interpretation is based on the fact that part-timers can be less attractive for business when the fixed costs of hiring and managing an employee are taken into account. The second interpretation—though in this domain the comparative studies are unreliable—is that part-time work is almost exclusively chosen in the countries of Northern Europe, while (despite low relative take-up) a high proportion of part-time workers in Latin countries would wish to work more hours. If the first interpretation pertained, then France could gain many jobs through a policy favoring part-time work. But the second interpretation would imply an increase in involuntary part-time work.

The government chose the first interpretation. The idea was not new, however. A decree of June 1984 had instituted aid for hiring a person under an open-ended contract who would be working between 28 and 32 hours a week. In 1986, the aid was reduced by half but extended to those working more than 16 hours a week. Little utilized, these arrangements were dropped in 1987. The assistance in a shift to part-time employment that was created in September 1989 did not inspire optimism, either. In 1990, only 168 employees took advantage of the scheme; in 1992, despite the turnaround in the labor market, the number was still only 1,169.

Aubry did change gears by introducing a standard deduction of 30% on employer social security contributions for hiring (or transforming a worker's job to) part-time; this corresponded to a drop of about 10% in labor costs. This measure would be revisited by subsequent governments (changed to a 50% deduction under Balladur, then back to 30%) before being eliminated in 2000 by the same Minister Aubry.

At first, this policy was a success: 100,000 persons entered into the arrangement in 1993, and they reached 400,000 in 1997. Within Europe, it was in France that the proportion of part-timers increased most rapidly during this period. Traditionally feminine occupations were particularly affected, with a quarter of such employees involved; in 1995, more than half of cashiers were working part-time. The case of retail distribution illustrates the long-term microeconomic impact of jobs policy measures. The number of peak hours in distribution is on the order of 25 hours a week, equivalent to part-time. But the flow of customers remains highly variable. Simplifying things, two models are offered to companies: either keep the current full-time employees, whose duties may sometimes be light; or manage (which is costly at best) part-time personnel according to the client flow (e.g. variable scheduling from one week to the next, or even one day to the next, with the ability to recall employees if needed, and so on). The Aubry scheme pushed firms to choose the second model, which could not lead to an overall increase in the volume of work-hours offered. This model is still dominant today, notably in large retail stores, despite the elimination in 2000 of the advantages linked to part-time personnel. In total, in full-time equivalent, according to the 2000 national accounts, employment in retail commerce did not grow at all: it was 1.229 million in 1997, compared to 1.230 million in 1991.

This mechanism is not confined to trade. It leads to a net increase in the proportion of part-time workers who declare themselves to be *under*-employed, meaning they wish to accede to full-time employment; and this figure reached almost 40% in 1997. The shift from part-time to full-time work also drastically slowed: while 20% of part-time workers in 1990 went to work full-time in 1991, this proportion dropped year by year, falling below 14% in 1997. Thus, the policy of enriching employment by encouraging part-time work contributed to increasing the number of poor workers in France.

"WE HAVE TRIED EVERYTHING."

In general, this legislature confirmed the ideological swerving of the Socialists between a Rocardism that was centrist and management-oriented and a Mitterrandism muted by technocrats without any clear ideology. While accepting a neoliberal market economy, the Socialists refused to offer any policy to change economic structures or welfare provisions. The Maastricht Treaty that instituted the European Union and had been pushed forward by François Mitterrand convinced a significant share of the electorate of the Left that the Socialists were abandoning themselves to European economic liberalism. Their disaffection would bring long-lasting sanctions on the Socialist Left during the 1993 legislative elections. Above all, the growth phase at the end of the 1980s had not been exploited to put in place any dynamic policy or to alleviate the job precariousness of young people in the labor market.

The approach of the 1993 elections, the cost of the employment policies, and the conjuncture all forced the Bérégovoy government to abandon budgetary rigor. The budget deficit reached 4.5% of GDP in 1992. In the end, the economic defeatism of the Mitterrand era was unambiguously affirmed during an interview the president of the republic gave on July 14, 1993. With respect to unemployment, he admitted, "We have tried everything.... Neither you nor I can do anything about it." Thus did the Left confess its tragic powerlessness.

NOTES

1. Olivier Blanchard and Laurence Summers, "Hysteresis and the European Unemployment Problem," *NBER Macroeconomics Annual* 1 (1986): 15–90.

2. Stephen Nickell, "Why Is Wage Inflation in Britain So High?" *Oxford Bulletin of Economics & Statistics* 49, no. 1 (1987): 103–28.

3. E.g. Mitterrand refused to sign an edict modifying the electoral map of deputies' districts, arguing that "the republican tradition states that the National Assembly should itself determine how deputies are elected."

4. To ensure some stability among shareholders, the government sold a portion of the capital to French firms that it selected under its own discretion.

5. Notably, it eliminated the Commission for the Transparency and Plurality of the Press, which had been precisely charged with controlling trusts in this sector.

6. After the taking of gendarmes as hostages by the Kanak independence movement on the island of Ouvéa (in the overseas territory of New Caledonia), Jacques Chirac (without informing François Mitterrand) ordered an assault that ended in the deaths of nineteen fighters for independence.

7. Jennifer Hunt, "Has Work-Sharing Worked in Germany?" *Quarterly Journal of Economics* 114, no. 1 (1999): 117–48.

8. The CSG is a "flat tax." It is assessed on almost all revenues of persons residing in France. Its rate was regularly increased. The amount levied is now much higher than that of the income tax.

9. Brigitte Dormont, Denis Fougère, and Ana Prieto, "L'effet de l'allocation unique dégressive sur la reprise d'emploi," *Economie et Statistique* 343 (2001): 3–28.

CHAPTER FIVE

1993–2002

"New" Effective Policies?

A few days after François Mitterrand's "we have tried everything" (chapter 4), the right-leaning government of Edouard Balladur inaugurated a new employment policy. It relied essentially on lowering the cost of labor to the neighborhood of the minimum wage. The election of Jacques Chirac in 1995 would accelerate this process. Then, as if to contradict the deceased president (Mitterrand would die in January 1996), the left-leaning government of Lionel Jospin, winner of the 1997 Assembly elections, added a sort of return to the original Mitterrandism by applying an ambitious reduction in working time, coupled with a series of innovative provisions. During this period France would enjoy remarkable job creation, offering hope for the end of mass unemployment, in the context of a euphoric international environment. But this splendid period was also one of France's relative technological decline and of a choice in favor of unskilled labor, while the major countries of the OECD were concentrating on the knowledge economy. Thus, France bequeathed to the decade of the 2000s both hopes and sources of disillusionment.

EXPERTS FOR A NEW JOBS POLICY

At the start of the 1990s, the OECD launched a vast study and a wide consultation of economists designed to construct a diagnosis and strategy for employment on the model of the Washington Consensus, defined at the end of the 1980s.[1] The OECD Jobs Study[2] would be published in 1994, but its findings were known in 1993. This approach was adopted in France by the Commissariat Général au Plan.

The OECD's reasoning rested on a "transatlantic consensus." The United States and Europe were experiencing the same type of shock: globalization and technological revolution. Both of these tended to reduce the relative demand for unskilled workers and above all to favor the highly qualified; their skills were necessary and rare in the new division of worldwide trade, as well as complementary to the new information technologies. A growing literature showed that these two factors were contributing to a clear rise in income inequality in the United States in the 1980s and early 1990s. It was thought that in Europe the "rigidities" of the labor market had prevented this natural process and had transformed wage inequality into inequality of access to employment. Moreover, these rigidities had an effect of hysteresis[3] on the labor market, which could only be reversed by a coordinated strategy. Here again we find the mechanisms stressed by economic research initiated in the 1980s.

Different rigidities were blamed in one country or another: a generous system of unemployment insurance, which discouraged returning to employment; a minimum wage, which prevented a downward adjustment of remunerations; job protection, which dissuaded employers from hiring; and so on.

This framework for interpretation was consistent with the facts as of 1990–1992. Most of the European countries (even, or especially, Scandinavia) had higher unemployment than that of the United States; everywhere, the least qualified workers and often the young were most affected. The crisis of 1993 lent credence to this interpretation. The unemployment rate was near or above 10% in many European countries—10% in Sweden, 11% in Denmark, with a peak of 16% in a Finland that was affected by the collapse of the USSR—while it was below 7% in North America.

Based on this diagnosis, empirically supported by numerous correlations, the OECD's Jobs Strategy[4] (the simplified version of 1996) advocated that countries:

- Set macroeconomic policy such that it both encouraged growth and, in conjunction with good structural policies, made it sustainable (that is, non-inflationary)
- Enhance the creation and diffusion of technological know-how by improving frameworks for its development
- Increase flexibility of working-time (both short-term and lifetime) voluntarily sought by workers and employers
- Nurture an entrepreneurial climate by eliminating impediments to and restrictions on the creation and expansion of companies
- Make wage and labor costs more flexible by removing restrictions that prevent wages from reflecting local conditions and individual skill levels, in particular those of younger workers
- Reform employment security provisions that inhibit the expansion of employment in the private sector
- Strengthen the emphasis on active labor-market policies and reinforce their effectiveness

- Improve labor-force skills and competences through wide-ranging changes in education and training systems
- Reform unemployment and related benefit systems—and their interaction with the tax system—such that a society's fundamental equity goals are achieved in ways that impinge far less on the efficient functioning of labor markets.

Thus, like the Washington Consensus for developing economies, the transatlantic consensus prescribed deregulation, but now for developed economies.

For France, the diagnosis concentrated on the cost of labor. The strong hourly productivity of labor in the Hexagon (metropolitan France) appeared as the corollary of this cost. Companies could only employ workers who were sufficiently productive, which excluded a significant portion of the available manpower. The relative weakness of personnel (in relation to the OECD average) in work-intensive sectors like trade or food services was seen as an illustration of this problem. The associated unemployment was thought to impose social expenditure (financed by social contributions) that would, in turn, accentuate the cost of labor.

Thus, growth in job creation had to go beyond developing job pools or targeted interventions and instead aim at a general cut in the cost of labor. Simulations of such a policy by economic institutions were promising. Qualitative studies pointed in the same direction; in particular, the leaders of small and medium-sized businesses saw in the lowering of labor costs an eventual lever for hiring in their firms.[5]

In January 1993, a few months before the elections, the experts almost unanimously pronounced in favor of lowering social security contributions. A report, *Choisir l'emploi* (Choosing Employment),[6] was prepared by two groups of the Commissariat Général au Plan: the "jobs" group and the "macroeconomic prospects" group. The backgrounds of their respective presidents summarized the exercise's revival strategy. Bernard Brunhes was a former advisor to Pierre Mauroy who had become a consultant in human resources, and Jean-Michel Charpin was a former director of the office of the state secretary of planning in 1983–84 and had become the director of economic studies at the Banque Nationale de Paris. This offensive would bear fruit.

BALLADUR AND JUPPÉ: ECONOMIC LIBERALISM, "EXPERTOCRACY," AND VOTE-CATCHING

In the legislative elections of 1993, France acquired a new majority. Splits within the Socialist Party and the ideological morass into which it had sunk allowed the RPR (Rassemblement pour la République, claiming the heritage of Gaullism) and the UDF (Union pour la démocratie française, a union of center-right parties) to form the biggest majority under the Fifth Republic. François Mitterrand decided (as in 1986) to remain president; this would be the second *cohabitation* between a president and a prime minister of opposite political parties. To concentrate on preparing for the presidential election of 1995, and with his fingers burnt by his *cohabitation* with François Mitterrand in 1986–88, Chirac pushed Edouard Balladur, his former minister of the economy, into the post of prime minister. The latter built a team with a strong centrist component, but the economic policy would indeed be neoliberal. In fact, the centrist minister of the economy, Edmond Alphandéry, was flanked by the powerful liberal Alain Madelin, minister for business and economic development; and the rising star of the RPR, Nicolas Sarkozy, became a budget minister who was also the government's spokesman, to which he would add (after July 1994) the portfolio of minister of communication. Work and employment were in the hands of Michel Giraud of the RPR.

The Balladur government realized the urgency for employment in July 1993. And its beacon measure was none other than the general easing of the cost of labor by an exemption from contributions for the family allocation portion of social security on salaries lower than 110% of the minimum, and 50% exemption for salaries lower than 120% of the minimum. This was the start of a particularly expensive policy, and it would become even more costly under all subsequent governments.

These measures preceded by a few days the submission of an "interim" report that served as the basis for the five-year law on employment, which was supposed to enrich economic growth in job creation. On his installation, Balladur had formed a working group on the obstacles to employment in France in order to orient his policy. This commission was headed by Jean Mattéoli, then president of the Economic and Social Council (a body assembling figures from business and industry, trade unions, and associations), a former minister of labor, and promoter of Barre's last plans for employment from 1979 to 1981. The twelve other members included godfathers of French business and finance like Claude Bébéar (then CEO of the insurer AXA) and Alain Minc (advisor to many French business leaders). The influence of experts was guaranteed by the presence of Jean-Baptiste de Foucault, the plan's commissioner, and of the current doyen of French economic expertise, Edmond Malinvaud.[7]

The Mattéoli Commission's patchwork of forty recommendations[8] was in line with the jobs policy overhaul advocated by the experts. It is useful to look in detail at this report because its paradigms have nourished the French debates about jobs policy that are still taking place.

The minimum wage and social protection are at the heart of an analysis that tries to make the labor market a market like any other, in which disequilibria arise principally from prices, in this case from net wages and the total labor costs. Even if the commission recognized that the "international comparison of the cost of labor in 1992 makes France appear in an average position compared to its principal partners," it directly targeted the way in which the minimum salary was fixed. The report noted that the minimum hourly wage had doubled in real terms from 1970 to 1983[9] before it went on to stagnate. For the commission, this situation had produced a strong concentration of salaries around the minimum (notably in personal services), had compressed the salary hierarchy, and had pulled the relative salary of qualified workers downward. Overall, the minimum wage would work against the hiring of unskilled persons and would deprive the averagely qualified of a salaried career.[10]

The commission proposed eliminating the indexing of the minimum wage to the growth of the average working salary, retaining only a simple price index; this would permit gradually lowering the relative cost of unskilled labor, and an ad hoc commission suggested some possible boosts. The apostles of this overhaul of the minimum wage also suggested that it would give margins of negotiation to both bosses and union organizations. It would also strengthen unions, whose presence in the private sector had just fallen below 10% of the workforce. Finally, the commission noted that to counter an overly high cost of labor, the state was obliged to lighten the costly tax burden for measures targeted at youth or part-time work—and now also at low salaries.

On the other hand, the commission set aside the idea of a "youth SMIC" (a lower minimum wage for the young), fearing it would devalue work among them, although it did assert that there was general agreement (among experts) that the SMIC was too high for this category; it therefore preferred to argue for a "lighter" minimum salary during the first two years of a career.

As proof of the astonishing inertia of economic ideas in France, despite the major changes in the economic environment and the advances in knowledge of international economics, and even the gradual slippage of the OECD doctrine, the ensemble of elements in this diagnosis—like the Mattéoli recommendations—would find themselves cloned fifteen years later in an influential report by the Council of Economic Analysis.[11]

While waiting for the mechanical relative erosion of the minimum wage to bear "fruit," Mattéoli suggested that exemptions from social contributions paid by companies should last at least five years and extend to hourly wages between 1.0 and 1.5 of the SMIC rate. Moreover, he thought it desirable to lower the weight of employer social contributions by financing them through taxes (on consumption or on income). Nevertheless, the avenue of financing social protection through VAT and not through contributions assessed on work (still not called the "social VAT") was again set aside, as it had been ten years previously, in favor of increasing the flat tax on revenue, the Contribution sociale généralisée (CSG).

Another recommendation relating to negotiations between management and labor, the total elimination of the fixed-term contract, was replaced by a unified open-ended contract, with the option to break it during the first eighteen months. This decision claimed both to resolve problems tied to the segmentation of the labor market and to give more flexibility to firms by inducing them to hire without resorting to fixed-term contracts, which implied paying a costly bonus for "job precariousness" when they were terminated. Here, too, the principle of a unified contract would reappear ten years later through the "single contract" advocated in a series of reports; and facility in breaking them would recur at the heart of the policy of the Villepin government, twelve years later (see the next chapter).

The final essential part of the Mattéoli report was a reduction in the duration of work to 1680 hours yearly (about 36.5 hours a week) for full-time workers, starting in 1998. However, this was principally conceived not as social progress but as a way of reducing the unit cost of labor, by aligning the duration of work with that observed in the Netherlands and Germany. This reduction in working time would in theory occur without hourly wage compensation and be accompanied by an annualization of working time (in accounting terms, the duration of work was measured not by the week but by the year), which would enable gains in productivity while reducing the recourse to costly overtime. (Extra hours in one week would be compensated for by reduced working time in another week of the year.) The Aubry Laws on the 35-hour week would adopt this logic. In parallel, the development of part-time work would be pursued.

Finally, the Mattéoli Commission wanted the new jobs policy to be freed from the fundamental obstacle posed by French social and cultural traits, in which insiders dominated to the detriment of outsiders: "Those who are active pay for the more and more inactive ones while trying to increase their own assets." "This equilibrium is untenable: even out of selfishness [of insiders], it is time to change it," concluded the report.

However, the deterioration of the job market was such that in the summer of 1993 the Balladur government had to resort to classic emergency measures and reinforce the many existing arrangements, in particular the Contrat emploi solidarité (CES). Thus workers were kept in subsidized jobs; in a year, the number of renewed CESs increased by more than half. Although the immigration flow was still low, that policy became even tighter, with a sharp restriction in visa conditions and the circulation of foreigners.

Meanwhile, Balladur and Sarkozy were sticking to a discourse of rigor. Despite its costliness for public finances, the launch of a national loan (and its success) functioned as a political referendum and paradoxically strengthened their image as good managers. In fact, the loan was presented as an advance on future privatizations, since holders of the bonds could exchange them for shares in the about-to-be-privatized companies. But the rise in the CSG in July 1993 and timid measures of budgetary economy, most particularly affecting research, could not compensate for the drop in fiscal returns and the additional cost of the new provisions. Thus, the government let the budget deficit go, confirming the change in paradigm of the French Right that had been initiated in 1986.

The deficit went from 4.5% of GDP in 1992 to 6.4% in 1993 and again to 5.4% in 1994, despite a return to sluggish growth and the promise of further privatizations. Suspended since the reelection of François Mitterrand in 1988, the privatization of more giants—BNP (bank), UAP (insurance), Elf-Aquitaine (oil and chemicals)—now brought 100 billion francs (1.25% of GDP) to the state.

The emergency measures were not without effect; they smoothed out the rise in unemployment. Combined with the absence of budgetary rigor, they made it possible to avoid a net deterioration on the job front. Although massive restructuring in

French industry was pursued, the pace was slower. In 1993, 200,000 jobs disappeared from manufacturing—but only 100,000 in 1994.

The rise in unemployment was even halted in 1994, thanks to the creation of nearly 140,000 jobs in public administration. The unemployment rate in the metropolis (in ILO terms) had grown from 9.6% in the first quarter of 1993 to 10.8% in the first quarter of 1994, and then waned to 10.1% at the start of 1995. This allowed France to post an evolution comparable to that observed in Germany or the United Kingdom.

But these relatively good results on the surface were accompanied by the largest budget deficits since the 1950s. The public deficit exploded: it went from 39.7% of GDP at the start of 1993 to 49.4% at the start of 1995—in two years, an increase equivalent to that observed during the Socialist governments of Mauroy and Fabius from 1981 to 1986.

Yet Balladur cultivated an image as a manager, strengthened by massive use of the French people's savings rather than of the financial markets, by means of a huge "Balladur loan." Relying on this managerial image, the government could pursue its neoliberal agenda. As a local result of the European consolidation process and of the Maastricht Treaty, the Bank of France became independent. In fact, not until the advent of the euro currency and of the European Central Bank would French monetary policy be really disconnected from French politics.

In tandem, the government made a substantial reform of pensions in the private sector. Since the aging of personnel was a demographic given, the financing of retirement became an inevitable issue. From an accounting standpoint, only four levers were available to the government: to raise contributions, to extend the financial base, to increase the length of the contributions period, and to reduce benefits. Since what predominated were the ideas that labor costs were too high and that capital had to be preserved, it was the last two options that seemed to be required. The Balladur reform of the general pension scheme (workers in the private sector) rested on three pillars that were carefully calibrated by French economic administrations: a gradual shift from 37.5 to 40 years of contributions for retirement at the full pension rate; calculation of pensions on the 25 best salary years instead of 10; and finally, indexing these years and pensions to prices instead of to average salaries.

The political debate focused on the forty years of contribution, although this was not the main point of the reform. It was the indexing on prices rather than salaries that was the major point. These effects were gradual—the average salary went up slightly more rapidly than did prices (which ensured political acceptability)—and yet massive, because they led to a continuous impoverishment of pensioners: a pensioner in 2010 with a completed career behind him or her received a fifth less than if the Balladur reform had not taken place.

From the point of view of jobs policy, on the other hand, the forty years of paying contributions was the most significant element. In effect, it pushed senior employees to remain in their jobs, which mechanically increased the size of the workforce. Yet, this effect seems to have been moderate, since employees were able to push back their retirement by only a quarter for an additional semester of contribution; women, in particular, were impelled by the obstacles to lengthen their careers.[12] This mediocre impact was consistent with firms' persistent habit of getting rid of seniors—a pattern catalyzed by the retirement policies in place since the start of the 1970s.

While the pension overhaul could be pushed forward, the same was not true of the application of most of the provisions of the five-year law on jobs passed in December 1993. Only the development of apprenticeships had significant success. Regional responsibilities for professional training were broadly extended, at the same time as firms benefited from both hiring subsidies and tax credits. In a few years, the flow of entries under apprenticeship contracts doubled, pulled up by more highly qualified apprentices, even including graduates of the engineering and business colleges. By the end of the decade, the number of apprentices had thus increased by 150,000, contributing to the significant rise in the employment rate among those younger than 25 (because apprentices had work contracts). Apprenticeships would spread to the service sector, especially for those obtaining post-*bac* diplomas. However, decentralization (from Paris to the regions) of management of apprenticeships would accentuate a strong heterogeneity among regions. The proportion of apprentices among young people varied massively from one region to another; the composition was also very different among regions, with some favoring work-study for "low" diploma levels, and others favoring higher-level diplomas. This heterogeneity suggests that not all regions were fully exploiting their potential to extend apprenticeship.

But labor and management did not agree on the annualization of working time, without compensation for employees. Thus, reshaping the labor market ran into strong opposition. Its symbol was the withdrawal of the Contrat d'insertion professionnelle (CIP)—which was quickly dubbed the "youth SMIC." The logic of this arrangement was the same as for the policy of lightening contributions: the promoters thought that an overly high cost of labor was harmful to employment in France. Young people were reputed to be less productive than their elders, and so the cost of their labor should be smaller. But with the general lightening of social contributions, the specific provisions for exemption of youth lost any relevance; thus, the lowering of the cost of labor had to occur through pay lower than the SMIC, as was already the case for work-study contracts.

The decree applying the five-year law was issued in February 1994. The CIP involved people under 26, with diplomas up to the new *licence* (three years of tertiary education). The CIP was a work contract of fixed length (between six months and a year), renewable only once; the pay was 80% of the SMIC. While other countries were using minimum youth salaries (the United States, New Zealand, the United Kingdom), those were generally based on ages under 20 or 22. The CIP was distinct in applying to a much larger class of young people. French youth protested, and in March the government—despite strong support from its legislative majority and from principal ministers including Nicolas Sarkozy—withdrew the plan.

Jacques Chirac (mayor of Paris at the time) was able to surf over all the discontent with this policy that merely adopted most of his own plan. While Edouard Balladur, supported by Nicolas Sarkozy and most of the center-Right, betrayed him by running for president in a key presidential campaign, Chirac transformed himself opportunistically into the champion of a struggle against "social fracture." Paradoxically, rivalries on the right allowed Chirac to misrepresent his political image, which assured him an easy victory in May 1995 over the Socialist Lionel Jospin.

Unshakeable in his support for Chirac, Alain Juppé, former minister of foreign affairs under Balladur, became prime minister. Possessing the same comfortable majority in the National Assembly as the preceding government, Juppé applied himself to pursuing the same economic policy, despite a rapid drop in his popularity.

This approach was marked by one important failure: to extend the degraded pension regime to public employees. Faced with large strikes in the public services, especially in transportation for several weeks in the winter of 1995, the project was withdrawn. However, the government could carry out most of its economic policy. One privatization followed another, of emblematic firms like AGF, Pechiney, and Usinor-Sacilor.

On the jobs side, changing work-time as called for in the five-year law of 1993 could not be applied on the ground. Instead, the government let the Robien law pass in 1996, which granted seven years of massive social tax cuts to companies that reduced work-time in exchange for an equivalent number of new hires. The Robien law would have a warm reception, essentially concentrated in the year 1997, before its abrogation by the subsequent government.

The Balladur exemptions from employer social taxes were extended under the "Juppé" reductions, at first for wages between 1.0 and 1.2 SMIC, then between 1.0 and 1.33 SMIC. Overall, the labor cost at the level of the minimum salary dropped sharply, on the order of 18% of gross salary, at the end of 1996. However, these measures were very costly for the state budget. Converted into euros, they would be 3 billion in 1995, 6 billion in 1996, and more than 7 billion (almost 0.6% of GDP) in 1997. As with the Robien law, this looming deficit would only have a noticeable impact on the labor market after 1997.

But clientelism would collide with this policy. Although the insufficient labor pool in large-scale distribution in France was one of the justifications for the policy of reducing social contributions, for several years the governments of Balladur and Juppé had deliberately slowed the expansion of the hypermarket chains—especially food supermarkets—and the associated jobs.[13]

In effect, the major French distributors now feared the rapid emergence of new foreign competitors, specifically the German "hard discounters" with stores of modest size (between 600 and 800 m^2). After a freeze period on new mega-stores that had been decided under Balladur, Juppé's trade minister, Jean-Pierre Raffarin, put through a law in 1996 on "commercial urbanism": it opportunistically lowered to 300 m^2 the sales area above which a distributor had to obtain authorization from a commission, on which sat one representative of small businesses and one from the incumbent large retailers in the customer catchment zone.

While retail trade in the United States and Germany had boosted job creation and growth, France had deprived itself for several years of this benefit. The effects of this policy were particularly noticeable under the subsequent legislature, when the creation of outlets could not meet the pent-up growth in consumption.

The end of compulsory military service (of ten to twelve months for young men) was also an important reform of the first two years of the Chirac presidency, and its impact on the labor market was significant. Pushed forward by the president, the elimination of military service was passed in November 1997, affecting men born after 1979. Thus, its effects would be gradual until the end of the 1990s. The first direct effect was that about 200,000 young men (corresponding to half the male cohort) would enter into employment without passing through military service, thereby increasing the size of the workforce.

The second effect was indirect. Young men had been prolonging their studies to delay or even avoid military service (there was dispensation for heads of families, etc.). Its elimination broke down this mechanism. Empirical studies with individual data confirm a significant drop in the length of men's education after military service was brought to an end.[14] In fact, we observe a decline of native-born male students in the universities between the academic years 1995–96 and 2000–01, which also increased the participation of the under-25s in the labor market.

The stronger presence of young men in the labor market until 2000 was accompanied by a slight increase in their unemployment rate, while the number of unemployed young women significantly declined. Overall, the elimination of military service significantly reduced the disparity in unemployment between young men and young women (figure 6).

In short, the Juppé employment measures and the end of conscription would essentially have impacts after 1997, and thus would enter into conjunction with the policies of Jospin's Socialist government.

THE PLURAL LEFT: BREAKS AND CONTINUITY FACED WITH THE NEW ECONOMY

Even as the Juppé government waited to see the fruits of its policy on the jobs front, Jacques Chirac decided to dissolve the National Assembly at the start of 1997 to ensure himself a majority until the end of his seven-year mandate in 2002. Apart from the favorable polls, the last year of the legislature was expected to be delicate, risking the chances of the majority if the legislative elections took place later, in 1998.

In fact, the economic forecasts were unanimously good at the start of 1997, noting a recovery of world and of French growth; yet they underestimated the level and durability of the recovery and of the associated fiscal returns. In July 1997 the government had to repay the enormous Balladur loan and to anticipate the

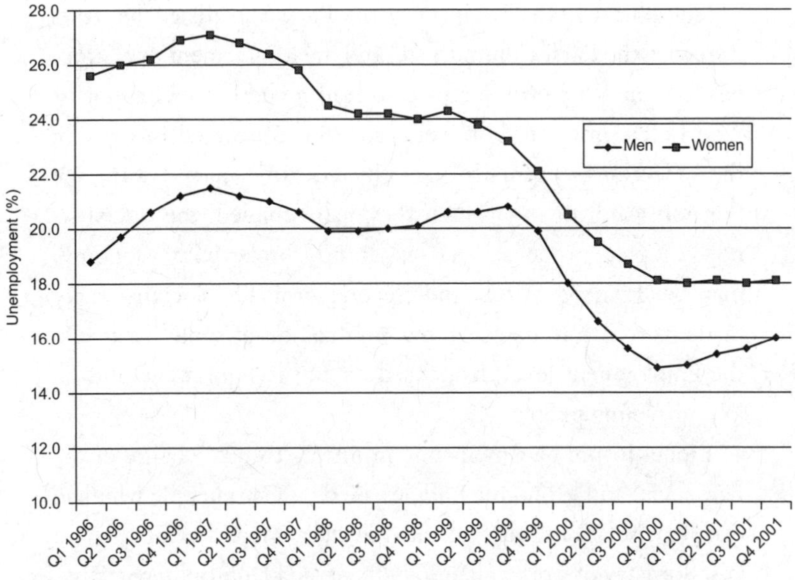

Figure 6. Unemployment rate (ILO concept) for 15-to-24-year-olds, Q1 1996 to Q4 2001, in France as a whole (including overseas territories). Employment evolution was more favorable to young women than to young men after the elimination of military service. Source: DARES-INSEE unemployment series. Note: The elimination of military service was projected in a November 1997 law and achieved at the end of 2001. But Jacques Chirac's announcement of it in February 1996 triggered a significant drop in the number of conscripts, which went from 201,000 in 1996 to 170,000 in 1997, falling to 17,000 in 2001.

application of European criteria under the Maastricht Treaty and adherence to the euro. Therefore, a policy of rigor was envisaged for the autumn of 1997. Public opinion was not wrong: the Right could not claim credit for the Robien law reducing work-time and simultaneously criticize the Socialists' flagship project, the 35-hour workweek. Their attempted political maneuver would be punished by a surprise defeat of the presidential majority.

The plural Left—comprising the Parti Socialiste, the Verts (Greens), the Parti Communiste, and the Mouvement des Citoyens (nationalist Left)—arrived to lead a comfortable majority. The Left's program, however, had been concocted in 1996 for the elections normally anticipated in 1998. Aware of the political gulf into which they had tumbled, the Socialists now adopted proposals that apparently broke with economy-manager François Mitterrand's second term. The Socialist Party made its return to power into a "civilization-at-stake" issue. On the employment level, it focused on the 35-hour week and on jobs for young people.

Lionel Jospin became prime minister. To take charge of the new social and economic policies, he chose two people who had excellent relations with business leaders. Martine Aubry got a vast ministry of work and employment, and Dominique Strauss-Kahn scooped up a super-ministry: economy and industry. The principal organization of employers, the CNPF, was at the time led by Jean Gandois, former president of Pechiney, where he was seconded by none other than Martine Aubry.

The longest growth cycle of the American economy had only just begun. But already, on the other side of the Atlantic, the first studies were seeing this growth as a new type of growth altogether. The economy was recovering strong growth and rapidly pushing back unemployment, yet there seemed to be no inflationary pressure. On the one hand, the combination of information technologies and innovative work modes had become sufficiently widespread to translate into important productivity gains, even in sectors like retail distribution, accompanying the emergence of the giant, Wal-Mart. On the other hand, the rapid progress of information technology itself, accentuated by the redeployment at the end of the Cold War of research effort to civilian uses, translated into tumbling prices for these goods. Meanwhile, a rise in the use of digital equipment by firms as well as households fed profitability and hence the product development of these new technologies. The dematerialization of the economy fundamentally carried with it a capacity to evade the tensions arising from physical markets: most wealth production would no longer depend on the supply of raw materials. The new industrial revolution (see chapter 1) could irrigate the whole economy. This same virtuous circle would reach European countries, from Great Britain, whose financial industry was a great consumer of ICT (information and communication technologies), to Finland and Sweden, which entered sectors of that market, especially infrastructure and then cell phones.

But at the start of 1997, nobody in France was talking about the "new economy," in the sense of the exuberant growth of the ICT sector and the Internet or of a new kind of growth without any apparent tension. In fact, France enjoyed neither Internet expansion nor visible productivity gains. Since the end of the 1980s, French firms had indeed begun to reorganize—but diffidently. This was the case with the creation of the Pechiney factory in Dunkirk, the ideal factory of Jean Gandois and Martine Aubry. Built on the debris of iron and steelmaking and of shipbuilding, it was supposed to become a factory from which aluminum would flow without defect or social conflict. Here we find all the canons of the "new productivity"—a flattened hierarchy and multitasking operators capable of performing several jobs. But tinted with paternalism (the obligatory use of the informal *tu* rather than the formal *vous*), this new organization style resulted in neither exceptional performance nor totally becalmed industrial relations.

With respect to organizational changes, France in 1997 was lagging behind the United States by five or ten years. Its volume of investment in commercial and household ICTs was comparable to that of America at the start of that decade. It thus found itself facing the new consumer economy from the situation of the American economy at the dawn of its rediscovered growth some years previously.

It was only a year later (mid-1998) that the notion of the "new economy" actually emerged in France, notably under the impetus of the minister of the economy, who would order from the Council of Economic Analysis, which was created by Lionel Jospin, a report on the same subject—that body's only report that included a direct commentary from a minister.

Optimism was thriving. The emergence of an Internet bubble (the one that would burst in 2000) was quickly identified. At the peak, Internet businesses would have had to represent 20% of the GDP of developed countries to justify their capitalization, which was totally unrealistic; in 2013, even the United States was well below that. But the bubble did not seem too worrisome: a simple correction would take care of it.

The fundamentals of the real economy were expected to be solid. Studies piled up (including mine)[15] suggesting a sort of transition phase from one industrial revolution to another, especially since we were witnessing a renewal of work productivity gains in Europe. At the end of the twentieth century, they were approaching American growth levels. At the end of 2000, when the Internet bubble had already burst, the goal of a return to full employment was realistically predicted in France for about 2005.[16]

As I have stressed when examining earlier periods, the perception of underlying economic phenomena and the theoretical understanding of them have different timings. And this largely explains the gradual slide of the Jospin government's policy. When it arrived in power, the economic program it was going to implement still assumed durable soft growth. This suggested that one had to continue to reverse the state's control of the economy in order to free up budgetary margins to maneuver. The government proceeded to make partial privatizations, which were modestly called "opening up" capital: France Télécom, Aérospatiale, Air France, and so on. In the midst of a bullish stock market, the revenue from these operations exceeded those of the Balladur and Juppé privatizations.

On the unemployment front, enriching economic growth in job creation remained top priority. Labor costs continued to be at the center of thinking about the problem. The commissioning of a report from the Council of Economic Analysis in April 1998 confirmed the continuity of views with the line followed by Balladur and Juppé.[17] First, the mission statement from Jospin was unambiguous: "*Taxation* of labor, especially unskilled labor, probably constitutes a factor that is unfavorable to the development of employment in our country."[18] Second, the prime minister entrusted the report to Edmond Malinvaud, who had become president of the Pontifical Academy of Social Sciences (whose goal was to promote the study and advancement of the social sciences, consistent with church doctrine). Thus, the report's conclusion was written from the start: it was necessary to accentuate the policy of lowering social "charges" on low salaries. The semantic slippage is revealing of the Left's ideological swerve: by "taxation" Jospin meant principally social contributions, which form the basis of social protection in France. But nobody mentioned "contributions" to the welfare state anymore, speaking instead of "charges," or "taxes" on businesses and employment.

Meanwhile, studies by Thomas Piketty on employment in France's services gave credence to the idea that France was suffering from a deficit of jobs in comparison to the United States in sectors that would always be labor-intensive, like catering and retail trade.[19] There, too, labor costs were advanced as the probable cause of this deficit—with no mention of the barriers to the development of retail trade.

In fact, the government did avoid making labor costs higher. The boost just given to the minimum wage (2.2% in July 1997) would not be repeated. Net wages would advance in 1998 by switching a portion of wage earners' contributions to the CSG, whose fiscal base was wider. The same logic, of better purchasing power without higher gross salaries, was continued.

Starting in 1997, studies (especially Piketty's)[20] helped inspire the idea of a negative tax, that is to say a monetary payment by the state to workers to induce them to take jobs and to sustain the purchasing power of low salaries.[21] This type of arrangement had been present in the United States since the 1970s. And it had been a pillar of the "Third Way" of the Labour Party of Great Britain, under the notable influence of sociologist Anthony Giddens and economist Richard Layard. Arriving in power in 1997, Tony Blair introduced a systematic tax credit for low salaries, most particularly for workers who were heads of families, on top of strengthening the job centers (accompanied by a system of financial sanctions in case of non-acceptance of some job offers).

In France, firms were beginning to report difficulty in recruitment, and so the prospect of full employment and the budgetary margins brought by growth finally opened the door to this policy for stimulating participation in the labor market. In May 2001, the Jospin government followed closely behind Britain and created such a bonus (the *prime pour l'emploi*, or PPE), despite the skepticism of some economists, who said that with the minimum wage the incentives to take a (full-time) job were already significant, and despite the hesitation of many on the left and in the unions, who stressed that it was up to employers to furnish decent remuneration.

Almost a decade later, *ex post facto* assessments could not manage to find a positive effect on job offers of this measure.[22] However, their methodologies were not trustworthy. Although several million people benefited from them, the successive increases in the job bonus did have a redistributive effect and helped make more tenable the relative stagnation of the lowest-income workers.

Preventing a rise in the unit cost of labor was also at the heart of the implementation of the 35-hour week. Simultaneously a social and an economic project, the 35-hour week was the emblem of the plural majority Left. It was probably the most discussed and analyzed of the economic policies in France; here I will tackle only the essential points of these controversies.[23] The commitment made by François Mitterrand during his 1981 election campaign was fulfilled, but under very different conditions from those envisaged at that time. Two Aubry Laws would set the framework for the shift to 35 hours. The first would lead to the resignation of Jean Gandois, claiming he was "fooled" by Martine Aubry, and the reorganization of French business leaders around MEDEF (Mouvement des Entreprises de France), a war machine against the 35-hour week. This opened a path for negotiations within businesses and sectors aimed at lowering the threshold for overtime hours from 39 to 35 weekly hours in 2000 for firms with less than twenty employees, and in 2002 for those below that. Negotiations concerned the whole organization of work schedules and salary scales. Any firm that participated by anticipating the legal date of the shift's passage and by creating or safeguarding jobs would benefit from incentives—on top of a lightening of social contributions at all salary levels, which would be long-lasting. This relief was calibrated by the government to make the shift to 35 hours neutral in terms of the average cost of labor. For a drop of 11% in working time (from 39 to 35 hours), nominal salaries would be maintained but undergo a "moderation"[24] of about 2%; the hourly gains in productivity were expected to be about 5%; and Aubry exemptions from the "charges" represented about 4% of the cost of labor—thus, overall, no additional labor costs for firms. This cocktail of provisions was meant to maximize the measure's effects on jobs.

However, one year later, the prospect of significant and durable growth, businesses' urgent need for software engineers, and the growing difficulties of recruitment reported by managers in various sectors had all changed the situation. The *réduction du temps de travail* (RTT), by its irreversible nature, was suspected of generating tensions in the labor market, especially among the highly qualified. Clearly, it was less relevant in an economy that was now creating many jobs.

The second Aubry Law of 2000 marked an important retreat from the 35-hour principle: firms could now apply the reduction in working time by modifying the calculation of working time! Thus, entire branches of commerce (like textiles and wholesale distribution) went to "35 hours" though the actual reduction was only 2 or 3 hours. Exemptions from social contributions and the possibility of offering flex-time were maintained.

Unlike the 35-hour workweek, the "new youth job services" did remain pertinent for the government, given the scope of youth unemployment and the reversible nature of this job creation. Open to those under 26 (at the signing date) who had known a period of unemployment, this was a matter of long fixed-term contracts (five years) for jobs essentially paid at minimum wage. It was intended to respond to the needs of non-market services, especially as support for those in higher education. These youth jobs arose from real collective needs; yet, although they quickly became "indispensable" on the ground, the government would not perpetuate them. The five-year period was not chosen by chance: it would allow youth to find opportunities on the labor market, or to pass public competitive exams (most of them quit before their contract ended)—but most especially, it corresponded to the duration of the legislature. In fact, with about 200,000 people enrolled in this arrangement (of whom half were under 26 in 2001), youth jobs contributed to lowering youth unemployment at the end of the century. But in addressing all youth, even those with qualifications, it would impose a "public" price on full-time young workers on minimum wage. Thus, young people were still condemned to precariousness. Despite the strong economic growth, more than 40% of the employed under 25 were in fixed-term contracts (apart from apprenticeships) or as temps, as opposed to 30% at the end of the 1980s.

Meanwhile, the number of those retiring dropped significantly. Yet, the state increased by the same proportion the dispensation for seeking employment for those over 55. Combined with the feeble effect of the Balladur pension reform, these communicating vessels resulted in a senior employment rate that barely budged.

Despite the cost of the jobs policy and the new social policies (principally the new universal medical coverage, started in 2000, which would benefit almost five million people starting in 2001), the fiscal returns would allow the public coffers to be somewhat replenished. The budget deficit fell by half, satisfying the Maastricht criteria and entry into the eurozone. In 2001, the deficit sank to 1.5% of GDP. This relative financial ease was facilitated by the Jospin government's choice to organize a shift to 35 hours in public services without new recruitment. Neutral in education and research (where the working time was not modified), this choice would profoundly disorganize hospitals when it came into effect in January 2002. Under Jospin, the share of public hospital services—apart from subsidized contracts—in overall employment declined.[25]

After the resignation of Strauss-Kahn, Laurent Fabius, the new minister of the economy, upset the Left's budgetary doctrine: he laid out a multi-year plan for lowering income taxes. Conceived to steal from the Right one of its political arguments, this plan would in fact open up an ideological avenue. Faced with salary moderation amid full growth, an income tax cut appeared at the time to be the only way to drive up French purchasing power. This fundamental of Reaganism would support the pillars of the Right's two subsequent victories in the presidential elections: Chirac held out the promise of a 30% cut in income tax, and Sarkozy used the slogan "work more to earn more" (that is, without being taxed on additional hours).

The "Fabius" Law of February 2001, designed to promote investment of employee savings in small and medium-sized businesses through fiscal advantages, had no visible effect on the total remuneration of employees. But by replacing basic salary increases, it would strengthen individual flexibility in remunerations, which was already very significant.[26]

RECORD JOB CREATION THANKS TO JUPPÉ'S REDUCTIONS AND THE 35-HOUR WEEK

Had the Left's new jobs policy achieved its purpose? France at the end of the century experienced an employment expansion

TABLE 6

A general drop in unemployment in the OECD, 1993–2001. All figures in percent

	1993	1997	2001
Germany	7.9	9.8	7.8
Denmark	10.7	5.4	4.2
Spain	22.4	20.6	10.5
United States	6.9	4.9	4.7
EU 15	10.7	10.6	7.4
Finland	16.2	12.6	9.1
France	11.1	12.3	8.8
Italy	10.0	11.6	9.5
Japan	2.5	3.4	5.0
United Kingdom	10.3	7.0	4.7
Sweden	9.3	10.0	5.0

SOURCE: OECD StatExtracts harmonized rate of unemployment.

that was exceptional in its history. The years 1998, 1999, and 2000 were the fourth, second, and first strongest years in job creation in the whole twentieth century. Of course the share of "atypical" jobs—subsidized contracts, fixed-term contracts, temps[27]—and of part-time work were increasing a great deal; but in absolute terms, the number of full-time open-ended jobs was progressing. France in 2001 had more than 25 million jobs, compared to 22.5 million in 1993.

But this performance has to be relativized. Employment improved in most industrialized countries between 1997 and 2001. The improvement in France was similar to the average of fifteen member states of the European Union (table 6).

The Scandinavian countries in particular, where labor costs were high, realized very good performance without challenging their welfare systems. These countries were proactive: Finland launched a technological policy and Denmark instituted a flex-security policy that was an alternative to the liberal strategy of the OECD.

In France, many microeconomic studies clearly showed that the new employment policy, centered at first on reducing the cost of labor to the vicinity of the SMIC, then later centered on the reduced working week, coupled with new exemptions, had helped to create jobs—at least in the short term.

These policies were addressed to all employers, and so their assessment is technically rather delicate since they use varying methods. The Balladur/Juppé measures employed rather disparate parameters, but most of their estimates fall close together:[28] on the horizon of 2000–2002, the Balladur and Juppé reductions would have created around 300,000 jobs at close to the minimum wage. Their effect was likewise visible in macro data. Between 1995–97 and 2000–02, France recorded a noticeable uptick in unskilled employment; its share in total employment plateaued and then rose. Concomitantly, French manufacturing had good export results, supported by renewed competitiveness.

Likewise, estimates of the impact of the Aubry Laws[29] on employment are convergent: creation of about 350,000 jobs, most of them concentrated around the "Aubry I" enterprises, that is, the pioneers that applied the most significant reduction in work time (RTT). The scientific and political debates concern which elements in the Aubry Laws caused this effect. Was it the reductions in social contributions, coupled with work-time flexibility, or was it the RTT? If the former is true, then Aubry can be considered an extension of Juppé. Fundamentally, this debate cannot be settled. Flexibility could never have been negotiated without the RTT, and firms would not have ventured into negotiations without financial aid provided by the state.

The impact of 35-hour employment can also be read as part of a spectacular evolution away from short-time work. In effect, firms' use of the RTT allowed them to avoid resorting to an arrangement that is always traumatic for an organization. In one decade, the number of days of short-time work fell by at least 2 million, compared to almost 12 million in 1995. Only the depth of the crisis that started in the last quarter of 2008 would make the margins offered by the RTT insufficient.

Elsewhere, the consequences of the 35-hour week went well beyond employment. Its implementation through negotiation translated into very heterogeneous conditions for employees, notably with respect to work-time flexibility and wages. It had a tendency to exacerbate unequal working conditions, since the rise in flexibility affected low-skilled jobs, particularly those held by women. In parallel, increased flexibility allowed companies to absorb shocks (negative or positive) and to resort less often to either short-time work or overtime hours. Above all, the 35-hour week offered additional holidays to half the employees who came under the scheme.

In total, the two main measures of the Balladur/Juppé and Jospin governments fostered the creation of around 600,000 jobs between 1993 and 2001. But they were very costly. For example, in 2000 the Balladur/Juppé reductions cost the state 6 billion euros. Based on the (consensual) hypothesis of 300,000 jobs created in that first period, then each job cost 20,000 euros (or at least 8,000 euros if we deduct the supplementary tax returns, welfare contributions, etc.). Thus, the financial return on these arrangements is far from remarkable. We have to raise a legitimate question: Did they not have the effect of eliminating alternative job-creation schemes—like for example creating more hospital jobs?

Furthermore, the estimates bear only on the short-term effects of these policies. To appreciate their long-lasting impact, we have to examine their consequences for the dynamics of the French economy. And one of its bases—innovation—dwindled in the last decade of the century.

BEGINNING A TECHNOLOGICAL DECLINE

While a new jobs policy was being constructed, research and innovation policy lacked any ambition. The relative decline of France with respect to research and development (R&D) occurred in two phases, under the Right and then under the Left.

The end of the Cold War had opened up important research opportunities. The need for military research could now give way to civil research that was directly oriented toward innovation for society and growth, particularly in countries like France and the United States, where military expenditure was considerable.

This opportunity was grasped by the Clinton administration, which inaugurated a new technology policy to accelerate American entry into the era of information technologies. The lever effect would be huge for companies in ICT, especially giants like Cisco and Intel, but also for the biotechnology sector, whose R&D expenditures rose dramatically. Startups flourished around Internet nodes.

The contrast with French leaders is striking. Of course, the new minister of research, François Fillon, did launch in 1993 a national consultation on research, but he merely concluded: "We have announced priorities for various sectors. But for me the essential thing is the realization of the deficiencies affecting the very structure of our research arrangements."[30] Fillon's goal was to solve them by means of a series of technical measures. The "priorities" took the form of a vast catalogue: heavy equipment, agribusiness, aerospace, transport, energy, developing countries, life sciences, environment, employment (*sic*), and the human and social sciences. Finally, military research should remain "privileged"!

Officially, civil and military publicly financed research was supported by budgets that had been voted to go up, but François Fillon let the budget minister of the day, Nicolas Sarkozy, apply drastic budget regulation. The negligible priority given to research was no longer hidden under Juppé: research did not have its own minister but only a secretary of state reporting to Education.

From 1993 to 1997, the share of R&D in the French GDP declined by 0.2 points, and this drop is entirely attributable to the state's withdrawal. France fell three ranks among the great scientific nations of the OECD, outstripped by Finland, South Korea, and Germany. Only Great Britain, despite its great universities, also opted for a decline in academic and industrial research, consistent with the choice of an economy dominated by a financial industry that siphoned off graduates.

The policy of the Jospin government was very different. The objective was to have France spending 2.5% of GDP on R&D by the end of the legislature. His friend, geochemist Claude Allègre—although already very controversial due to his denial of the danger of asbestos[31]—took over the research portfolio and was supposed to lead a reconquest of preeminence.

Despite its decline under the previous governments, the share of state-funded research in the GDP was still in France one of the highest among countries that were intensive in R&D. This situation could give rise to two interpretations: either for structural reasons R&D in France had to be propelled by strong public spending, or else the country would have to wait for a privately financed dynamic without enlarging the role of the state.

The government chose the second option. The fall in public expenditure was simply checked, though recruitment resumed in the universities, which had been chronically understaffed since the start of the 1990s because of the flood of students. On the public research side, as under Fillon, Allègre's priority was to restructure the sector. But this resulted in such chaos that Jospin was forced to replace Allègre in 2000. To nourish private research, the 1999 law on research and innovation simplified the creation of startups by researchers working in the public labs and gave them the ability to acquire patents.

The French wait-and-see attitude was unlike the dynamic innovation policies in many other countries. In fact, the new economy was reshuffling the world's technological cards so that both nations and companies could grasp them. Battered at the start of the 1990s by unemployment rocketing from 3% to 16% in three years, Finland is emblematic of this situation. In 1992, Nokia, a private company led by a former banker, decided to abandon its traditional activities (paper, rubber boots) and concentrate on mobile telephones, for which the market was then limited; faced with the tightness of the Finnish financial market, Nokia in 1994 joined the Nasdaq in New York. By the end of the century, Nokia alone accounted for 40% of Finnish research, and it had become the world leader in a key technology of the information economy. After that, all Finnish actors chose the knowledge society. The public universities followed the needs of business by markedly increasing the number of doctorates. This comparison has its limits, though: the key role of a single enterprise, Nokia, proves that we cannot regard a small country (5 million inhabitants) as a model that can be transposed to the major European economies; and in any case Nokia's difficulties in the 2010s show the limits of such a strategy.

In France, it was short "professional" courses (two years at universities) that were privileged. Already structurally limited by the French specificity of a separation between the *universités*, where research training was concentrated, and the *grandes écoles*, which drained a large share of the best students, faculty and resources, doctoral programs were further undermined by the paucity of their number and by the decline of the real amount of allocations to finance theses. The number of PhDs had stagnated inexorably since 1993. Thus, firms had to deal with a pool of high-level scientists that was even more limited because the engineers coming out of the *grandes écoles,* from whom they tended to recruit their researchers (often without a PhD), were turning to the lucrative opportunities offered by a French (and European) economy in expansion, accompanied by strong growth in careers in finance in the second half of the 1990s.

Expenditure on research by foreign firms in France was generally content to follow the growth of GDP. The same was true of expenditure by French firms on the home territory. The latter were even less inclined to innovate, because the policy of reducing labor costs and the overall neutrality of the 35-hour rule allowed them to gain in competitiveness without any innovation.

Germany would not experience this sequence. The drop in salaries and the liberalization of the labor market—the Hartz Laws—conducted by chancellor Gerhard Schröder followed an effort by German business toward innovation that had been initiated in the second half of the 1990s. Thus, Germany was able to hand on an economy—although depressed on the domestic market—that was ultra-competitive in exports in the first decade of the twenty-first century.

In contrast, France was obsessed by the development of low-skilled employment that the experts called for, and was blinded

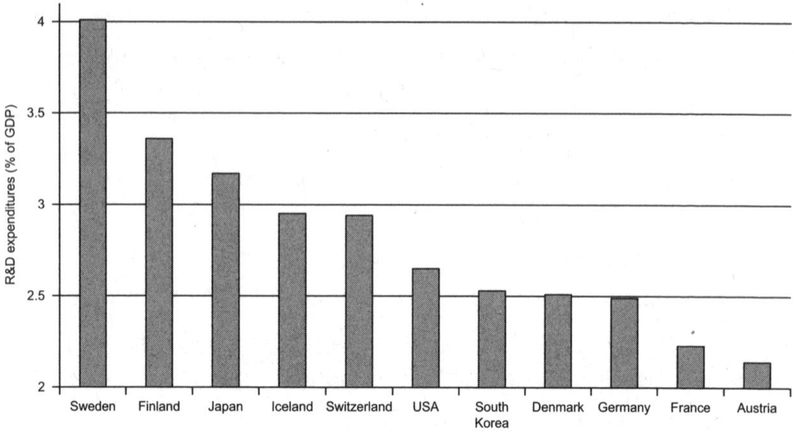

Figure 7. France misses the knowledge-economy train: 2002 R&D expenditures (2004 for Switzerland) as a percentage of GDP in OECD countries with intensive research. Source: OECD StatExtracts (http://stats.oecd.org).

by the recovery of growth and the containment of unemployment, and so it did not fully enter into the knowledge society. In 2002 (figure 7), in terms of R&D intensity, it ranked tenth among OECD countries, hotly pursued by Austria and left far behind by the leading countries, including the three prime world economies at the time (the United States, Japan, and Germany).[32] While full employment seemed around the corner, this relative decline would bequeath to the first decade of the 2000s a French industry that was structurally weakened and a deficit of jobs with high value added, even though (contrary to what many claimed) clear flexibility in the labor market had been attained in practice.

NOTES

1. It consisted of a series of recommendations constructed by experts at the World Bank and the IMF, and was especially aimed at

the countries of Latin America. The World Bank and the IMF were to make their loans contingent on the adoption of policies inspired by the consensus: budgetary discipline, financial liberalization, liberalization of trade, massive privatization of public enterprises, and the deregulation of markets for goods and services. This liberal purge would play out in painful failures; see Dani Rodrik, *The Globalization Paradox: Democracy and the Future of the World Economy* (New York: W. W. Norton, 2011). There was gradual abandonment of the Washington Consensus in the 2000s, before it reappeared in the European crisis of the 2010s.

2. *OECD Jobs Study: Facts, Analyses, Strategies* (Paris: OECD, 1994); *OECD Jobs Study: Evidence and Explanations*, vols. 1 and 2 (Paris: OECD, 1994).

3. Recall that the idea of hysteresis arises from physics and refers to persistent—even irreversible—impacts of a policy (see chapter 4).

4. *OECD Jobs Strategy: Pushing Ahead with the Strategy* (Paris: OECD, 1996).

5. Bernard Gazier and Rachel Silvera, "L'allègement du coût du travail a-t-il un effet sur l'embauche ? Quelques résultats d'une enquête auprès de dirigeants d'entreprise," *Travail et Emploi* 55, no. 1 (1993).

6. Commissariat Général au Plan, *Choisir l'emploi* (Paris: La documentation française, 1993).

7. As I noted in previous chapters, Malinvaud had directed the forecasting department of the statistical bureau, INSEE, when it made critical errors in economic diagnosis in 1974 and in 1981, before he became the holder of the economics chair at the Collège de France.

8. *Rapport d'étape à M. le Premier Ministre sur les obstacles structurels à l'emploi* (July 1993), printed by the Service d'Information et de Diffusion du Premier Ministre; available in a few French librairies, e.g. the Céreq documentation center (www.cereq.fr).

9. One-third of this evolution was due to the automatic rule of indexing on half the hourly wage rise; two-thirds was due to the "nudges" left to the discretion of successive governments.

10. If the minimum wage were lower, then initial salary would be lower, too, allowing employers to gradually increase remunerations as employees gained experience.

11. Pierre Cahuc, Gilbert Cette, and André Zylberberg, *Salaire minimum et bas revenus: Comment concilier justice sociale et efficacité économique?* CAE report no. 79 (Paris: La documentation française, 2008).

12. Antoine Bozio, "How Elastic is the Response of the Retirement-Age Labor Supply? Evidence from the 1993 French Pension Reform," in *Pension Strategies in Europe and the United States,* eds. G. de Ménil, P. Pestieau, and R. Fenger (Cambridge MA: MIT Press, 2008), 37–85.

13. Philippe Askenazy, Jean-Baptiste Berry, and Sophie Prunier-Poulmarie, "Working Hard for Large French Retailers," in *Low-Wage Work in France*, eds. Eve Caroli and Jérôme Gautié (New York: Russell Sage, 2008).

14. Eric Maurin and Theodora Xenogiani, "Demand for Education and Labor Market Outcomes: Lessons from the Abolition of Compulsory Conscription in France," *Journal of Human Resources* 42, no. 4 (2007): 795–819.

15. Philippe Askenazy, *La croissance moderne* (Paris: Economica, 2002).

16. Jean Pisani-Ferry, *Plein emploi,* CAE report no. 30 (Paris: La documentation française, 2000).

17. Edmond Malinvaud, *Les cotisations sociales à la charge des employeurs,* CAE report no. 9 (Paris: La documentation française, 1998).

18. Mission letter of the Prime Minister to Edmond Malinvaud, No. 8853, April 6, 1998, in Edmond Malinvaud, *Les cotisations sociales à la charge des employeurs: analyse économique*, CAE report (Paris: La documentation française, 1998).

19. Thomas Piketty, "L'Emploi dans les services en France et aux Etats-Unis: une analyse structurelle sur longue période," *Economie et statistique* 318 (1998), 73–99.

20. Thomas Piketty, "La Redistribution fiscale contre le chômage," *Revue française d'économie* 12, no. 1 (1997) 157–203; Thomas Piketty, "L'impact des incitations financières au travail sur les comportements individuels: une estimation pour le cas français," *Economie et prévision* 132–133 (1998) 1–35.

21. This income supplement is intended to make work more economically attractive than minimal welfare, and thus to induce people to resume work rather than living on income from transfers. It presumes that a large part of unemployment is voluntary.

22. Marion Cochard, Bérengère Junod-Mesqui, Franck Arnaud, and Sébastien Vermare, "Les effets incitatifs de la prime pour l'emploi: une évaluation difficile," *Economie et statistique* 412 (2008): 57–80.

23. For more details, see Philippe Askenazy, "Working time regulation in France 1996–2012," *Cambridge Journal of Economics* 37, no. 2 (2013), 323–47.

24. Even employees at the minimum wage experience an erosion in real terms. Their nominal salary is maintained but is partially deindexed from inflation.

25. Philippe Raynaud, "L'emploi public est tiré par la fonction publique territoriale," *Economie et Statistique* 369–370 (2004): 75–92.

26. While the end of the 1990s was marked by strong growth, between 20% and 30% of full-time employees experienced a drop in pay from one year to the next (within the same company): Pierre Biscourp, Orietta Dessy, and Nathalie Fourcade, "Les salaires sont-ils rigides? Le cas de la France à la fin des années 1990," *Economie et Statistique* 386 (2005), 59–89.

27. Between 1993 and 2001, fixed-term and seasonal work went from 5% to 6.8% of employment, and temps from 0.6% to 2%, but traineeships, subsidized contracts, and apprenticeships remained stable at around 3.1%. Young people were the most affected by this decreasing job security, which was largely linked to provisions of the employment policy.

28. For a synthesis, see Benoît Ourliac and Cyril Nouveau, *Les allégements de cotisations sociales patronales sur les bas salaires en France de 1993 à 2009*, Document d'Études Dares No. 169 (Paris: Dares, 2012).

29. See Philippe Askenazy, 2013, "Working Time Regulation in France 1996–2012", *Cambridge Journal of Economics* 37 (2013), 323–47.

30. Proceedings of the Assemblée Nationale, second session, June 21, 1994.

31. The controversy around Claude Allègre was further illustrated by his later criticism of the Intergovernmental Panel on Climate Change, which he called a Mafia-like system maintaining the myth of global warming linked to human activity.

32. China in 2002 was not yet the second-largest world economy.

CHAPTER SIX

2002–2007

The Decay of French Economic Policy

The first decade of the twenty-first century opened with bad news: the bursting of the Internet bubble and the attacks of September 11, 2001—the latter, a human tragedy that triggered a geopolitical cataclysm. Paradoxically, these events would strengthen belief in the solidity of a capitalism capable of absorbing major shocks and sustaining rapid global growth. This optimism would then implode in 2008.

However, none of this prevents us from detecting the consequences of new national employment policies in Europe—policies that were devised precisely because of the stability of the macroeconomic context at the start of the 2000s. In the first years of the twenty-first century, each country tried to resolve its major economic problem, whether it was the working poor in Great Britain or unemployment in Germany. And although France was hoping finally to defeat mass unemployment, that scourge was more significant than ever. Even before the crisis of 2008, France shared with Spain and Germany a worrying level of unemployment—clearly above 7%.

This persistent unemployment retrospectively challenged the policies applied during the second presidential mandate of Jacques Chirac. After a constitutional reform, the presidential term of office changed from seven to five years, in this case running from 2002 to 2007. This was a key period, falling between the upsurge of the end of the century and the Great Recession. Chirac's policies were characterized by a messy proliferation of new measures—the byproduct of sclerosis in analyses of the labor market and of saturation in the leading measure in the preceding period: the reduction of labor costs for low-paying jobs. After the 1990s (when this policy had demonstrated a certain stimulation of job creation), impotence and confusion seemed to return. Yet, overall, the macroeconomic environment had been favorable.

THE "GREAT MODERATION"

Whether real or merely expected, the rapid growth of companies engaged in the "new economy"—notably the domain of the Internet—was accompanied by the formation of an Internet bubble in the securities markets at the end of the twentieth century. The bubble started to burst in March 2000, triggering a rapid collapse of the Nasdaq. This outcome was not a surprise. Economic decision-makers, notably the central banks, had anticipated this shock. In fact, a drop in interest rates, especially in the United States, and an injection of liquidity very quickly enabled the crash to be contained. This entrained a consolidation of sectors of the new economy around the most robust actors, without major macroeconomic consequences. The financial authorities, led by the Fed and the European Central Bank, demonstrated that they had anticipated the situation.

A few months later, their capacity to react forcefully was tested by an event that nobody could have anticipated: the 9/11 attacks. Here again, they resorted to a massive injection of liquidity to restore immediate confidence.

Macroeconomics was triumphing. Empirical studies were devoted to the "great moderation," meaning the attenuation of macroeconomic fluctuations, and even the disappearance of global macroeconomic risk. Though lacking the power to prevent regional crises, the authorities were thought to have the tools necessary to ensure worldwide financial stability, especially in key economic zones. This stability was judged to be all the easier to realize because the deregulation of finance, its globalization, and its worldwide sophistication would allow smoothing out the risks. And on this scale, the danger appeared almost null, since the world had not experienced a global recession since the end of the Second World War. Moreover, given what was happening in the real economy, nothing presaged a slowdown in global growth. Great demographic powers like China and Brazil were moving from emerging status to that of economic giants. In the rich countries, R&D expenditures (except for France) continued to fly high, while growth in productivity, although running out of steam in Europe, remained high in North America. European integration was being pursued, unleashing a process of Eastern Europe's catching up. World trade was exploding. Even tensions over the prices of raw materials (especially oil) seemed incapable of undermining world growth, which according to IMF figures surpassed 5% in 2007, the highest point in three decades.

This whole edifice would be brought down in financial tumult with the collapse of the American bank, Lehman Brothers, in September 2008; we will return to this in the next chapter.

POLICY CROSS-CURRENTS IN EUROPE

While the "great moderation" dominated the macroeconomic environment, European leaders were still trying to respond to disequilibria in their national economies.

Action on the primary division of revenue between labor and capital began in the British Isles at the start of the decade. Ireland was facing a slide of up to 15 percentage points in the share of labor in value added over a few years. The Celtic Tiger had indeed enjoyed very strong economic growth. But this occurred thanks to the implantation of many foreign firms, which were attracted by an advantageous social and fiscal environment. Hence the "Pfizer Effect," named after the manufacturer of Viagra: production took place under license, which required that a great part of the resultant wealth serve to pay for these licenses, remunerations that therefore returned to the home base, meaning (generally) abroad. To reverse the collapse of the share of labor, in 2000 the Irish Centrist-Nationalist government introduced a minimum wage, which was quickly raised to the French level. One year previously, the Blair government had also established an hourly minimum wage that for most workers was also comparable to France's. The result of this policy was a significant drop in the proportion of low-hourly-wage work in the British private workforce.[1] At the same time, the British government had greatly expanded employment in the public services, long neglected by the preceding Conservative governments, thereby generating hundreds of thousands of jobs. This largely contributed to a low level of unemployment in Britain, until the 2008 crisis.

Blair's policy contrasted with the one applied in Germany by the Social-Democrat Schröder. The end of his first term had been marked by an upturn in unemployment to the level of the start of his term. Re-elected in 2002, the German chancellor was convinced by the liberal wing of his supporters that he had to introduce a new jobs policy. A super-ministry was created, merging the Ministries of Economy and Labor; it was directed by Wolfgang Clement (who would leave the Social Democratic Party in 2008 before supporting the liberal Free Democratic Party in 2009). The Hartz Commission, named after its president (a former human resources manager of Volkswagen), was asked to propose mechanisms for a liberalization of the labor market in order to finally control German unemployment, which was now comparable to France's.

Packages of major reforms were undertaken starting in 2003. Dozens of new provisions favored "mini-jobs" (very short-term part-time jobs) and "midi-jobs" (based on half-time). Thanks to a simplified procedure, an employer could hire anybody—someone with or without work already—for a low salary, not covered by collective agreements, and paying reduced inclusive contributions. The holder of this job paid neither taxes nor contributions based on his income, but he or she had only limited rights to social welfare. The measure had immediate quantitative success. From 2003 to 2004, two million new mini-jobs were created; a majority of those hired were already employed. Nevertheless, the sectors that were intensive in low-skilled and part-time work, like bulk distribution, took advantage of the measure to employ women in mini-jobs. The result was a surge, mostly affecting women, in low-paying jobs in Germany.

But these initial measures did not attack the long-term unemployment problem that was affecting almost half the Germans out of work. For these "difficult" people, Hartz led in January 2005 to the creation of the "Ein-Euro-Job" (paid at one euro an hour)—essentially, assisted community service jobs. In parallel,

Hartz aimed at a "modernization" of the German labor market through the "activation" of social expenditure. This resulted in a rise in the demand for jobs. But ultimately, despite this complete overhaul of the institutions of the labor market, the unemployment rate continued to rise until the electoral defeat of Schröder at the end of 2005. Many microeconomic assessments suggest that the Hartz Laws had a weak short-term impact. Even economists who promoted the policy were obliged to find a silver lining: "While these reforms have also led to the introduction of many new instruments which have now been proven to be ineffective, they have been able to enforce a thorough evaluation of the labor market programs—something the academic community has called for."[2] Small consolation for millions of impoverished workers! Thus—at least in the first phase—the policy of creating precarious jobs was no more effective across the Rhine than it had been previously in other countries of Continental Europe (like Italy).[3]

Yet managers in France supported the idea that these reforms had contributed to a drop in wages in Germany that favored the competitiveness of its manufacturing industries. The Hartz Laws had in fact affected salaries, but principally in the service industries where precarious jobs were concentrated. The impact was only indirect in manufacturing industries, which were covered by collective agreements negotiated by powerful unions. In 2007, according to data from the American Bureau of Labor Statistics, the hourly cost of German labor in industry remained 32% higher than in firms in France; this differential reached 59% in the automobile industry that year, or barely less than the 63% observed in 2002, before the Hartz package. Most especially, the appreciation of the euro raised the cost of the German manufacturing worker to 153% of the American level and

191% of the Japanese level. German competitive costs were built not just on internal salaries but also on opportunistic subcontracting in countries with low wages, particularly in Eastern Europe.[4] We will come back to these points in the following chapters, with the debate about the differential competitiveness of France and Germany and the German "employment miracle" that in 2012 came to the forefront of political preoccupations.

THE EUROPEAN STRATEGY

In this first decade of the new century, the point in common between British and German policies was their disconnection from the European jobs strategy, elaborated by the European Commission, which was supposed to guide national policies. This strategy was a component of the Lisbon Strategy proposed in 2000, whose goal was to make Europe "the most competitive and dynamic knowledge-based economy in the world."[5] The guiding light of the jobs strategy was to "promote flexibility combined with employment security and reduce labour market segmentation."[6] The Scandinavian countries, which had experienced a net decline in unemployment since the middle of the 1990s, were promoted as a model. Moreover, now that the OECD recognized in its revised jobs strategy that there was no obvious link between the performance of the labor market and its deregulation (which it had called for ten years previously), the European strategy would attract some interest in France. Reports piled up that advocated innovative work contracts or alternative financing of unemployment benefits. Apart from the experts, politicians (on both left and right) were also thinking about the matter, as were management and labor. This would inspire certain measures in the second half of Jacques Chirac's five-year term, even if the French citizens showed their reluctance regarding the European strategy by rejecting via referendum in 2005 the "constitution" for Europe. The first half of Chirac's term, on the other hand, was governed by the desire to halt the process of converting to the 35-hour workweek and to revert to the policy conducted under Balladur and Juppé, whether lowering labor costs or pension costs.

UNDOING THE 35-HOUR WEEK

The reelection of Jacques Chirac in 2002 occurred in a very particular context: the elimination in the first round of the prime minister, Lionel Jospin, and the consequent face-off with the leader of the extreme Right, Jean-Marie Le Pen. Chirac's success by default (with more than 80% of the votes)—confirmed by a victory in the legislative elections over a demoralized Left—did not prevent him from conducting an uncomplicated right-wing policy that prefigured that of Nicolas Sarkozy (to whom the next chapter will be devoted).

Until the end of May 2005, the prime minister was a Centrist, Jean-Pierre Raffarin, former minister of trade. He led three successive governments. Two heavyweights from the majority succeeded each other in the vast Ministry of Social Affairs and Labor, François Fillon and then Jean-Louis Borloo. Francis Mer, president of the French Steel Federation and member of management's principal organization, MEDEF, became minister of the economy in the first government. He would leave this post in 2004, replaced by Nicolas Sarkozy, former budget minister and brother of the vice president of MEDEF. Sarkozy would be replaced by Thierry Breton, one of the major French bosses of the CAC 40.

Unsurprisingly, their policy combined the aspirations of MEDEF with a desire to undo the symbols of the preceding legislature. The first symbol was youth jobs. The scheme would not be renewed, although it arose from social needs. The second and more fundamental symbol was the process of reducing working time, which would be halted in several stages.[7] Firms could maintain a work schedule of 39 hours a week, or return to that if they had already transitioned to 35. Small companies overwhelmingly chose the first option, while most of the larger ones would continue to apply the 35-hour agreements they had negotiated. The heat wave of the summer of 2003 and its 15,000 deaths justified the creation in 2004 of an additional day of unpaid work "in solidarity with old people" (employers would pay a tax to subsidize air conditioning in nursing homes, for example). The government reached its goal: the drop in work-time duration halted and even began to be reversed.

Firms were all the more motivated to do this because the "Aubry" subsidies were abandoned. Starting in 2003, all firms, whatever their work schedules, would benefit from the Fillon discount for between 1.0 and 1.6 of the SMIC (minimum wage), that is to say, a reduction in the social contributions paid by firms for hourly wages lower than 1.6 times the SMIC. This measure would cost about half a percent of the GDP as additional public effort. The government was hoping it would produce a significant impact on employment. Since the Balladur-Juppé discounts in the 1990s had created around 300,000 jobs, this current extension could not help being significantly favorable to employment, especially in small firms, where the wages were lowest. This reasoning was also supported by most of the experts. It appeared so obvious that the national statistical bureau, the INSEE, forgot its obligation to be neutral. In the midst of the electoral campaign at the start of 2002, it published a study by two of its economists that suggested an even greater effect from the "alleviation of charges."[8] This study was immediately taken up by the candidate Chirac and played a significant role in the credibility of the outgoing president's economic program. And today (a decade later), this "evidence" is still the main obstacle to proposing an alternative jobs policy in France. Therefore, we should take the time—and I would say the scientific risk—of impeaching this dominant paradigm.

Theoretically, the massive effect of a supplementary layer of "alleviated charges" is far from evident, even when using the model favored by its promoters. Let's look at the logic underlying these measures. Excessive cost of labor eliminates workers whose marginal productivity is lower than this cost.[9] But the distribution of labor costs in countries without a minimum wage (or low wages) forms a bell curve (figure 8); following the theory, the cost being equal to marginal productivity, the latter also follows such a curve. This means that the proportion of people with the very lowest productivity—let us say, between 8 and 10 euros an hour (which we can call the tail end of the distribution curve)—is less than that having low productivity—let us say, between 10 and 12 euros an hour (nearer the middle of the distribution). Thus, a first wave of exemption that lowers the minimal cost from 12 to 10 euros would be much more effective than a second wave that makes this cost drop from 10 to 8 euros. This is all the more true since, to avoid low-wage traps, the greater the "lightening" at the level of the minimum wage, the more the discounts should affect a larger base of employees with a productivity that is still higher than the minimum wage.

This is exactly what was observed with the Aubry exemptions. While the Juppé discount went up to 1.3 SMIC, most of the

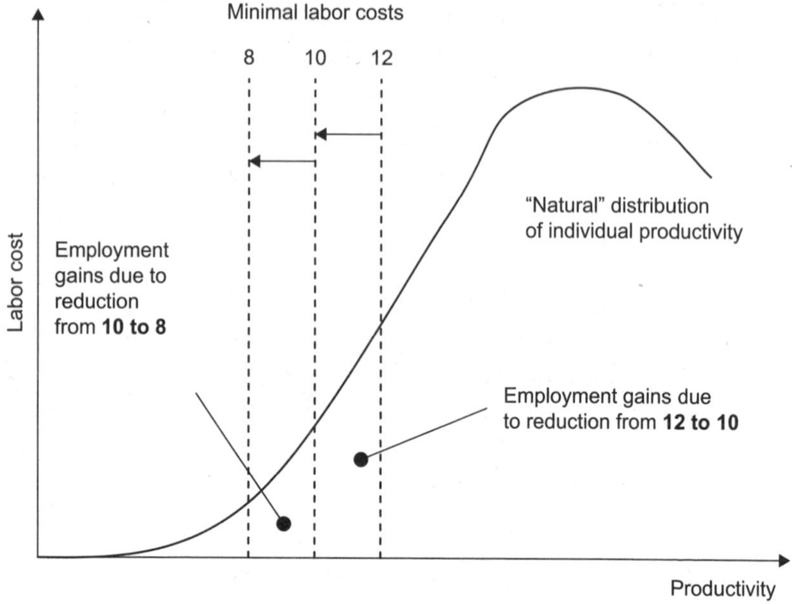

Figure 8. The employment effect of reducing labor costs at the minimum wage, according to the "theory" that cost = productivity.

Aubry exemptions went all the way to 1.8 SMIC. Similarly, the employment effect of the latter assistance was lower than that estimated for Juppé's. In effect, in 2002 the Aubry measures cost as much as the Juppé exemptions. Reduction of working time plus massive subsidies were expected to create many more jobs than the Balladur-Juppé measures. Now, the overall impact on employment in 2002 of the 35-hour week was estimated at 300,000, or as much as the Balladur-Juppé policy.

Moreover, supplemental "lightening" measures worked to cannibalize other aspects of the jobs policy. For example, if the cost of labor was lowered for everybody, the relative advantages of employing young people or hiring in certain geographical zones consequently lost their attractiveness.

What were the consequences of the Fillon plan? Strangely, very few studies have been published on this subject since it was implemented. The minister of labor commissioned one from a team at the INSEE, but this work remained in a drawer. In reality, it had no significant impact on employment, but this absence of "significance" is attributed to insoluble methodological problems—which are however of the same nature in the studies that ascribe massive effects to the Juppé plan! Still, the INSEE decided to publish, in 2010, in its journal *Economie et Statistique*, a study by researchers at the Centre d'études de l'emploi, which estimated an elasticity in the cost of labor 4 to 5 times smaller than that generally used for Balladur-Juppé, even applying the same type of method.[10]

Finally, in aggregate series, we observe no change in tendency. Recall that after the Juppé plan there was an upsurge in unskilled labor. This time, there was nothing of the kind. Small businesses were the principal beneficiaries of the Fillon measures, and yet the share in employment of the largest firms continued to rise.

Yet it is regularly claimed that the Fillon discount avoided the destruction of jobs linked to the rise in the minimum wage to secure the 35-hour workweek. The implementation of 35 hours had generated a multiplicity of minimum hourly wages according to when a firm had shifted to this régime. Jean-Pierre Raffarin had decided in favor of a convergence "upward." Thus, between 2002 and 2005, the minimum hourly wage in companies that had remained at 39 hours progressed by 11% in real terms. Still, this "generosity" is wholly relative. Workers on the minimum wage in companies who were the last to shift to 35 hours would not experience any increase in their basic hourly wage for three years. Finally, comparison with the years when the

Balladur-Juppé discounts were effective ends up destroying the argument: back then the minimum wage had increased by 7% in real terms, for everybody, between 1994 and 1997.

In any case, taking into account the cost in public expenditure of the Fillon exemptions, the consequences for employment were very disappointing. The key jobs policy, conducted continuously since 1993 with the first Balladur measures, had reached its limits. Moreover, on the eve of the Great Recession, the cost of labor at the minimum wage was at a level comparable to that of the minimum wage in Great Britain, where the existing studies have detected no clear deleterious effect on employment, just a little on the profits of employers in low-wage sectors.[11]

CONTINUITIES

While the most visible Jospin measures—youth jobs, the 35-hour week—were dismantled by the Right majority elected in 2002, several parts of the policy advanced since 1997 were adopted, both by the Raffarin governments and the Villepin government that succeeded them in May 2005. (Villepin would keep the same ministers of economy and labor.)

Research remained a non-priority. While the ministers of labor and the economy were the heavyweights in the legislative majority, the same was not true of the four junior ministers for research who succeeded each other. In fact, we find again the principles enunciated in 1993 by François Fillon when he was minister of research. In the first place, public research was suffering not from a lack of resources but from poor organization and steering. To get around existing structures, new bureaucracies were now established! At the end of the legislative session, under the impetus of the prime minister, an embryonic reassembling of academic structures appeared, which prefigured the policy during the following presidential term. The second recurrent principle was to bring universities and the business world closer together. The government's instrument for moving in this direction was the *pôles de compétitivité* (clusters of competitiveness), which grouped in the same geographical area firms, establishments of higher education, and public and private research bodies—all with a mission to work in synergy on economic development projects that encouraged innovation. Dozens of clusters of this kind were created and financed—but with dubious economic impact.[12] In total, France's relative decline in this area (now on a par with Austria) continued. R&D expenditure as a share of GDP fell below 2.1%. The gap with Germany was inexorably widening.

Much more ambitious (and much more costly) was the pursuit of lower taxes initiated by the Socialist Laurent Fabius. A push by President Chirac for a one-third cut in income tax was underway. In total, the drop in the scale was around 20%. This amputation cost the public treasury 0.6% of GDP, which represented, roughly speaking, half the reductions in France's military expenditure after the end of the Cold War. In 2007, income taxes fell to a fifth of the state's revenues. The fall was slowed, though, by the takeoff of very high incomes: even if the wealthy knew many ways to avoid taxes, their soaring incomes sustained the national revenue from taxes. Mechanically, the progressivity of income taxes diminished. It would be partially re-established by the pursuit of another policy initiated by the Jospin government. Even if it did not seem to have a clear effect on economic behavior,[13] the *prime pour l'emploi* (working tax credit) was firmly revalorized. In 2007, 9 million households benefited from an average tax credit of 500 euros, or a little less than 4% of their working income.

THE FILLON REFORM OF PENSIONS

Early retirement financed by the state continued to be phased out. The extinction of the main retirement scheme (the *Allocation de remplacement pour l'emploi*) was confirmed, as well as special allocations from the National Labor Fund, in effect since 1995. Only workers exposed to asbestos remained able to quit work immediately. In effect, France wanted to meet the Lisbon agenda, which aimed at half of those aged 55–64 remaining in employment by 2010. To reach that goal, the government was counting on the Fillon pension reform of 2003, which was also supposed to solve the financing of these pensions until 2020. It envisaged that regular discussions between management and labor would make only minor adjustments to guarantee a balance among pension schemes.

Workers were encouraged to remain at work by means of a premium/discount system.[14] Combining work with drawing a pension was facilitated. Early retirees were taxed. Alignment with the general scheme, based on the length of public employees' contributions, was set for 2008. The length of contributions for a full pension would gradually be extended for all those at work at age 41 in 2012. The law automatically linked the duration of contributions with gains in life expectancy in subsequent years.

Opposition from the labor unions somewhat softened the Fillon law, but this softening broke the united front and bore the signature of one of the largest trade unions, the CFDT (French Democratic Confederation of Labor), which followed a strategy of independence from parties of the Left. Neither special schemes nor the legal minimum age for retirement (60) were touched. The very lowest pensions would be raised to guarantee that an employee who had had a complete career at the minimum wage (SMIC) would earn a net pension of at least 85% of the SMIC at the moment of departure. The provision for long careers also moved in the direction of some social justice. Employees and non-employees on aligned schemes who had started work young (between 14 and 16 years old) obtained a right to anticipate leaving for retirement before age 60 if their length of contributions was sufficient. In practice, the pension reform widely exceeded the government's expectations. Around 100,000 workers would take advantage of it each year from 2004 to 2008, under the general scheme alone. This take-up was all the more important in that it counterbalanced the marginal positive effect on rates of activity among seniors exerted by other provisions in the Fillon law. The average age of retirement declined, rather than increasing, but access to this right would be severely restricted by a law passed in December 2006.

A commitment to do something to alleviate the painfulness of retirement would not be honored. Management and labor had eighteen months to find an agreement before the government took over. But management was snared in sterile discussions due to hostility from MEDEF, and the unions remained inactive.

On the other hand, management and labor did reach an agreement on the creation of a senior contract, which was ratified by a decree in 2006. This contract was for 18 months, renewable once (that is, a maximum of three years), for employees over 57. This provision relied on the notion that it was impossible for unemployed people over 57 to find a job—which was due to the range of work contracts offered by firms. The standard fixed-term contracts lasted only 18 months and did not permit reaching the retirement age of 60. Economic model simulations of the senior contract were very optimistic; they relied on models of search and matching in the labor market, one of the dominant paradigms in labor economics, which make contractual matching difficulties the major cause of unemployment. This new contract was expected to enjoy major success and to boost the employment of seniors. The ministry of labor even created a statistical team to follow the evolution of the contract numbers. However, one year later, the team was quietly dissolved because only a few dozen senior contracts had been signed. Although unused, this contract still figured among French work rights as of the end of 2014.

A desire to clean up provisions concerning seniors led to the elimination of the Delalande contribution, a tax on dismissing workers over 50, which had been introduced twenty years before (under the second Chirac government) and whose effects on the employment of seniors had been roundly criticized.

THE DISINTEGRATION OF THE JOBS POLICY

There were now hiccups in French economic growth. It was only 1% in 2002, and 1.1% in 2003. A glimmer in 2004, 2.5%, dimmed to 1.9% in 2005. These rates were insufficient to bring back full employment by 2005, as a number of experts had hoped at the end of the 1990s. Worse, after three years of Raffarin governments, metropolitan France had 300,000 more unemployed; the young people who had widely benefited from youth jobs under Jospin were the first to be affected.

A new impetus had to be given to the employment policy, which became concrete in the first pillar of the Borloo Plan for Social Cohesion presented in June 2004. It was less a policy than a rag-bag of recipes. Economic administrators were mobilized to gather any good ideas that were easy to put into practice. Thus, the plan included eleven programs for employment, each with an average of five measures each. For example, there were programs for status as "student-apprentice," as well as for reactivating aid to unemployed persons who created small businesses. New types of subsidized contracts took the place of the old ones. The total cost of the jobs pillar of the Borloo Plan was thus low—for an impact on employment that was potentially positive but unquantifiable.

More costly was the territorial policy. New zones were created in which firms benefited from generous tax and welfare contribution exemptions. The arrangements piled up, sometimes even overlapping in electoral districts with influential legislators: free urban zones (ZFU) were a subset of zones of urban "redynamization" (ZRU), which themselves included sensitive urban zones (ZUS); job pools for redynamization (BER) were included in aid for regional purposes zones (AFR); BER communities could also be zones of rural redynamization (ZRR), and so on. The effects on employment were uncertain at best.[15] For example, the ZFUs seem to have benefited from job creation, but a good share of this came from displacement of economic activities from other geographic zones. Moreover, the cost per job was exorbitant. One can only wonder about the strange logic of this policy. To be a ZFU, an area had to have an outstanding proportion of unqualified youth. Instead of making a public investment to correct this situation, the state was subsidizing private enterprise. What is worse, such a town would now have no interest in improving the situation of its residents, because to do so would be to risk losing fiscal attractiveness!

The whole set of these measures could not have better than negligible effects on unemployment—but this, the French people were not told. More jobless people being crossed off the administrative list of the unemployed meant that the government could claim that unemployment was falling, according to the figures from the National Employment Agency. This biased evolution "validated" the policy to the government's satisfaction, especially in the Ministry of Labor. Those in power then decided to put pressure on the INSEE to not publish the true figures on unemployment in France, although France's institute shared European commitments to the truthfulness of statistical information. Public statisticians mobilized to denounce this antidemocratic manipulation of data during the approach of elections. In short, France made itself look ridiculous. Meanwhile, the European statistical bureau, Eurostat, assumed its responsibilities and published the true figures for France—but too late to influence the presidential campaign of 2007.

THE FAILURES OF THE CNE AND CPE

Dominique de Villepin compounded this surreptitious manipulation of statistics with a second deliberate violation of France's international commitments in the creation of the New Hiring Contract (Contrat nouvelle embauche, or CNE) in 2005. The CNE was a open-ended contract reserved for companies with less than twenty employees. For an indemnity of 8%, the employer could fire the employee without justification within the first two years, that is to say, well beyond the usual probationary period. The idea for this contract came from labor economists who were obsessed with parity models—the same models that predicted success for the senior contract. This framework of analysis had become dominant within economic departments, especially because it permitted data simulations. It always promoted flexibility in the labor market as the way to foster employment; "rigidities" supposedly generated unemployment. Moreover, the CNE specifically was seen as the first stage in the creation of a "single contract," one with simplified firing and progressive rights to compensation. The single contract would permit resolving both the dualism of the labor market and a good portion of unemployment—yet with significant nuances. Reports piled up to ensure that the plan was promoted;[16] even the IMF asserted: "The CNE's effectiveness in reducing unemployment will be the larger the fewer limitations it has in duration and scope, and the sooner it leads to the adoption of recent proposals to integrate all existing contracts into a single one, with internalization of the social costs of layoffs and as little legal uncertainty as possible."[17]

Unsurprisingly, the government announced that the model simulations predicted the eventual creation of 90,000 jobs thanks to the CNE. But were these effects actually observed? We will never know. The decree instituting the CNE was immediately attacked on the grounds that allowing firing within two years for any reason violated Convention 158 of the International Labour Organization (ILO) and Article 24 of the European Social Charter. These documents, ratified by France, required that any firing be for good reasons. Strangely, the Conseil d'État (the administrative supreme court) rejected this argument and approved the text of the law. The *conseils de prud'hommes* (labor courts), for their part, ruled in favor of employees and international documents, and therefore condemned the employers who used the contract. The organization of small and medium-sized firms alerted all of its members to the legal risks, which put a brake on the use of the CNE; thus, instead of reducing uncertainty for firms, the CNE exacerbated it.

The government then launched into procedural moves to delay the judicial process. It succeeded: the Courts of Appeal would not rule until the end of the legislature, and hence after the elections. On November 14, 2007, the ILO concluded by consensus that the CNE was incompatible with Convention 158. It would be definitively abrogated in June 2008, and all the CNEs would be converted into standard open-ended contracts.

Similarly, the First Hiring Contract (Contrat première embauche, or CPE) would have been just as contested as the CNE. Without even informing the economic administrations or his ministers, Dominique de Villepin, convinced by the experts, announced the creation of the CPE out of the blue in January 2006. It adopted the principles of the CNE but applied it to people under 26 who were recruited by firms of any size. This youth "subcontract" provoked opposition among students, especially those in *lycées,* a protest movement reminiscent of the one against the "youth SMIC" advanced under Balladur. Ultimately, the result was the same: the measure was withdrawn. More precisely, those in power chose a strange procedure. The law was promulgated, but in a TV speech on March 31 the president of the republic asked the government "to take all necessary measures so that in practice no contract could be signed."

At the same time, neither the unions nor the government and its experts saw that a large segment of the French labor market was experiencing a deep change. In joint decisions on November 26, 2003, the Cour de Cassation (Supreme Court) simplified the use of short-term contracts in sectors like restaurants and entertainment where it is "customary practice" not to employ open-ended contracts; thus, a single worker can be repeatedly hired on short-term contracts (*CDD d'usage*) as many times as the employer needs that worker. The result would be a dramatic rise in very short-term contracts in the next decade (see the last chapter).

The creation of new advisory bodies to the government (like the Centre d'analyse stratégique, erected on the ashes of the

Commissariat au Plan) could not mask the disintegration of economic and social policy at the end of Jacques Chirac's second term. In five years, growth had never taken off. A decade of lagging behind in the battle for innovation was beginning to weigh on the performance of businesses. Foreign trade surpluses transmuted into deficits, especially in relation to Germany. The employment policies put in place at the end of the century had reached saturation and were costing more and more for less and less effectiveness. According to Eurostat, the unemployment rate reached 8.8% in the first quarter of 2007, compared to 8.4% five years previously. Between feeble growth and pressure on employment, the salaries of most workers progressed only slowly, as job requirements became ever more burdensome. According to a European survey of working conditions, France was among the highest in Europe in the proportion of workers reporting that they were insufficiently paid for the efforts demanded of them.

In 2007 the French people would become passionate over a presidential campaign that would oppose for the first time two dynamic candidates who had not experienced the Second World War: Nicolas Sarkozy (a conservative) and Ségolène Royal (a socialist). The campaign unfolded without the least consciousness of the specter of a looming financial crisis. The French chose the candidate who better understood their expectation of greater buying power, as expressed in his remarkable slogan, *Travailler plus pour gagner plus*: Work more to earn more.

NOTES

1. Jérôme Gautié and John Schmitt, eds., *Low-Wage Work in the Wealthy World* (New York: Russell Sage Foundation, 2010).

2. Werner Eichhorst and Klaus F. Zimmermann, "And Then There Were Four … How Many (and Which) Measures of Active Labor Market Policy Do We Still Need?" *Applied Economics Quarterly* 53, no. 3 (2007), 243–72.

3. Gianna Claudia Giannelli, Ursula Jaenichen, and Claudia Villosio, "Have Labour Market Reforms at the Turn of the Millennium Changed Job Durations of the New Entrants? A Comparative Study for Germany and Italy," *Journal of Labor Research* 33, no. 2 (2012), 143–72.

4. This strategy was paradoxical: it implied that as the euro appreciated the competitiveness of German industry improved. In effect, Germany's principal market remained the eurozone, especially France. With appreciation of the euro, Germany firms could buy the components for their products more cheaply, and thus could lower the prices of these products for the rest of the eurozone, thus winning larger market shares.

5. Presidency conclusions, Lisbon European Council, March 23—24, 2000.

6. Council Decision 2005/600/EC (July 12, 2005) on guidelines for the employment policies of Member States.

7. For a thorough analysis of this question, see Philippe Askenazy, "Working Time Regulation in France from 1996 to 2012," *Cambridge Journal of Economics* 37, no. 2 (2013), 323–47.

8. Bruno Crépon and Rozenn Desplatz, "Evaluation des effets des dispositifs d'allégement de charges sur les bas salaires," *Economie et Statistiques* 82, no. 3 (2002), 231–45.

9. The marginal productivity of a worker is the quantity of additional production generated by an additional hour of work.

10. Mathieu Bunel, Yannick l'Horty, and Fabrice Gilles, "Les effets des allègements de cotisations sociales sur l'emploi et les salaires: une évaluation de la réforme Fillon de 2003," *Economie et Statistique* 429 (2010), 77–105.

11. The lastest reports are available on the Web where the Low Pay Commission regularly posts them (https://www.gov.uk/government/publications/low-pay-commission-lpc-research-2014); earlier reports are online in the National Archives (http://webarchive.nationalarchives.gov.uk/20130708092703/http://lowpay.gov.uk/lowpay/rep_research_index.shtml).

12. Gilles Duranton, Philippe Martin, Thierry Mayer, and Florian Mayneris; *The Economics of Clusters: Lessons from the French Experience* (Oxford: Oxford University Press, 2010).

13. Marion Cochard, Bérengère Junod-Mesqui, Franck Arnaud, and Sébastien Vermare, "Les effets incitatifs de la prime pour l'emploi: une évaluation difficile," *Economie et Statistique* 412 (2008), 57–80.

14. The discount was a lowering of the pension when the number of contributing quarters was insufficient. The premium was an increase in the pension for every additional year, which was intended to encourage workers to pursue activity beyond when they had earned the full rate.

15. Roland Rathelot and Patrick Sillard, "Zones franches urbaines: quels effets sur l'emploi salarié et les créations d'établissements?" *Economie et Statistique* 415–16 (2008); Adrien Lorenceau, "L'impact d'exonérations fiscales sur la création d'établissements et l'emploi en zone rurale: une approche par discontinuité de la régression," *Economie et Statistique* 427–28 (May 2010), 27–62; Laurent Gobillon, Thierry Magnac and Haris Selod, 2012, "L'effet des zones franches urbaines sur le retour à l'emploi," CEPREMAP Working Papers (Docweb) no. 1209.

16. Pierre Cahuc and Francis Kramarz, *De la précarité à la mobilité: vers une sécurité sociale professionnelle,* rapport au Ministre de l'Economie et au Ministre de l'Emploi (2004); Michel Camdessus, *Le sursaut: vers une nouvelle croissance pour la France* (Paris: La documentation française, 2004).

17. International Monetary Fund, *France—2005 Article IV Consultation Concluding Statement of the Mission* (July 2005).

CHAPTER SEVEN

2007–2014

From Optimism to the (Not So) Great Recession

> What victorious majorities should especially fear is wanting to do everything at once, at the risk of confusing everything and compromising everything.
>
> Léon Gambetta, 1875[1]

At the beginning of 2007, the world economy was running full tilt, but France remained partially on the margins of this prosperity, which reinforced French lassitude after twelve years of the presidency of Jacques Chirac. Nevertheless, a new president of the same political stripe would be elected, at a time when an alternation of parties had become the norm in major European countries.[2]

The election of Nicolas Sarkozy came with enormous expectations due to his promise of a return to forceful political action. Yet within two years unemployment had once again become the prime preoccupation of the French, or rather their foremost anxiety. The Sarkozy years were marked by an avalanche of measures, in a world economic context that had rapidly deteriorated. But France was far from experiencing either a deep recession or an exceptional surge in unemployment.

In the end, Sarkozy was more undermined by scandals than unseated by his economic performance when he lost the presidential elections in May 2012 to the Socialist candidate-by-default, François Hollande. The latter, whose campaign slogan was *Le changement c'est maintenant* (Change is now), lamely followed in the footsteps of his predecessor on some key economic dimensions, both domestically and on the European scene: satisfying employers' petitions and accepting the European leadership of Angela Merkel.

This chapter examines only the essential elements of the economic policy of recent years. The absence of historical distance and the shock of the worldwide Great Recession make this examination necessarily more impressionistic than those in previous chapters.

CRISIS OF CAPITALISM, CRISIS OF IDEAS

Perspective is also lacking for an analysis of the crisis that began in 2008—not to mention the failings in economic science, of which significant portions will have to be rebuilt. This operation will probably take a long time. Without this new knowledge, I must be content to describe some of the mechanisms that are destabilizing capitalism these days, although I cannot claim to be able to isolate the most determinative mechanisms.

The collapse of an American investment bank, Lehman Brothers, immediately provoked the evaporation of markets situated at the heart of capitalist economies, such as the inter-banking market (exchanges between banks), and made the foremost world economy totter. Though it was supposed to serve as insurance, the interdependence of financial systems turned into a contagion and precipitated capitalism's rush to the edge of the chasm. Massive public interventions to take the place of the defaulting markets did arrive to save the worldwide financial system. But the authorities were incapable of avoiding the shock's being transmitted from the financial sphere to the real economy through the abrupt tightening of credit. In 2009, the world experienced its first recession in seventy years. In its wake came an unprecedented crumbling of global trade (despite the absence of protectionist measures) and a spectacular rise in unemployment in most of the Western economies. The crisis became known as the Great Recession—in reference to the Great Depression of the 1930s.

What happened? Just as with the crisis of the 1930s, decades of research will be necessary to answer this question with any clarity. Although some economists had previously warned of the dangers of financialization, of the proliferation of exotic financial instruments, and even the risk posed by subprimes, nobody had anticipated such a worldwide subsidence. Thus, the science of economics, too, entered into crisis. Fundamentally, the question is: What's wrong with macroeconomics? To answer this, we should first try to understand the dysfunctions of capitalism that engendered the Great Recession. Several "explanations" are tangled together.

In the first chapter, I developed the hypothesis of the (at least transitory) exhaustion of the productivity gains issuing from the revolution in information and communication technologies. This exhaustion preceded the collapse of Lehman Brothers by several years. The shortcomings of finance would then come from the search in the "casino economy" for profits that the real economy could no longer offer. Getting out of the Great Recession would require rebuilding a new productive momentum.

Another factor that we have already tackled, the rise of inequality in income and inheritance, is also blamed for the deviations in the financial sphere. But the growth in inequality of consumption, at least before the crisis, and especially in the United States, was much smaller.[3] The low-income and middle classes did take part in American prosperity, and acquired property "thanks" to the use of modern tools of indebtedness; in return, these tools allowed the financial sector to offer the risky but highly profitable products demanded by those with large inheritances and incomes. Unless the motor of consumption is set aside, we must accept either a private indebtedness that is unsustainable in the long term, or the growing indebtedness of the state, in the absence of fiscal instruments capable of redistributing the income of the wealthiest. Thus, capitalism could be restabilized either by revamping the fiscal instruments or by taking action on the primary distribution of income—for example, by strengthening the negotiating power of workers.

Thus, most analyses stress the financial system, in and of itself. They point a finger at the myopia of the financial markets. Though the United States, Spain, and the United Kingdom experienced real estate bubbles, the premiums for risk on the lending financial institutions did not rise. Financial markets do not obey the normal law of supply and demand, where demand falls when prices increase. On the contrary, a rise in the price of real estate—immediately resalable—attracts buyers in search of quick profits. Thus, speculation is inherent in the financial world.

But are market actors really myopic *by nature?* Or are they in some way responsible, but not guilty? Maybe they have an interest in remaining *rationally* "myopic." This voluntary risk-taking behavior arises from an asymmetry regarding traders that has long been denounced: when stock prices rise, their profits are enormous, but when prices fall, their losses are low. What is true of the traders is also true of the financial institutions that employ them: investment banks and hedge funds. The private cost of their speculation is much lower than its social cost. Thus, sophisticated financial instruments, especially securitization,[4] permit them to transfer the final risk to savers. The financial institutions therefore have a kind of insurance that allows them to take major risks. This is all the easier because accounting methods ("off the books") allow them to get around the constraints of regulations, which are thus rendered inoperative.

Even more perverse is the anticipated role of government authorities. Speculators know that if a crisis emerges, government intervention to limit its effects can be massive. At worst, some firms will disappear, but most will benefit from the ultimate insurance: the State. Bailout plans will be organized to limit the scale of the recession. Structurally, the risk is thereby transferred to the government. In such a framework, private financial actors will try to take the same risks simultaneously, to be certain that the government will be obliged to intervene to save the economy—and this is exactly what happened. The abrupt halt to trading between banks revealed that it was not a single bank in particular but rather most of the banking actors in the world who were implicated in the taking of risks—which indeed necessitated interventions by governments in all the Western economies.

Worse, the principal financial actors seem to have captured the regulatory bodies, by directly giving the regulators the model for their own regulation! The principal American bankers dictated the Paulson Plan of 2008, named after the former CEO of Goldman Sachs who had become treasury secretary under George Bush. The exorbitant scale of the plan—2,500 billion dollars, or 100 times the sum committed to help homeowners who were under property foreclosure—as well as choices like the absence of partial default on the guarantees of AIG—can be explained by this takeover of the supposed watchdogs.

In short, instead of weakening them, the consolidation of the financial sector after the crisis left actors who were even bigger and more powerful, as well as profits and bonuses that returned to the record levels of before the collapse of Lehman Brothers.

These perversions of the financial system were now recognized by a majority of economists and demanded profound changes in regulations. But the absence of clear understanding of the processes made the task of constructing restorative regulation arduous. Each interpretation of the crisis suggested its own prescription. More than five years after Lehmann Brothers fell, and despite taxes on traders' bonuses, new prudential ratios (Basel 3), and new financial and banking regulations in the United States and Europe that have been spread over a decade, the fundamental mechanisms of the crisis are probably still at work. After the Great Moderation, a great instability dominates.

THE CRISIS OF SOVEREIGN DEBTS IN THE EUROZONE

Moreover, a major new factor of instability emerged in Europe—more precisely, within the euro area: the crisis of sovereign debts. It emerged at the start of 2010, and the first link in the chain was Greece. Other countries that would succumb were Ireland, Portugal, and Spain. The humiliating acronym PIGS (Portugal, Ireland, Greece, and Spain) appeared in Northern Europe. The Great Recession exposed the weaknesses of these countries within the eurozone; but these weaknesses were different from one country to the next. Portugal had one of the least advanced economies in Europe. The Celtic Tiger was injured in saving a hypertrophied banking system and by the bursting of the real estate bubble. The Spanish real and financial economies were threatened by an even larger bubble, in which the savings banks were involved. Greece had only managed to enter into the euro through fudging its national accounts, which had been structurally affected by tax evasion on the part of the major ship-owners, by the fiscal privileges of an ultra-rich Orthodox Church, by an archaic administration, and especially by extravagant military expenditures resulting from its latent conflict with Turkey.

It would be simplistic to attribute the sovereign debt crises to these national frailties alone. To accuse Germany of maintaining a sluggish domestic market while drowning the rest of Europe with its products is equally unsatisfactory.

The Italian case is particularly instructive. From the end of 2010, PIGS became PIIGS. Italy saw the interest rates on its national debt soar. Yet, the specific situation of Italy could not justify this degradation. Certainly, Italy was affected by the Great Recession, but it possessed a diversified economy, including a north that was competitive and exporting. There was no real estate bubble, and few financial institutions were unstable. Nor had public finance deteriorated: the national debt was massive, but for decades Italy had shown its ability to pay interest on such a debt, thanks to a primary surplus.

If Italy was attacked, it was because eurozone institutions were incapable of acting, and the political response to the Greek crisis had been inappropriate. The institutional construction of the eurozone had been carried out under the sway of a belief in the Great Moderation. Without the prospect of a major economic crisis, one could hand the keys to budgetary discipline to the judgment of the financial markets. This would allow escape from the sanction mechanisms foreseen by the Maastricht Treaty, which were overly dependent on intergovernmental negotiations. (Moreover, when Germany and France had not respected the Maastricht criteria in the first half of the 2000s, no sanctions had been applied.) Thanks to such treaties, the markets possessed total freedom of action, and the European Central Bank (ECB) could not directly acquire title to the debts of member states. It could speculate on paper about the debts; but it did not do so before the Greek crisis. On the contrary, just as the Maastricht sanctions were virtual, nothing suggested that in the event of a speculative attack there would be any intervention by the ECB or other member states. Until 2007, debt rates throughout the euro area countries converged.

Pandora's Box was opened at the start of 2010. Hostile speculation was directed at Greece as it revealed the truth of its accounts. Yet, a few billion euros would have sufficed to save it. Angela Merkel demonstrated a fatal political blindness. Faithful to a sober line and anxious not to commit Germany financially, she refused to help. Sarkozy followed in her footsteps—people referred to the couple as "Merkozy." The Spanish leader (Zapatero) and the Italian leader (Berlusconi) were already too weakened to intervene. The markets now knew that they could speculate on the debts of European nations without risking immediate intervention. The sovereign debt crisis would henceforth rebound and rebound, from the last-chance plan to the ultimate plan. New instruments were created in this catastrophe: the European Financial Stability Facility, then the European Financial Stabilisation Mechanism, which was replaced in

2013 by the European Stability Mechanism, and so on. The ECB slowly modified its doctrine by buying up public debt on secondary markets.

The rescues were made all the more necessary because the affected countries had engaged in a suicidal policy of austerity. Austerity had plunged them into a recession that made them incapable of keeping their budgetary promises. This suicide can only be understood through the ideological strategy of the troika appointed to solve the problem, composed of the ECB, the IMF, and the European Commission (specifically the Directorate General for Economic and Financial Affairs). These institutions were charged with the recovery of the affected countries, yet they had all demonstrated their limits. The IMF was busy downsizing; the European Commission, which was expected to check government accounts, had seen nothing of (or had not wanted to see) Greece's cooking its books; and the Central Bank had no awareness of the risks of the crisis—to the point of increasing its prime interest rate a few weeks before the fall of Lehman Brothers. The troika saw the European crisis as a remarkable window of opportunity for achieving the conversion of Europe to a neoliberal model of the economy. Although the situations of Greece and Ireland were fundamentally different, the troika proposed a common interpretation of the sovereign debt crisis and a single solution: governments were spending too much; their role was too large. The solution was to balance public accounts as fast as possible, to reduce the number of public service employees, to slash social programs, to launch privatization programs—and so on. Studies by the IMF were unveiled to support these measures, which in the short term were not supposed to entail recession but to restore growth and confidence. In 2010, teams of economists in Europe denounced this policy and these IMF studies as based on absurd hypotheses.[5] They were not heeded. (Neoliberal economists applauded the studies.) The foremost academic economists initially remained silent. Probably scalded by their inability to anticipate either the financial crisis or the sovereign debt crisis, and at a loss to explain the facts, they did not speak up, although in private some (though not many) expressed worries about the policy. At best, at the end of 2011 (and for the majority, at the end of 2012), economists did begin to express views, given the evidence, that peripheral Europe had been plunged into a deep recession. But it was too late; the train had left the station.

The final cost of this European debacle was incommensurable in human terms—unemployment, poverty—as well as in purely economic terms; and yet, it was a debacle that France escaped. The fear of a scenario like Japan's—two decades lost for the eurozone—is quite real. Worse, the crisis made bedfellows of the extremes, in particular the extreme Right in democracies that were still young. Recall that barely four decades previously, Portugal, Greece, and Spain were all still military dictatorships. The European political project seems to have come to a halt, of which a cut in the multiyear European budget is only one illustration.

INITIAL OPTIMISM

Let's go back to 2007. Nobody had imagined such a crisis, especially not in France. After the elections of May and June 2007, France had one of the biggest government majorities of the Fifth Republic. It was composed essentially of those faithful to President Sarkozy, including prime minister François Fillon. There was no longer a Ministry of Work and Employment, but a

Ministry of Work and Solidarity, in charge of issues having to do with working conditions and pension reform, and a secretary of state for employment under the Minister of the Economy, Christine Lagarde (who became director of the IMF in 2012). The Ministry of Labor was experiencing instability unparalleled under the Fifth Republic: in less than three years, four ministers succeeded each other. This instability had little impact on policy, however, because policy was essentially set from the Elysée Palace, where the social advisor at work was Raymond Soubie (the advisor to Chirac and to Barre, back in the 1970s!). The same was true of economic and research policies. Of course the government opened a door to some personalities on the left, adopting a concept utilized by Michel Rocard in 1988. Former Socialist Prime Minister Rocard himself would accept missions and preside over commissions, before being appointed in 2011 to the astonishing post of France's ambassador to the Arctic and Antarctic—but the comparison stops there. On the one hand, the conduct of policy was much more dynamic than at the end of the 1980s; on the other hand, it was clearly partisan.

In May 2007 the lights were green, the forecasts were optimistic. In the half-yearly forecasts of April 2007, the IMF saw a growth of 2.4% starting in 2008 and accelerating, while the budget deficit would regress back to well below 3%. This promised significant budgetary margins while remaining within the Maastricht criteria. Despite a TV speech (September 21) by François Fillon on "France in bankruptcy," the government would completely use up these virtual margins, devoting them to a "fiscal package" whose inspiration was more ideological than economic. This was expected to produce a vague good: "the shock of confidence." The gross cost to the permanent welfare regime of this package—made concrete by the TEPA (*tra-*

vail, emploi, pouvoir d'achat) law—was around 1% of GDP. But the almost zero growth in 2008 and the recession of 2009 quickly transformed the hope of room for maneuver into a very strong contraction of public revenue. The contraction was even more violent because since 2002 the state had sharply reduced income taxes, and that revenue was not very sensitive to the cycle. However, the Fillon government would not go back on its law. On the contrary, imitating the European Commission, it would opportunistically use the conjunction of the crisis and its policy: digging the deficit a little deeper would help push measures to restrict public spending and a "harsh" overhaul of pension schemes.

BETWEEN IDEOLOGY AND PRAGMATISM, TO A MACHO POLICY

Passed under emergency procedure, TEPA contained many measures that relied on a single rationale: inequalities in income and in wealth are legitimate and an engine of economic activity (the trickle-down theory). TEPA introduced a "fiscal shield" at 50%: your total direct taxes would not exceed half of your annual income (net of various allowances and exemptions); if they did, the government would send you a rebate check. Capital investment in small businesses was exempted from the wealth tax, which though not eliminated was sharply reduced. Certainly the stated purpose was to promote small businesses and to ensure the "return of fiscal exiles," but according to the statistics we have, neither goal seems to have been achieved. In total, almost half a billion euros was returned each year to the largest French fortunes, including many financial supporters of the government in power.

TEPA also set the presidential slogan, "Work more to earn more," to music. It introduced a symbolic measure for parents of students who were liable for tax by exempting their revenue—thereby returning to a measure in force in the Middle Ages! The law also introduced an arrangement for bonus hours that was unique in the world. Overtime was exempt from income tax and from almost all social contributions. In total, each additional hour earned more for the employee and cost less for the company than a normal hour of work. This amounted to the death of the very principle of referring to working time. Now, in all countries *except* France, the legal duration of work—officially 35 hours in France—was not a maximum but rather the threshold at which one started to count overtime, whose cost was much higher for companies.

The extraordinary character of this system prompted immediate and unanimous opposition from unions and experts, although a good number of the latter had publicly supported Nicolas Sarkozy's candidacy. It cost several billion euros, and it had an odd economic effect: the arrangement subsidized hours at the end of the day, which are in general less productive.

It also contributed to gender inequality. Consider a couple in which the husband works full-time and the wife part-time. (About a third of women work part-time—though many would like to work more—while more than 90% of men work full-time.) Within a company, the financial choice between offering bonus hours at full-time and a longer duration of part-time is inverted by this arrangement: it is now more costly to transform a part-time job into full-time than to grant bonus hours to a full-time worker. The same reasoning will occur in the household. In the division of domestic tasks, it is much better for the husband to work for a tax-exempt income supplement than for the wife to increase her working hours, if she is working part-time. Data from the French labor force survey are consistent with this inegalitarian tendency from the first year of the application of the overtime bonus. The annual effective duration of work by part-time employees declined by 1% between 2007 and 2008 and again by about 1% between 2008 and 2009. Male full-time employees experienced an increase in work time in 2008; in 2009 this returned to the 2007 level.

Apart from this machismo, TEPA came at a bad moment. The crisis had not only drastically reduced the budgetary margins of maneuver, but it had also reduced the overall hours of work offered in the major developed economies. In France, once the RTTs were exhausted, arbitration between short-term employment and duration of work had to occur. In a decentralized way, companies in Great Britain and in Germany had reduced the working time of employees in order to best preserve the jobs necessary for the economic upswing as soon as it appeared. Of course the French state had favored part-time unemployment, which is a form of short-term job sharing; but here again, this tool was much less widely used than in Germany—to which we shall return.

France thus found itself at cross-currents with Europe, with an increase over several quarters in the declared number of overtime hours, even as economic activity was collapsing. According to European studies of labor forces, the effective duration of work by a full-time employee did not budge in France between 2007 and 2009, while it fell by 0.7% in Great Britain and by 2.2% in Germany.

The creation of an arrangement for the self-employed was another leading measure in the "work more" program. This was meant to simplify access to independent worker status.

Administratively, signing up was very simple (a few minutes on the Internet); social and fiscal contributions were calculated automatically and linked to turnover. This arrangement enjoyed enormous success, with hundreds of thousands of people benefiting.

For now we have only tidbits of information about the consequences of self-employment. But the trend is already observable. Firms in various realms were externalizing/outsourcing their employees—for example, copyeditors in publishing. The firm benefits from total flexibility, and the ensemble of risks falls on the person who has become precariously self-employed. This trend had been observed in Italy, where a form of self-employment had been fostered in the 1990s. It led to a reform in 2004 that created the status of "entrepreneur dependent on the granting of commissions"—a status that opened up benefits financed by the giver of the commission, especially for maternity leave. Thus losing its attraction for employers, the status of "entrepreneur" in Italy has sharply declined.

However, in most cases, the quarterly turnover of the *auto-entrepreneurs* is low—and often nil. They come into competition with artisans and tradespeople, but they have lower contributions and guaranties, and hence work at a lower cost, especially the many self-employed who are already salaried and are earning extra income, obeying the injunction to "work more to earn more."

SLASHED PUBLIC SERVICES

To finance part of TEPA, the state as employer launched into a vast reduction in personnel, pompously baptized the Révision générale des politiques publiques (General Review of Public Policies). Initiated slowly under the previous Chirac mandate, the non-replacement of public workers going into retirement approached one in two. Apart from Research and Justice, all ministries were involved. The "turn to austerity" in mid-2010 was in fact a continuation of this policy. National education, the principal component of public services, was directly affected. Destruction of teaching and ancillary posts was massive, on the order of 30,000 per year; this reduced by around 5% the job opportunities for those under age 30, who constituted most of the recruits. The non-replacement rule was applied in most cases without considering current or future needs. The mini baby boom France had experienced since the 1990s translated into an increase in the number of students in secondary schools, just when teaching personnel were declining rapidly. To fill the gap, training was skipped: new teachers went directly in front of classes.

Despite the politicians' security discourse, by 2010 the number of police had fallen to its 2002 level, while the French population had grown by several million. Here in fact we find the same political logic as given during the public service amputations performed by Margaret Thatcher and David Cameron; but it would take several years for the deterioration of public services to be troubling to the citizens. After 2010, the budgetary problems of the countries of Mediterranean Europe would push them to follow France—but with even greater cuts. Yet, the financial gain for the state was relatively limited. For the full year of 2011, it represented about 1.5 billion euros in the Hexagon.

The effort demanded of public workers did not stop there. The Fillon government froze their salaries, which meant a drop in their real wages. In 2011, the drop reached 0.8% among workers in local government, 0.6% in the hospitals. Only senior civil servants escaped, because their bonuses increased.

While the majority of workers in the private sector were men, women held the majority of public service jobs. This amounted to almost three-quarters of personnel in public hospitals, though women remained in the minority among senior administrators. Thus, the drop in the salaries of public agents and job opportunities in government automatically enlarged the income inequality between women and men.

URGENT MEASURES

The conjunction of the crisis and these public policies triggered a rapid rise in unemployment. The rescue of the banking system was ensured by overwhelming taxpayer assistance, comparable to what was done in the rest of continental Europe. It was facilitated by liquidity injections from the ECB. A single major bank, the Franco-Belgian Dexia, specializing in credit to local administrations, would be dismantled over several years. As elsewhere, the financial giants came out of it bigger still. Thus, BNP Paribas absorbed Fortis to become the largest bank in the eurozone.

Very quickly the government tried to break the spiral of unemployment—lower consumption—lower economic activity. It resorted to the same principles as those applied under Balladur in 1993, treating unemployment through state-supported jobs. The recovery plan of 2009 provided a number of assisted open contracts in the non-market sector (the *contrat d'accompagnement dans l'emploi,* paid for at least 90% by the state; the *contrat d'avenir*), which rose from 230,000 to 380,000. Subsidized mercantile contracts (*contrat initiative emploi*) were doubled, to reach 100,000 over the year 2009. Authorizations for short-time work were widely granted and the compensation lifted to about 90% of net salary; in short, contrary to the large-scale use of short-time work in Germany, on average only 200,000 French employees were involved in any quarter, with little effect.[6]

Despite well-known windfall effects, the government introduced exceptional measures to try to avoid a crumbling of the youth market—which it had itself precipitated by reducing the recruitment of public employees. Let us give a few examples. Apprenticeship was in free fall but had been supported by "zero social contributions" for twelve months for the hiring of an apprentice and a bonus of 3,000 euros for a hiring by a company with less than fifty employees. Recruitment of an intern under a contract of indeterminate length was also worth a bonus of 3,000 euros. Still more generously, any hiring under a contract of more than one month gave the right to assistance of 185 euros a month (for a maximum of one year) to companies with less than ten employees.

The government also tried to limit the collapse in consumption in 2009 by multiple measures, from a cash bonus when purchasing a new automobile to an exceptional bonus of 150 euros in June 2009 for 3 million low-income families. The acceleration in the implementation of the Revenu de solidarité active (RSA) was in the same spirit of lifesavers offered to the worst off, but now it was perennial. The RSA was composed of a "plinth" and a new "activity" complement. The "plinth" replaced the single-parent allowance and the RMI (Revenu minimum d'insertion). The "activity" was meant to strengthen the financial gains of the "working poor." While intended as an experiment, the RSA was generalized in 2009, even before evaluations were completed. It is true that the arrangement finally adopted was less generous than the one that was tested. The paltry financial gains—usually a few dozen euros per person—combined with a form of stigmatization of the "working poor" on assistance, and cumbersome administration, explain why half of those eligible for the RSA "activity" do not apply for it.

Generally speaking, though, these measures contributed to the relative maintenance of consumption and enabled the recession to be less severe than in Great Britain or Germany. But they could not stop unemployment from growing. In parallel, the government acted head on with a series of pragmatic structural reforms that had been discussed for many years. These concerned the markets for goods, the "public service" of employment, and the "social dialogue."

LONG-TERM REFORMS: DECEPTIVE IN THE SHORT RUN

The crisis did bury many recommendations from the commission presided over by Jacques Attali, a famous but controversial French essayist who was a "special advisor" to François Mitterrand. The Commission for the Liberation of French Economic Growth occupied and flattered many experts and academics; it allowed the Fillon government to supervise the ideas they put forward. A block of proposals to open up regulated professions (taxi drivers, hairdressers, etc.) was quickly forgotten, although it merited deeper reflection. The law on economic modernization that did pass in 2008 merely adopted the recommendations that were electorally the least dangerous for the majority. The most significant was the continued dismantling of laws that restricted the construction of commercial retail outlets; with consumption depressed, it was difficult to evaluate the consequences of this policy.

Similarly, they hoped for a positive long-term impact from the creation of a single unemployment office—the Pôle emploi—in the image of British job centers, which had demonstrated a certain efficacy in a phase favorable to reducing unemployment. In fact, the Pôle emploi was soon overtaken by the crisis and a rapid rise in the number of people out of work. The spectacular rise in economic activity, combined with major and rapid restructuring, translated into deterioration of the services offered to the unemployed. The new system was obliged to resort to costly private providers to serve hundreds of thousands—and the providers proved ineffective.[7] In parallel, the firing of workers on open-ended contracts was simplified. An employer and an employee could agree on their separation (*rupture conventionelle*). Unlike a standard firing, the agreement per se is taken as a legitimate reason for the firing. Unlike a dismissal, the employee retains the rights to unemployment benefits. In 2012, such separations accounted for 16% of the total losses of open-ended contracts.

The reform of union representation promised a long-term transformation of the bargaining situation in France. The goal of a law passed in August 2008 (approved by management and by the two major union confederations, the CFDT and the CGT) both affirmed powerful and representative unions and encouraged the emergence of new and innovative unions. Company agreements were now subject to a double majority: validation by organizations representing at least 30% of employees (according to the most recent professional elections) and the absence of opposition from unions representing 50% of the votes. The automatic representation of the five great confederations introduced in 1966 gave way to representation based on votes in company elections. A 10% rate had to be reached in the first round (now open to all unions) of an election by members of the company committee (or else the sole delegation of the personnel) for a union to be considered as representing a company's employees; at the branch level, the threshold was 8% (aggregating the results of elections throughout the firm). The process of transition was completed in 2013.

The fears of blockage of negotiations due to a split majority were not realized. But a complete remaking of the syndical landscape did not take place. At the national level, the five "historical" trade unions all met the representation threshold, and they were the only ones to do so.

AN INEGALITARIAN REFORM OF PENSIONS

Apart from this wide-ranging policy on the labor market and work relations, the other great "reform" of the Sarkozy term had to do with pensions. This was an additional stage in the strategy initiated by François Fillon as minister of labor in 2003. It took place in two phases: so-called special regimes, and then the general and public-employee schemes. A multiplicity of special regimes, from the Banque de France to the railway company, the Société Nationale des Chemins de Fer (SNCF), were modified in 2007–2008 to "converge" around the general regime. Though presented as a great victory by the president of the republic, the convergence was only partial. For example, at the SNCF the length of contributions for a full pension would go from 37.5 years to 41 years in 2018, but the age of eligibility for a pension remained fixed at age 50 for drivers and at 55 for other railway employees, and periods of parental leave were incorporated. In 2011, convergence gave way to divergence. In effect, special regimes were only involved in the second phase: major modifications in 2010 affected the general and public regimes. Special regimes kept to the "calendar" set in 2007–08.

From the start, the debate was vitiated by hasty international comparisons and misunderstanding of the underlying financial bases. Politicians and the media (using OECD data) proclaimed that the legal age of retirement in France was very low, 60 as opposed to the usual 65, notably in Germany. So France had finally made *the* reform, as other countries had been able to do, again including Germany. Let us linger over the comparison between France and Germany.

Reforms were fastidious in both cases. Germany significantly modified its pension schemes in 1992, 1999, 2001, 2004, and 2007, and it would continue to do so. Several legal ages of retirement coexist in both countries. In France, before the Fillon reform, the minimum age was 60 (lower for those who had started work young), and the age for a full-rate pension was 65. (The former is the age a worker can assume pension rights; the latter is that which allows him to obtain a full pension, even if he has not contributed for a sufficient number of annuities.) In Germany the reform of 2007 eliminated (after 2012) the possibility for Germans who had contributed for at least fifteen years to retire at age 60; they now fell into line with workers who could take their pension at 63 if they had 35 annuities. Thus, the minimum age in general was well below 65 in Germany. Sixty-five corresponded to the age necessary for a full pension; the reform underway would raise this to 67 in 2029. And a full pension at 63 would require 45 annuities; but this length of time was relative, since many workers had started work at 15 as apprentices.

Once these figures are examined, we discover that the French reform was much more severe for future retired workers than the one across the Rhine, although the demographic situation is much less dramatic in France, where the birth rate is more dynamic. The minimum age for receiving a pension (62) will be the norm in 2018, and the length of contributions moderately increased. Full-rate pensions were delayed to age 67—but as of 2023 in France, compared to 2029 in Germany. And this is the essential parameter. The generation that is going to retire in the 2010s is that of the crisis, most of whom experienced difficulty entering the labor market and then had chaotic phases in their careers. They would be unable to have a full pension at age 62 but would have to wait until they are 67. And since 67 is the expected length of a healthy life for a blue-collar male worker in France, he would therefore statistically have zero valid years of pension, compared to 10 years for a manager, who has statistically a far longer healthy life expectancy. But the first people to be affected by the reform were women: already, a third of them had to wait until age 65 to retire, because of their choppy careers. Despite that, the average pension for women is 40% lower than for men. Half of them, potentially, will reach age 67 by 2023. Taking the daily benefits of maternity leave into account in the calculation of pensions of mothers (as foreseen in the law's plan) would be of little practical help: it would apply only to new children, and hence the first women who would benefit are women who are currently 45 at most and who will take retirement around 2030—and nobody knows if this "advantage" will still exist then.

Women are also affected by the pseudo-convergence between government workers' contributions and employees in the private sector. The contributions of the former are only an accounting game; there is no pension fund for government workers—even virtually—that might equilibrate pensions and contributions. The increase in government workers' pension contributions therefore amounts to a drop of around 3% over a decade in the salary of these public employees—on top of which comes the salary freeze.

All three of the emblematic "reforms" of Sarkozy's term that affected labor—overtime, trimming of public services, and pensions—were harmful to women. It is unlikely that this was by deliberate political will. On the other hand, this common feature shows that apart from the symbolic goals at the level of the economic elite—for example, that corporate boards should be 40% women—equality between women and men was absent from policy thinking.

Nevertheless, the reforms of pensions, the taxation of early retirement, and after 2010 the impossibility of pensioning off an employee before the age of 70, profoundly changed the situation of working seniors. Thus, in 2012, only 3% of people aged 58 were in early retirement, compared to 19% in 2006. In total, the employment rate of those aged 55 to 64 grew in France from 38.1% in 2006 to 44.5% in 2012, despite the crisis and the rise in general unemployment. The comparison with the United Kingdom (whose demography is close to France's) is illuminating. The rate of employment of French seniors remains far from the British level, but the gap between the two countries is narrowing: 13.6% in 2012, compared to 19.2% in 2006 (European Labour Force Survey data).

The other ways of financing of pensions foreseen until 2018 are likewise illuminating. The biggest is the trimming of 2 billion euros from Fillon's 2003 social contribution alleviations (see the previous chapter); without saying so, François Fillon recognized the ineffectiveness of the arrangement he had imagined seven years before. The most surprising is the immediate use of the Pension Reserve Fund, which was not to be touched until after 2020. The durability of French pension schemes is absolutely not guaranteed.

COSTLY VOTE-CATCHING MEASURES

To find financing was all the more necessary because Sarkozy was taking care of his supporters. A good illustration is that of French expatriates. First, the national constitution was modified in 2008 to permit during the legislative vote of 2012 the election of eleven deputies (2% of the total) to represent French citizens abroad. Then, the state made French *lycées* abroad free for the children of expatriates (apart from government functionaries)—most of who did not pay taxes in France. Apart from its cost, this measure provoked a flood of applications by French teenagers, which resulted in the eviction of foreign pupils, although the goal of French *lycées* is to spread French culture outside the borders of the Hexagon.

But the principal beneficiaries of these measures were businesses. An electoral base of the French Right, restaurateurs obtained a drop in VAT (5.5% instead of 19.6%) in restaurant meals starting in July 2009; this became the lowest VAT in this sector within the European Union (except Luxembourg). This reduction was only possible with agreement from the European Union; the alignment of President Sarkozy with the European policy of Angela Merkel was a direct counterpart of the acceptance by Germany of this lower VAT. At an annual rate, the lost revenue to state coffers was between two and three billion euros. The "contract" signed between the government and business representatives from the restaurant sector assured that this sum would be "returned" to consumers in the form of lower restaurant prices, and to employees in the form of higher salaries and more staff. On the first promise, according to INSEE data, only half the restaurateurs lowered prices, and these only on a few items. On the second commitment, a sector agreement was applied in March 2010; the salary and benefit advantages represent less than a third of the fiscal gain for firms in this sector. In short, job creation was modest. Taking into account this sector's dynamic, the effect of reduced VAT on employment (full-time and part-time) probably did not exceed 10,000. The gross cost to the state for the employment created in restaurants might be estimated at a minimum of 100,000 euros per year per position, or about 4 to 5 times that of a starting nurse working full-time.[8]

Still more "ambitious" was remaking the *taxe professionnelle*, which was a tax based essentially on productive investment (in stock and flows) and which had been decried, practically since its creation in 1976, as a burden on the manufacturing industry and as accelerating company relocations. The suppression of this tax had been planned for several decades by governments of both Left and Right. But this had not been done, because of two obstacles. The first was total uncertainty about the impact of its suppression on investments in firms: there was no prior solid estimation, and firms did not seem to want to see it as a significant determinant of their decision where to settle or their activity in France, more so because the local taxation of companies occurred in many European countries, including manufacturing in Germany.[9] The second obstacle was the cost of eliminating the professional tax, which had become an essential source of financing for local government. Nevertheless, the president's commitment was maintained. This has meant a loss of more than twelve billion euros in tax revenue since 2010. The financing of this measure largely relied on increased local taxation of individuals (excluding the beneficiaries of the "fiscal shield"). The suppression of the professional tax was supposed to change the behavior of companies and to favor employment. Four years later, admittedly in the context of recession, no significant change was detectable.

RESEARCH AS A PRIORITY?

Meanwhile, the Fillon government modified French research policy. Early fear that research would be abandoned, with the presence in power of the two former ministers (Fillon in Research, Sarkozy in Budget) who had initiated the decline of state-funded research in 1993, proved unfounded. Under the impetus of the director of the president's office at the start of his term, a majority became aware of France's lag in the knowledge economy, and particularly its decline in R&D. France was the only major industrial country that had experienced such a collapse between 2002 and 2007, and two-thirds of this was attributable to a withdrawal of R&D expenditure in private firms. This awareness, combined with lobbying efforts by the major corporations for improved fiscal treatment of their research activities, became the lever of a supplementary tax sprawl. The Ministry of Research became a strong ministry again; Valérie Pécresse combined research and higher education.

Public research had experienced since 2005 an upheaval in how it was financed. The research bodies saw their endowments reduced, to the profit of a new emerging actor: the National Research Agency, which distributed upon tender major financing for projects over periods from two to four years. The government extended this by increasing the competitive arrangement in the framework of "great loans," that is to say by resorting to indebtedness, to endow the chosen projects with capital. The cost of the interest on the loans, estimated at between 800 million and 1 billion euros, was offset by reductions in state expenditure, notably in recurrent endowment of research bodies. The result expected from these communicating vessels was the emergence of major research nodes with worldwide visibility—to the detriment of many universities. It was facilitated by another managerial reform consisting of giving presidents of universities greater autonomy in management.

The government also claimed to give more value to jobs in research, now that this had become a priority. But by "priority" it meant the one-for-one replacement of researchers who were retiring. The return of young French researchers from abroad was also a priority—but with only 25 specific contracts per year. Bonuses (*primes d'excellence scientifiques*) were offered. For university teachers, they adopted the existing bonuses. For researchers, the budget's allowance represented 2% to 3% of the wage bill, that is to say, equivalent to the diminution of net salary imposed by the pension reform. One gets lost in the arrangements for "excellence": campuses of excellence, bonuses for excellence, laboratories and networks of excellence, equipment of excellence, initiatives of excellence, and so on.

It is still too early to measure the scientific impact of this promotion of research. For one thing, the administrative responsibility of research teams to obtain national financing was increased so much that participation in tendered European bids diminished. Universities that had become autonomous were obliged by budget increases to recruit managers. In 2013, a number of universities thus found their budgets so hard-pressed that they had to reduce teaching volume and freeze research-teaching posts. It was the "poles of excellence" that now benefited from major financing. In fact, the reform of research proceeded according to the Sarkozy ideology of favoring the strongest.

A GENEROUS RESEARCH TAX CREDIT

While managers of public research were focused on constructing "poles," the government carried out a spectacular remake of the research tax credit (*crédit impôt recherche*, or CIR), which in two years became the state's major fiscal rebate (*niche*). It was also the spearhead of research policy in France, and so must be examined more closely. The CIR had already been modified many times. Created in 1983 and before the 2000s confined to firms with growing expenditure on R&D, it was extended under the previous term to a limited portion of stock expenses. The CIR thus offered initially a tax credit on the *increase* in a firm's R&D expenditure; in fact, the main beneficiaries were innovative small businesses that were in rapid development. An evaluation of tax credits—found in various countries like the United States and Japan—is always delicate. The rare French studies suggest they were relatively effective, with 1 euro of fiscal expenditure able to generate more than 3 euros in private R&D in the long term.[10]

This encouraging result gave rise to an enormous error of interpretation. Though it referred only to *old* CIRs, it would be extrapolated to the new CIR introduced in 2008, in which the credit offered by the state was based on total expenditures rather than on their increase. Nevertheless, it is logical to expect that a tax credit that a firm receives even if its effort is fading cannot have the same effect as a credit extended only if the effort is increased. This misunderstanding led to fantastical estimates prior to its implementation. For example, at the start of 2009, the General Directorate of the Treasury and Economic Policy—whose work was usually careful—estimated that the CIR on its own would enable reaching an objective of 3% of GDP in domestic spending on R&D.[11] This would necessitate the recruitment of 25,000 researchers between then and 2020, including 10,000 in 2009–2010, all accompanied by an annual increase in the salaries of researchers that might reach 3% per year. Public statements were equally astonishing. The Ministry of Research claimed that the CIR functioned well because it cost a lot. The yearly cost of the CIR is more than 4 billion euros, almost twice the state's subsidy to the CNRS (the overall research body) and its 12,000 researchers. While France is a midget compared with Japan or the United States with respect to private research expenditure, the cost of the CIR is similar: less than 4 billion euros in the United States and almost 5 billion in Japan (in purchasing power parity terms). It is much higher in cost than the British CIR. Germany simply does not have such a tax credit. In fact, the French CIR is the most fiscally generous arrangement in all the OECD countries.

Moreover, the perverse effects had been underestimated. The first was the administrative fattening of fiscal advice: corporations, even the largest ones, if they did not have a specialized internal service, secured their "CIR." Accounting and tax law offices were remunerated at between 10% and 20% of the fiscal savings; the CIR thus produced potentially several hundred million euros in fiscal mediation. The second effect was linked to the application of European law. Firms benefited from the CIR even if they subcontracted their research to other countries in the EU.

Again out of a concern to bring the university and business together and to "foster" public research, the CIR was also doubled when a private firm subcontracted to an institution of public research or higher education in France. This meant that 60% of the expenses were reimbursed by the state to the firm—and that the net cost of subcontracting to them was a third less than keeping research internal. The risk was that the former would replace the latter. Since public research could not increase its statutory personnel, the danger was now the eviction of basic and independent research for the sake of research directed at corporations. This was a major danger in the long term, because it is basic research that fosters the innovations of the future and hence will help shape growth in the years 2020–2030. But already, in the decade of the 2010s, the absence of an ambitious educational policy would affect the current generations of children and adolescents who will arrive on the labor market.

Here again it is too early to estimate the ultimate impact of the CIR. However, the first signals suggest that instead of researchers' being recruited, it is leading to the elimination of positions due to the communicating-vessels phenomenon. For example, the French champion in R&D (for vaccines against the flu), Sanofi Aventis, in subcontracting part of its activity to public laboratories, eliminated its internal research positions. A first evaluation of the new CIR is edifying: for every 1,000 euros in lower taxes, firms spent 700 more euros on R&D.[12] Furthermore, this evaluation does not take into account the fact that to finance this policy the state reduces its own research effort. Overall, progress in domestic R&D expenditure is slow: 2.25% of GDP in 2011, compared to 2.11% in 2006, according to the OECD Main Science and Technology Indicators (May, 2014). Worse, the gap *vis-à-vis* Germany is growing (it spent 2.89% in 2011, compared to 2.54% five years earlier). First estimates for 2012 confirm the gap: 2.98% for Germany, 2.29% for France.

FRANCE FRACTURED BUT UNEMPLOYMENT CONTAINED

Thus, we see that all measures since 2007 have had the same characteristics: voluntarism, an enormous cost for public finance, redistribution toward businesses or the most wealthy, machismo, crumbs for the most modest, and speed in implementation—with a correlative absence of reflection on possible perverse effects.

The policy results were visible by the time Sarkozy left office. The many gifts to enterprise allowed non-financial corporations to pay out under his five-year term—amid full economic crises—the highest net dividends to their shareholders since the end of the Second World War.

Of course inequality in income and wealth has been dug deeper. In 2010, the best-off 1% of households owned almost 20% of the nation's total wealth, or about 2.5 times more than the 50% of households below median income. After a drop in 2009, the 1% highest net income earners started to rise again in 2010, at a pace of 5% per year in real terms. At the same time, poverty was exploding. With the freeze on the minimum wage, salary inequality at the bottom of the scale widened. By the latest available statistics, the number of poor people (below 60% of median income) went from 7.8 million in 2006 (including 2.4 million children) to 8.6 million in 2010 (including 2.7 million children). The fracture is also territorial. Towns that were already poor, like Dunkirk in the north, are getting poorer. At the other extreme, Neuilly-sur-Seine, a chic community on the west of Paris (of which Nicolas Sarkozy was mayor until his election as president), seems to have totally escaped the crisis: between 2008 and 2011, according to INSEE data, the median income there grew by 2,000 euros, and the 10% highest incomes grew by more than 7,000 euros—the record in France.

While they have reinforced inequality—which was their goal—Sarkozy's policies have not sucked France into the strategy of forced austerity, as occurred in southern Europe. The budget deficit in 2009 reached its worst point since the end of the Second World War: 7.1% of GDP (INSEE National Accounts, base 2010). It remained significant in 2010 (6.8%) and in 2011 (5.1%). Correlatively, the French national debt soared to 84% of GDP at the end of 2011.

By historical chance, Nicolas Sarkozy was budget minister during the preceding yawning deficits. The accumulated deficits when he was budget minister between 1993 and 1995, finance minister in 2004, and president of the republic from 2007 to 2012, together represent about half of the current French public debt! In some respects, Nicolas Sarkozy was a Keynesian. Of course France was in recession in 2009, but only by 3.1%, as compared to 3.8% in Spain, 5.2% in the United Kingdom, 5.1% in Germany, and 5.5% in Italy (OECD StatExtracts, August 2014). Modest growth returned in 2010, and even accelerated in 2011, to 2% of GDP. At the end of the five-year presidency, France and Germany were the only major European countries to feature a GDP higher than in 2007, just before the Great Recession.

The results on the employment front were astonishingly good. Of course the unemployment rate grew significantly; yet, it remained contained. At almost 10% at the start of 2012, it was thus much lower than in 1997, four years after the crisis of 1992–1993, which was much less profound than the Great Recession. In fact, macroeconomic models from the economic administrations, as well as institutes, were incapable of explaining this phenomenon. France ought "normally" to have about half a million more unemployed. Could this containment be attributed to the policy of Nicolas Sarkozy? Some mechanisms, including the dramatic improvement in the education of the French workforce in the past two decades, seem to explain much of this performance.[13] Other countries experienced this anomaly as well, especially the United Kingdom and Germany.[14] Correlatively, the three main European economies all presented sluggish work productivity. The black spot remains in France: youth unemployment had reached 23% when Sarkozy left office.

HOLLANDE, OR THE FALSE ECONOMIC CHANGE

François Hollande was well aware of this in 2012. The Socialist candidate for president constructed his campaign around two priorities—youth and fiscal justice—and his slogan was "Change is now." The victory of Hollande in May 2012 was confirmed in the legislative elections in June 2012, when the Socialist Party obtained an absolute majority. As with Mitterrand in 1981, Hollande named as prime minister the mayor of a large provincial city (Nantes): Jean-Marc Ayrault. He formed a vast government, including as many women as men, plus ecologists and leftist radicals (center-Left). But it was strangely unbalanced. A giant Ministry of Social Affairs and Health was entrusted to Marisol Touraine. At the opposite extreme, economic, industrial, trade and financial affairs were split among four ministers, plus three junior ministers. The historically most powerful person in France (after the king in the Ancien Régime and after the president in the Fifth Republic), the minister of economy and finance, found himself eclipsed by the bustling minister of productive recovery (*sic*), Arnaud Montebourg.

The new majority immediately found itself faced with major challenges. Although it intended to deliver change, it was looking at a stagnant economy, a recession in the euro area (France's principal client), and total uncertainty about the future of Europe (and France's position in it)—plus the nation's budgetary commitments. On the other hand, it had perhaps (on paper) important margins of maneuver by attacking the many fiscal gifts made by Sarkozy.

The first measures before the summer pause of 2012 corrected the most flagrant points of the policy of the previous majority. The fiscal shield was abrogated. Fiscal exemptions for overtime hours were almost eliminated; on the other hand, the conversion to the 35-hour workweek was not resumed. Budget savings enabled most of the financing of relaxed access to retirement at age 60 for those who began work very young, the re-establishment of teacher training, and resumption of recruitment of primary and secondary school teachers. The self-immolation of an unemployed person in front of a job agency pushed the government to immediately recruit hundreds of agents to help the jobless in their efforts to find work. Yet, the continuity with Sarkozy's policy was evident. The freeze on public employees' salaries was maintained, as well as the suppression of positions (outside education) and the reduction in administrative budgets, including research; infrastructure projects were postponed. Similarly, the minimum-wage tweak in July 2012 was wholly symbolic and transitory until January 2013.

Continuity was also evident in European policy. Though Hollande could have constructed a coalition with Italy and Spain within the eurozone, he refused any confrontation with Angela Merkel, even though she had openly supported the re-election of Nicolas Sarkozy. France accepted the budgetary pact (officially, the Treaty on Stability, Coordination and Governance—TSCG) written by the European Commission and Merkel, with prior approval by Sarkozy. The ratification of this new treaty was a retreat from France's sovereignty and a major limitation on the power of Parliament, which was henceforth under the tightened supervision of the European Commission in the elaboration of France's budget. Hollande was placing a dual wager. On the one hand, following his diplomatic advisors, he had to maintain France's credibility while waiting for a hypothetical weakening of Merkel during the German elections of September 2013. On the other hand, the TSCG placed at the core of budgetary policy a new criterion to reach under pain of sanctions: a "structural deficit" of less than half a percent of GDP. But the definition of the structural deficit—the level of deficit if the economic conjuncture was average—was far from unanimous among economists, and the method of calculation even less so. In practice, the results differed widely; worse, sometimes several years later, economic institutes and administrations drastically revised their estimates. Hollande's political calculation was thus: France could sign the treaty, because in practice it would be inapplicable.

Despite the triumphal re-election of Merkel, the economic conjuncture partially validated Hollande's strategy. Recession in the eurozone persisted, and a new major macroeconomic risk appeared: deflation. Inflation fell well below the ECB goal of 2% annually. There was panic in the corridors of members of the troika. The IMF acknowledged the evidence in January 2013: the austerity policy in Europe was killing growth and trapping countries in a vicious circle. The European Commission granted a supplementary delay to several European countries, including France, to adjust their public finances. Finally, the ECB lowered its rate of refinancing to 0.5% in May, then to 0.25% in November 2013.

This delay allowed Jean-Marc Ayrault's government to smooth out the household tax increases. Nevertheless, the list of these kept getting longer, and they now affected most households. One of the most noticeable was the hike in VAT scheduled for January 2014. In the last moments of his presidency, Nicolas Sarkozy had set this hike for October 2012, but it was immediately suppressed by the new majority, only to be re-established with different parameters. Like Sarkozy, Hollande and Ayrault imposed (in the autumn of 2013) a new pension adjustment: a tiny reduction in current pensions, a longer period of contribution and an increase in contributions paid by both employees and employers. But unlike Sarkozy, François Hollande courted the trade unions, engaging in "contractual policy-making." Thus, the government regularly organized conferences to which all unions were invited. Employer and employee organizations were asked to modify large slices of the labor law and the organization of professional training. A first national agreement was signed between a majority of unions and management in January 2013; Parliament faithfully transcribed its many provisions into the law. The key element was the possibility of a "job competitiveness agreement": if an agreement with a union counting for more than 30% of the votes (without opposition from another counting for more than 50%) was found, then the firm could lower the workers' salaries. Workers who refused to take wage cuts could be fired (the refusal was considered a legitimate cause). First acknowledged as a major change of French regulation, this reform seems to be as little used as the senior short-term contract (see previous chapter): only five firms had signed job competitiveness agreements in one year.

Aware that such a remaking of the "right to work" would have uncertain effects on employment, the Ayrault government pursued the social treatment of unemployment. The youth jobs utilized by the Jospin government were reintroduced under the name of "jobs of the future." A second tool, the arrangement for "generational contracts," sailed forward. Simplifying, this meant that a firm received a subsidy for three years for hiring someone under 26, if at the same time it did not fire someone over 57 (hence the name). However, youth unemployment began to slowly decline during 2013. At the end of 2013, according to the

ILO definition, about 650,000 French youth were unemployed, compared to 0.9 million in Great Britain.

Hollande and Ayrault especially hoped for success from their central policy: the Tax Credit for Competitiveness and Employment (Crédit d'impôt pour la compétitivité et l'emploi, or CICE). The genesis of this measure is fascinating. From the start of his term, Hollande was convinced that a shock was necessary to restart the French economy. Wanting to break with the ideologue Sarkozy, Hollande consulted widely. Louis Gallois, former CEO of the aeronautic giant EADS, was in charge of diagnosis and proposals for recovering France's competitiveness in the autumn of 2012. Into this opening immediately flooded employer lobbies and a procession of some of my fellow economists, both liberals and self-proclaimed social democrats.

A comparison with Germany is again necessary. German growth was barely better than France's (1 point more in 2011, 0.7 points in 2012). But unemployment had returned to a level lower than before the crisis. France's trade deficit *vis-à-vis* Germany had become a chasm, going back to its relative level of 1982. Correlatively, French manufacturing industry was declining much more rapidly. Finally, while the deficit in the French budget remained large, Germany had a surplus.

Where did the German success come from? If we speak of the "German miracle," it is precisely because it is still hard to grasp the key factors, or more precisely the relative weight of the various mechanisms at work. Germany may be in a phase that is demographically favorable for now, with few children who are costly (in education) and not yet many old people (pensions, health). It may be benefiting from its geographically central place in Europe, in direct contact with the "new Europe." While the Hartz Laws might appear disappointing at the microeconomic level, they caused real sacrifices among a significant portion of German workers. Germany may also be harvesting the strategies of innovation in its businesses that were launched in the mid-1990s, and the conquest of emerging markets.

The absence of a central scenario validated by scientific literature left space for an intellectual blitz between August 2012 and October 2012. This calls for a look at the causes of the France–Germany differential in terms of competitiveness.

On the one hand, France had missed the mark in competitiveness with respect to innovation. Out of incompetence or susceptibility to lobbies, the duo in power let itself be convinced that this implied that the tax credit for research should be preserved for the whole duration of the legislature. On the other hand, French firms were said to be hampered by inflated salary costs. The problem is that the hourly cost of work in the manufacturing industries was similar on both banks of the Rhine. So they had to find another argument: manufacturing also uses services, which must be much more onerous in France. Certainly wages in services are much higher in France, but nothing proves that this is the case for most services used by factories. Recall that the very low wages in Germany are in occupations like hairdressing, restaurants, and retail. To convince those in power, statistics on the profits of non-financial companies were put forward. The gross margin (gross operating surplus divided by value added) was 8 to 12 points higher in Germany. But this comparison is doubly fallacious. First of all, the majority of German small businesses are partnerships: their members do not receive salaries but dividends that are accounted at the marginal rate. This status is little used in France. Second, because manufacturing is more intensive in capital, it would be normal that Germany had greater margins. A serious diagnosis would require access to the fiscal data in both countries.

But a truncated diagnosis was possible. France required an immediate policy to restore the competitive cost of French firms by lowering the cost of labor, and this time not only for those close to the minimum wage. The decision was made at the start of November 2012 to measure most financial margins with a single tool, the CICE. This tax credit is equivalent to a cut in payroll taxes (for wages up to 2.5 times the minimum) of 4% in 2013 and 6% in subsequent years. This signifies (in permanent annual flow) 20 billion euros as gifts to business. This one stroke is equivalent to all the reductions in social contributions granted by the Balladur, Juppé, and Raffarin governments. France was thus entering into the non-cooperative and deflationary strategy followed by numerous European countries: raising cost competitiveness against its partners.

This decision was far from convincing all the deputies in the majority. But they did pass the CICE, with a commitment to evaluate it, and possibly challenge it. (A few days after the announcement of the CICE, I was named to the Council of Economic Analysis.[15] In July 2013, I became an independent expert for the committee to follow up the CICE, which is supposed to pilot its evaluations and to report on them to Parliament.)

The apparent ease of imposing the CICE on his Socialist majority convinced François Hollande to go further in tax cuts for companies and in wage freezes. Despite the introduction of a minimum wage in Germany and the 11% increase in the UK minimum wage scheduled in 2014 and 2015, France did not raise its minimum wage. In the presidential address to the nation at the start of 2014, he clearly explained that his policy was to reduce the "charges" paid by firms to create jobs. In saying "charges" instead of "social contributions," he was sticking to the vocabulary of the employers' organizations. On January 14, 2014, this leader who claimed to be a Social Democrat announced the removal of the employers' contribution to the family portion of social security by the end of his mandate in 2017. This represents about 4% of labor costs. Basically, private employers' contributions will decline to where they were before the sharp increases instituted by Raymond Barre in the 1970s. The amounts transferred to firms are so huge that the government will have to dramatically cut public spending and probably a portion of social benefits. To ensure the acceptance of this policy by citizens, MEDEF, the main employer organization, promised that its members would create hundreds of thousands jobs in France; Hollande proposed creating an observatory of what he called the "responsibility pact." In effect, the Socialist Party definitively abandoned the pretense of conducting economic affairs; meanwhile, MEDEF claimed to be able to control French capitalism.

Despite the worst defeat of the Socialist Party in local elections in March 2014, Hollande confirmed his policy, simply reorganizing the government and replacing the prime minister, choosing Manuel Valls, who represents the right wing of the Socialist Party. The Green Party quit the government. Valls announced additional reductions in company taxes and cuts in public spending. His plan was validated by the National Assembly in late April 2014, but with merely a relative majority. Late August, the government was revamped with the eviction of the minister of economy, Arnaud Montebourg, who supported consumption stimulus. Valls' plan followed the same path as the Conservative policy in the United Kingdom. But contrary to Cameron, who claimed that "reducing tax and regulation is not enough" and implemented a "modern industrial strategy,"[16] Valls did not propose a clear industrial strategy associated with his fiscal policy.

Will this policy succeed? And will it live up to the stakes? The uncertainties—both negative and positive—are large, both nationally and within the European Union. What is certain is that François Hollande has used all his budgetary margins of maneuver, and will not have a second opportunity—unless he jettisons his key policy. In its reiteration of the history of the last four decades, the wager by Hollande seems to rest on a superficial diagnosis of the state of France. Without claiming to be exhaustive, the next chapter will lay out some of the dimensions of the difficulties and advantages of France within Europe.

NOTES

1. Léon Gambetta, *Réflexions de M. Gambetta sur la situation politique: lettre adressée aux lyonnais, le 25 octobre 1875* (Paris: Ernest Leroux Editeur, 1875), available at http://gallica.bnf.fr.

2. José-Luis Zapatero marked the return of the Socialists in Spain in 2004; Angela Merkel became German chancellor in 2005; and Romano Prodi assumed the presidency of the Italian Council in 2006.

3. Dirk Krueger and Fabrizio Perri, "Does Income Inequality Lead to Consumption Inequality? Evidence and Theory," *Review of Economic Studies* 73, no. 1 (2006): 163–93.

4. Securitization is a financial technique that transforms assets for which there is no actual exchange market (for example, debts) into valuables that are easily negotiable.

5. The optimistic estimates of the IMF were based on the impact of national policies of austerity in isolation, but Europe was entering into a *coordinated* policy of budgetary austerity.

6. Pauline Gonthier, "Why Was Short-Time Work Unattractive during the Crisis?" IRLE Working Paper No. 130–12, Institute for Research on Labor and Employment, Institute of Industrial Relations, UC Berkeley (2012).

7. L. Behaghel, B. Crépon, M. Gurgand, T. Kamionka, L. Lequien, R. Rathelot, and P. Zamora, "L'accompagnement personnalisé des demandeurs d'emploi: les enseignements de trois expériences contrôlées menées en France," *Revue française d'économie* 28 (2013), 123–58.

8. The calculation used here is conservative: the minimal fiscal cost of the measure (2.3 billion euros), less the branch agreement (1 billion euros, at most, over a full year), less the drop in prices (300 million euros, at most, "given back" to consumers). Total: 1 billion euros for 10,000 jobs.

9. See for example Raymond Bernard, Hubert Jayet, and Dominique Rajaonarison, "L'environnement souhaité par les entreprises," *Economie et Statistique* 326 (1999).

10. Benoît Mulkay and Jacques Mairesse, "Une évaluation du crédit d'impôt recherche en France (1980–1997)," *Revue d'Économie Politique* 114, no. 6 (2004).

11. DGTPE, "Les effets économiques de la réforme du Crédit d'Impôt Recherche de 2008," *Trésor Eco* 50 (2009). This error would be reproduced by the Inspection des finances in its report on the CIR of September 2010: *Mission d'évaluation du Crédit Impôt Recherche*, N°2010 M 035 02 (Paris: La documentation française, 2010).

12. Benoît Mulkay and Jacques Mairesse, "The R&D Tax Credit in France: Assessment and Ex Ante Evaluation of the 2008 Reform," *Oxford Economic Papers* 65, no. 3 (2013): 746–66.

13. Philippe Askenazy and Christine Erhel, "The French Productivity Puzzle," mimeo (Paris: CEPREMAP, 2014).

14. See ILO, *Euro Zone Job Crisis: Trends and Policy Responses,* Studies on Growth with Equity (Geneva: ILO, 2012). This question has been explored in many studies in the United Kingdom, which advance a multitude of hypotheses without an emerging consensus. See for example Richard Disney, Wenchao Jin, and Helen Miller, "The Productivity Puzzles", in *IFS Green Budget* (London: Institute for Fiscal Studies, 2013), ch. 3.

15. This is an independent, non-partisan advisory body reporting to the French prime minister. Its fifteen members come from the academic community and are chosen by the prime minister.

16. David Cameron, Lord Mayor's Banquet speech, November 12, 2012.

CHAPTER EIGHT

The State of France

Four Decades After the First Oil Crisis

After four decades of struggling against unemployment and adapting to globalization, where does France stand these days? Reading the *New York Times* or the *Economist,* the answer is categorical.[1] France is the sick man of Europe—as was the United Kingdom in the 1970s and Germany in the 1990s. France is too big to be saved; it is burdened with a spendthrift state; the French people do too little work and are addicted to their advantages; the citizenry is averse to reform. Even academic studies see French society as distrustful and unhappy.[2] In this chapter I offer a portrait of France, necessarily impressionistic, that interrogates some of these clichés. Just as the French no longer wear berets but still buy baguettes, these clichés only partially convey a nuanced reality.

In the first place, I hope that an attentive reader of this book will be convinced that France is reforming. Indeed, the French are coping with an avalanche of reforms and counter-reforms. Their apparent aversion to reform (highlighted in international surveys) is probably more like a symptom of an overdose of half-hearted reforms and their adverse impacts. The overdose is made possible by a constitution that gives the leader of the majority party (or coalition) a freedom of maneuver that is much wider than the American president has. And the trade unions can no longer play the role of a counterweight to the power of the employers; some of them are content to go along with the government in power.

IS FRANCE REALLY IN DECLINE?

The question reappears regularly in the French national debate, in the media and in foreign capitals. Such worries reached their first paroxysm after the 1981 election of Mitterrand, the first Socialist president of the Fifth Republic. There was a second wave of panic with the election of the second Socialist president, Hollande, thirty-one years later.

Without entering into the psychology or culture of the French people (or the media), the key economic data show a France hit hard by crisis since the end of 2008. But here the situation is not obviously different from that in the two major English-speaking economies, the United Kingdom and the United States (table 7). Growth is sluggish but slightly positive for the period 2009–13; unemployment is massive but contained (although it started from a high level); and foreign exchange is in the red, but not excessively so.

Even youth unemployment has not exploded. One year after the election of François Hollande, 700,000 people under 25 were unemployed, much as in the spring of 1982, one year after the arrival of Mitterrand. Their number even began to decline in 2013; and the proportion of youth "not in education, employment, or training" (NEET) was similar to the proportions in the United Kingdom and the United States.

While France has lost position with respect to R&D, we have seen that this situation is shared with the United Kingdom and is rooted in the first half of the 1990s. On the other hand, in the Shanghai ranking of world universities in 2014, the United Kingdom had six universities among the first ten in Europe, France had two—and Germany, none.

One country stands out more than France: Germany. Despite the crisis of the euro area, its current account is largely in surplus, and it enjoyed a sharp drop in unemployment. Its manufacturing sector remains powerful: at the start of 2014, according to labor-force surveys, Germany had almost 1 manufacturing job for every 10 inhabitants, compared to 0.5 in France, and less than 0.5 in the United Kingdom and the United States.[3] But the other side of the coin is that Germany is in demographic decline and will have fewer inhabitants than France or the United Kingdom by around 2045. In 2012, the fertility rate did not even reach 1.4, as in Spain, while it slightly exceeded 2 in France, just above the United Kingdom and the United States. In Europe, only Ireland is doing better than France in fertility.

French demographic dynamism explains one part of the schizophrenia of the financial world. On the one hand, France evokes constant fear in comparison with "model" Germany; and on the other, its public debt is attractive. France is the only country that regularly dares to test the confidence of very long-term investors by offering 50-year treasury bonds. Thus, a few weeks after the election of François Hollande, a test float of 0.7 billion euros at 50 years drew a demand of 1.6 billion, for a final interest rate of only 3.27%.

TABLE 7

Major economic indicators before and after the Great Recession (average percentage of GDP)

	France		Germany		UK		US	
	2000–08	*2009–13*	*2000–08*	*2009–13*	*2000–08*	*2009–13*	*2000–08*	*2009–12*
Annual growth	1.8	0.2	1.6	0.7	2.7	–0.1	2.3	1.2
Unemployment	8.6	9.5	9.2	6.3	5.2	7.8	5.1	8.7
Current account	0.2	–1.6	3.5	6.8	–2.1	–2.8	–4.7	–2.7

SOURCE: OECD StatExtracts, extracted August 24, 2014

IS FRANCE CRUSHED BY TAXES—BUT EGALITARIAN?

One of the principal arguments for concern about the survival of the French economy is the high rate of taxes and the correlatively massive social transfers. This "model" was already made more fragile by globalization and would become untenable in a Europe in crisis. The statistics are indeed striking. In 2011, tax revenue exceeded 44% of GDP in France, as opposed to 37.5% in Germany, 35.5% in the United Kingdom, and only 25.1% in the United States. While France is far behind the "good student" in the eurozone, Germany, France's deductions avoid the colossal budget deficits of Great Britain and (even more) the United States. Above all, they enable the effective financing of social transfers that are far superior to those practiced in the three other countries. However, this assessment needs refinement.

Let's start by breaking down the tax burden in France. Table 8 shows some important figures for 2011. (Tax increases passed in 2012 and 2013 will not significantly alter these.) Among the accepted ideas that circulate both in France and abroad are that businesses and households are being pummeled and that the wealth tax is confiscatory. The first is easy to dispose of. In 2011, France's income and profit taxes were the lowest of the four countries, barely 10% of GDP. As I have stressed in the preceding chapters, income tax has been sharply cut since the start of the 2000s. Similarly, though the fiscal tax rate on companies is much higher than in the three other countries, the multiplicity of tax credits (such as the Crédit d'impôt recherche) reduces the total bill spectacularly, especially for the largest firms. This is one factor that explains why France receives as much direct foreign investment as Germany (40 billion euros in 2011, compared to 54 billion for the United Kingdom).

More surprising, wealth taxes are not exorbitant compared to Great Britain or the United States, which like France enjoy an overall wealth much higher than the Germans (about 600% of GDP as against 400% in Germany). One illustration will enable us to understand the gap between what is taken as common knowledge and the reality of the fiscal provisions in France. The wealth tax is normally payable on any household wealth worth more than 1.3 million euros. Take the Durant family. The two parents are owners of their own architectural office, valued at 2 million euros. They have inherited a Picasso worth 500,000 euros, and are owners of a cottage in Normandy worth 500,000 and an apartment in Paris worth 1 million. Thus, they possess wealth (*patrimoine*) valued at 4 million euros. What will be the taxes on this wealth? They pay property taxes: about 1,100 euros per year in Normandy and another 1,300 in Paris. Their wealth tax is nil. Professional property—including minority shares—is not assessed (the architectural office), nor are artworks (the Picasso), nor are woods and forests. Only the principal residence is taken into account, and only at 70% of its value, in this case 700,000 euros. In total, their taxable wealth is only 1.2 million—which is below the threshold. The total tax on their *patrimoine* thus amounts to 2,400 euros on 4 million—or 0.06% per year.

Such taxes only become significant for very large fortunes, and again only on the fraction that is used for personal use or pure rents. The tax liability is far from being confiscatory for median fortunes; so inequality in wealth remains marked, and is increasing. According to the INSEE study of wealth for 2010, the net median wealth of a household whose head is an unskilled worker is less than 6,000 euros, compared to 28,800 for a skilled worker, 214,500 for an office worker, 482,600 for an independent professional (e.g. a lawyer), and 539,200 for a farmer.

TABLE 8

Principal taxes and transfers in 2011 (% of GDP)

	France	Germany	UK	US
Social transfers	35.6	28.7	29.1	21.8
Budget deficit	–5.2	–0.8	–7.8	–10.1
Total tax revenue	44.2	37.5	35.5	25.1
Taxes on income and profit	10.1	11.0	12.9	11.8
Contributions on wages	16.8	14.3	6.7	5.7
Taxes on wages	1.4	0	0	0
Taxes on wealth	3.7	0.9	4.1	3.0
Taxes on consumption	11.0	10.8	11.6	4.6

SOURCE: OECD StatExtracts, extracted September 1, 2013

Another illustration of the relative complexity of the French fiscal system is that taxes on salaries counted for 1.4% of GDP in 2011—while in the three other countries, they do not exist. But large portions of these taxes replace the VAT. France does not impose VAT on a whole series of activities: finance and insurance, as in the rest of Europe, but also cooperative property ownership, non-profit organizations, health, and so on. To compensate, a tax is deducted from salaries in these sectors. In most international comparisons, this tax is added to labor costs. But this is not a matter of an accounting convention. Explicitly replacing the VAT, it could instead be added to consumption taxes. The total taxes on consumption would then exceed those in the United Kingdom and Germany; but France would still roughly fit the European model,[4] which is distinct from the United States.

In short, the average fiscal pressure in France seems in accounting terms very close to that of the United Kingdom. The real difference concerns social pressure: the welfare contributions paid by employees and employers. These were 10 percentage points higher than in the United Kingdom in 2011. The CICE (Tax Credit for Competitiveness and Employment) and the scheduled removal of the employer's contribution to the family policy would reduce this gap by half. In the meantime, these contributions finance vast social transfers. And these give France a poverty rate, after taxes and transfers, that is the lowest of the countries under consideration, though before taxes and transfers, it is the highest (table 9). This is especially striking with regard to seniors. The concentration of the national effort on this population is clear when we look at the minimal allowances paid by the French state to a single person in 2013: 787 euros per month for someone 65 or older, 483 euros for someone 25 to 64, and nothing for someone under 25.

If we use OECD calculations and the Gini index, in 2010 inequality is lower after transfers and taxes; of all these countries, Germany has the best performance. Overall, the French system is not exceptionally redistributive, whatever indicator of inequality is used.

This is explained by the many transfers that benefit the middle classes but also the better-off classes. The following example of the Martin family illustrates the rules in force for income and expenditure in 2013. (This example will appear very complicated to many readers, yet it is "simple"—although it allows me to no more than sketch the Byzantine French tax system.) The Martin family has a child, age 7. The two parents have comfortable incomes, at least 100,000 euros per year each (or about 250,000 dollars for the household, a symbolic level in the American debates). Having only one child, this family gets no family allowance. However, it benefits from an income tax reduction of

TABLE 9

Poverty (share of population below 60% of median income) and inequality in 2010

		France	Germany	UK	US
Poverty rate	Before tax and transfers	0.396	0.356	0.354	0.329
	After tax and transfers	0.144	0.153	0.172	0.242
	Before tax and transfers, age 65+	0.861	0.860	0.693	0.411
	After tax and transfers, age 65+	0.132	0.209	0.182	0.221
Gini index	Before tax and transfers	0.505	0.492	0.523	0.499
	After tax and transfers	0.303	0.286	0.341	0.380

SOURCE: OECD StatExtracts, extracted September 1, 2013

1,500 euros. For after-school periods, the family uses the services of a caregiver employed by a specialized company. This amounts to 35 hours per month, for a cost of 700 euros. The jobs policy provides a tax credit on half of this expenditure, or 350 euros per month. Thus, income tax reductions add up to 5,700 euros per year. Now suppose that a happy event occurs on January 1 with the birth of a second child. The tax reduction for two children is 3000 euros. With two young children, the family gets family allowances of 128 euros per month. The baby goes to the *crèche*, and there is a tax credit on the nursery school fees of 1,150 euros. The caregiver is now looking after two children (after school and *crèche*). Thanks to the family policy, and since both parents are working, the family receives financial aid for this employment of 595 euros per month. The cost of the caregiver for the family is now only 1,260 euros per year; plus there is a tax reduction of half that sum, or 630 euros. The result is that the Martin family benefits from a tax reduction of 630 + 1,150 + 3,000 = 4,780 euros, and from social transfers of (595 + 128) × 12 = 8,676 euros.

Here we see the generosity of the French system, even for those who are well off. The birth of the baby generates an increase in disposable income of more than 650 euros per month for the Martin family. This is more than the net salary of a half-time worker on the minimum wage (560 euros), or the minimum guaranteed allowance paid to a pregnant woman without an income (620 euros). We also see from this simple example the entanglement of social and fiscal provisions. The fact of receiving more in social transfers with the birth of the second child generates a rise in income tax of more than 900 euros for the Martin family.

The case of the employment of the caregiver is illuminating, as well. She is employed by a specialized company (most of the insurance companies offer this service to their clients). The VAT is 3.5 euros; the company's profit margin is 1 euro and the labor cost for the company of one hour of work is 15.5 euros. In French statistics (as in international comparisons) it is this 15.5 euros that is used as the labor cost. But on the Martin family's side, with its two children, the cost (net of transfers and tax reductions) is only 1.5 euros (about 2 dollars) per hour. The very high labor costs, like the transfers, are thus partially an accounting phenomenon. Without even calling for a fiscal revolution, the state could decide to make all its provisions more transparent. In the case of the Martin family, one would eliminate the financial aid—and as a counterpart, the reduction for such jobs of 5 euros per hour in the employer's contributions—and increase the income tax credit to 90%. The result would be strictly similar for public finances and for the money in the pockets of the family, the employee, and the company. But in the statistics, the weights of taxes and contributions and the costs of labor and transfers in France would all diminish. And this would give a more accurate image of the French system.

In short, the image of a France crushed by taxes yet very egalitarian is more virtual than actual. This myth hides an accumulation of transfers that necessitates a multitude of taxes—especially on transfers!—and a relative bias in favor of seniors. And even this bias should gradually evaporate in the coming decades as a result of the pension reforms that have taken place since 1993 (see the preceding chapters). This accumulation has allowed all governments to claim that they are looking after the French.

The opaqueness and complexity of the socio-fiscal system are probably the real economic obstacles. And this realization permits some optimism. France could gain much from a simplification of this system, lowering both public expenditure and revenue, without this being translated into an explosion in inequality.

On the other hand, it would clearly be more arduous to tear down the many costly public policies "in favor" of employment and business. We have seen in the preceding chapters that these often cannibalize each other and are prone to major windfall effects. But some actors would inevitably lose out in any such remake, especially the major French multinationals. The latter possess powerful connections on both the right and the left of the political spectrum; they effectively control the principal organization of French employers.

A HEALTHY HEALTH SYSTEM AND A FAILING EDUCATION SYSTEM?

Beyond inequality in wealth, French society is riven by other fundamental inequalities: in health and in education. However, the French health system is often put in the positive balance scale for France. It relies on *juxtaposition* between a largely liberal urban medicine, with mainly public hospitals and public coverage of long-term illnesses. The results seem clear. French life expectancy significantly exceeds that of Americans, British, and Germans. Consistently, one measure of the global efficacy of a health system, "amenable mortality" (i.e. premature deaths that would not occur in the presence of effective and timely care), is in France the lowest of all OECD countries, ahead of the Scandinavian countries; it is about half of that in the United States.[5] France attracts patients: within the European system of compensation for social security expenditure, it presented a surplus of 800 million euros in 2012. Yet current French expenditures for health (11.6% of GDP in 2012) are equivalent to those of Germany (11.3%), and much lower than American levels.

On the other hand, access to care is highly dependent on social hierarchy. For example, inequality in breast cancer detection is as high in France as in the United States. Inequality in access to a doctor, in particular to a specialist, is likewise much higher than that observed in the United Kingdom or Germany; this is the direct consequence of out-of-pocket expenses of around 40% for specialists whose rates are well above what is reimbursed by social security. The split is also spatial, because doctors have the freedom to practice anywhere. In the various *départements*, the density of urban doctors varies by 1 to 2, and that of specialists by 1 to 8. Doctors tend to be concentrated in well-off and sunny towns!

In total, the high average life expectancy hides important disparities.[6] A male office worker's life expectancy is 7 years longer than a laborer's—10 years longer for living in good health. And while life expectancy continues to grow, the expectation of life in good health has been stagnating since the middle of the 2000s. The French health system performs well and is of moderate cost, but it is also part of the country's social inequalities.

Inequality also afflicts the educational system. For example, according to the 2012 PISA study, average reading scores among young Americans, French, British, and Germans are equal. But it is in France that the typical social gap is widest and getting wider. Along with New Zealand, France is the country where the social origin of the parents is the most striking predictor of children's test results.

Educational democratization in undeniable, since the proportion of young people with diplomas in higher education in France has reached British and American levels. But the summit has become inaccessible. Thus, the proportion of the children of blue-collar workers and clerks in the four largest French *grandes écoles* (the École nationale d'administration, ENA, produces political and administrative elites; the École des hautes études commerciales, HEC, produces financial and corporate elites; the École normale supérieure, ENS, produces intellectual and scientific elites; and the École polytechnique, or "X," produces industrial elites) has gone from around 30% in the 1950s to less than 10% today. The competitive examination that is the most demanding in terms of cultural baggage—social sciences at the ENS—takes only 25 students per year, and up to 20 of them come from the same class at Henri IV, the most prestigious *lycée* (public and therefore free) in France. This establishment looks out on the Place du Panthéon in Paris, the most expensive real estate in France—and lies 700 meters from the ENS.

As with health, public investment in education is spatially inegalitarian. Public teachers can choose where to be assigned as a function of points, linked notably to their seniority and to assessment of their teaching. The youngest teachers are therefore assigned to the most difficult schools. The result is that in 2010, the state spent 9,300 euros per student in the Paris *lycées*, compared to an average of 6,300 in the Créteil academy, the eastern suburb of Paris. This inequality of funding would be bearable if education were not eroding. But as a principal expenditure of the state, education does not escape efforts to economize. In 2012, total domestic expenditure on education represented only 6.9% of GDP, compared to 7.3% in 2000. Expenditure per student is now similar to that observed in the United Kingdom.

The accumulation of inequalities—although overall much less marked than in the USA—translates at the end of the causal chain into massive inequality in access to employment, which has been even worse since the start of the crisis. But, although they are depressing, these facts can again be read as a glass half-full. In Europe, France still has large margins of maneuver to improve the level of education and the state of health among entire sections of its population, by finding out how better to spread its resources, or rather by inverting the transfers that currently go toward the most privileged.

DO THE FRENCH REALLY WORK SUCH SHORT HOURS? ARE THEY REALLY SO PROTECTED?

The implementation of the 35-hour workweek in the 1990s contributed to the belief that the French work few hours, while being very productive for each hour worked. Even in France, the crystallization of the political debate over the 35-hour week—which is considered deadly by the Right but a social achievement by the Left—has supported this idea. Yet, as we have seen in the preceding chapters, the 35-hour week has never been fully applied.

It remains true that the data—especially from the OECD—suggest that the annual average duration of work is much lower: in 2012, it was 1,479 hours in France, compared to only 1,397 in Germany, but 1,654 in the United Kingdom, and 1,790 in the United States. But these data are somewhat misleading. In effect, the sources vary from one country to another. The national accounts in Germany and France use a complex model based essentially on reports from employers. American data are also based principally on employers' statistics. On the other hand, the British make use of workers' claims in the European Labour Force Survey. In the United States, employees report working longer than what their employers report. This is also the case in France. If we apply the British methodology in France, we obtain the same annual work duration in France as in the United Kingdom. (The design of German Labour Force Survey does not permit performing the same exercise.) Similarly, according to the INSEE's time-use survey,[7] the image of the French perpetually on vacation is erroneous. Unskilled blue-collar and in-house personnel take, on average, five weeks of vacation per year. On paper, office workers have two weeks more, but a traveler from London to Paris will observe that London pubs are filled with jolly office workers at 5:00 PM, while on the other side of the Channel, numerous offices do not empty until after 7:00. In short, the duration of work in France lies within the European norm,[8] which is quite distinct from that in the United

States (which combines a long day with very short—or even nonexistent—vacations).

Another assertion does not totally survive analysis: that the French benefit from an exceptionally protective labor law. OECD data on employment protection place France in the lead for temporary contracts and just behind Germany for regular contracts. On paper, these comparisons are probably correct: it is almost impossible for a French employer to fire an employee within the span of a temporary contract (beyond the trial period). But can we really speak of a constraint for the employer and protection for the employee when we observe that out of 4.6 million temporary private contracts (apart from those of temp agencies) that were concluded in the first quarter of 2014, 3.8 million were for less than a month, and most for less than eight days?[9]

For regular workers, the law is apparently protective, but nothing prevents an employer from (for example) modifying the work schedule of an employee or her workplace; and if this is incompatible with the worker's family life, then the employer may propose an "amicable" separation (*rupture conventionnelle*). Single women with children are particularly vulnerable.

In fact, the progressive adjustment of French labor law and the inventiveness of firms' human resources departments offer a labor market that is increasingly flexible. As with the German market under the Hartz Laws, it is gradually approaching that of the English-speaking countries. Here, too, one might wish for simplification. However, as we have seen in the preceding chapters, to touch the labor laws would amount to tampering by a sorcerer's apprentice, since the mechanisms at work and their heterogeneous effects are so complex. Good intentions could translate into an explosion of inequality, with no gains in efficiency.

Our portrait of France up to now is rather "reassuring" in terms of the adaptability of the French economy and institutions to the constraints of globalization, despite their failure to immediately grasp the opportunities of a changing world and despite some deleterious policies. However, France faces two challenges: real estate and Europe.

OVERPRICED REAL ESTATE?

The strong performance of real estate prices in France is usually presented as to its credit. It has carefully avoided the calamity of subprimes, as in the United States, or dependence on short-term interest rates, as in Spain.

The comparative evolution of residential real estate prices in France, Germany, the UK, and the US is spectacular (figure 9). In line with its demographic decline, Germany experienced a collapse of real estate prices before the Great Recession. In contrast, the United Kingdom and France underwent (until 2008) a boom in residential real estate prices, much larger than that observed in the United States. The implosion of the property bubble brought American prices back to a level lower than at the start of the 2000s. The adjustment was also significant in the United Kingdom (but prices have been recovering since 2013). It was much less severe in France, where prices remained historically high.

Demand exceeds supply due to factors that are demographic, sociological, and related to desirability. The growth in the French population is sustained. Purchases of secondary residences or *pieds à terre* by foreigners are still dynamic. The success of alternating child custody after divorce—rotation from week to week between parents—requires both parents to have

Figure 9. Housing prices relative to disposable income in France, Germany, United Kingdom, and United States, Q1 2000–Q1 2013 (scale set to 2005 = 1). Source: International House Price Database, Federal Reserve Bank of Dallas (http://www.dallasfed.org/institute/houseprice).

larger lodgings. The growth in real estate prices has an impact on rentals, too, which since the start of the century have risen 1% faster than retail prices.

These high prices hinder France's competitiveness in several ways. While studies of the French case are still ongoing, work on the United Kingdom and Ireland underlines the fact that an increase in the cost of real estate for households requires employers to pay higher salaries.[10] German salary moderation during the 2000s, like the drop in real salaries during the Great Recession in the United Kingdom, coincided with periods when the price of real estate fell.

The price of business real estate seemed to soar to levels not seen since the end of the Second World War in France.[11] For firms that owned their premises, the impact was mixed: on the one hand, their investments were more costly, but on the other, they benefited from significant collateral that facilitated obtaining credit, a significant advantage during the financial crisis. But with their equity increasing spectacularly, firms were encouraged to increase the dividends paid to stockholders. This mechanism can explain why French businesses claimed to have insufficient profit margins and at the same time still distributed historically high dividends on shares (see the preceding chapter). On the other hand, the cost of real estate is clearly an obstacle to the creation and development of new businesses. The levers possessed by the state to affect the price of these assets are limited.

FRANCE IN EUROPE

The biggest uncertainty about the future of the French economy relates to the European environment. Over the last four decades, French leaders have clearly bet on Europe. Mitterrand definitively converted the Left to this project, and Chirac erased the last Gaullist pretentions to independence. Between 1974 and 2014, the European Commission was presided over by a French statesman for thirteen years; since its creation in 1999, a French citizen has governed the European Central Bank for eight years.

Moreover, France has been the motor of the major stages in European economic—but also political—integration. It fought to keep the United Kingdom inside political Europe by accepting the "money back" rebate on the United Kingdom's participation in the European budget;[12] it let Germany implement an accelerated policy of convergence after reunification, despite the economic impact on the rest of Europe; and it fought for the entry of Greece into the eurozone.

But it seems now to have lost its singular political hand within the eurozone, tagging along behind Germany, while the sovereign debt crisis is not resolved. This weakening is not the expression of resigned acceptance of a European economic strategy that does not respond to the heterogeneity within the union. I have already stressed the demographic heterogeneity that intra-European migratory flows are incapable of eliminating. The German budgetary efforts of the 2010s may be coherent from the perspective of a declining and aging population, because they imply that in the coming decades public expenditure will rise sharply. Conversely, the French birthrate requires increased investment *today* in return for reduced needs for finance in the long term. Thus, this heterogeneity is obviously economic. While the search for competitiveness through lower costs—notably salaries—suits European manufacturing economies, it is not suited to the service economy, in which one of the paths to growth is through improved quality. Historical heritage is also profoundly heterogeneous. The trauma of Nazism limits the emergence of extremes in Germany. But low confidence in Europe bolsters the extreme right in Greece, Denmark, and France; as well as populism in Italy; and even the radical Right in the United Kingdom.

NOTES

1. The article by Steven Erlanger in the *New York Times* of August 24, 2013, is a summary of the clichés about France:

Changing any country is difficult. But the challenge in France seems especially hard, in part because of the nation's amour-propre and self-image as a European leader and global power, and in part because French life is so comfortable for many and the day of reckoning still seems far enough away, especially to the country's small but powerful unions. . . .

In a more competitive world economy, the question is not whether the French social model is a good one, but whether the French can continue to afford it. Based on current trends, the answer is clearly no, not without significant structural changes—in pensions, in taxes, in social benefits, in work rules and in expectations....

The warning signs are everywhere: French unemployment and youth unemployment are at record levels; growth is slow compared with Germany, Britain, the United States or Asia; government spending represents nearly 57 percent of gross domestic product, the highest in the euro zone, and is 11 percentage points higher than Germany....

When the French work, they work hard; labor productivity, perhaps the single most important indicator of an economy's potential, is still relatively high, if dropping. But with long holidays and the 35-hour week, the French work fewer hours than most competitors, putting an extra strain on corporations and the economy....

Ninety percent of French companies have 10 or fewer employees and fear expansion because of extra tax burdens and strict labor regulations.

2. Yann Algan and Pierre Cahuc, *La société de défiance: comment le modèle social français s'auto-détruit,* CEPREMAP collection (Paris: Éditions de la rue d'Ulm, 2007); Claudia Sénik, "Why Are the French So Unhappy? The Cultural Dimension of Happiness," Working paper no. 2011–34, Paris-Jourdan Sciences Economiques.

3. The breakdown by industry of employment in household surveys is less contingent on divergences in method than the breakdown in the national accounts.

4. This is indeed a European Union model, since in the name of an integrated market, European directives control the VAT.

5. Juan G. Gay, Valérie Paris, Marion Devaux, and Michael de Looper, "Mortality Amenable to Health Care in 31 OECD Countries: Estimates and Methodological Issues," OECD Health Working Papers, no. 55 (2011).

6. Philippe Askenazy, Brigitte Dormont, Pierre-Yves Geoffard, and Valérie Paris, "Towards a More Efficient Health System," *Les notes du Conseil d'analyse économique,* no. 8 (July 2013), http://www.cae-eco.fr/IMG/pdf/cae-note008-en.pdf.

7. Fella Nabli and Layla Ricroch, "Enquête Emploi du temps 2009–2010," *INSEE résultats* no. 130 (Paris: INSEE, 2012).

8. For the long series see Richard Blundell, Antoine Bozio, and Guy Laroque, "Extensive and Intensive Margins of Labour Supply: Working Hours in the US, UK and France," IFS Working Papers, no. 11/01 (2011).

9. Very short contracts are also successful because they enable getting around another protection in work rights: the rule against signing more than two fixed-term contracts with the same worker except after a delay of at least one-third of the duration of the contract. For example, with a contract of five days from Monday to Friday, the delay is two days (or the time of a weekend), so a firm (open seven days a week) may rehire the same worker on Monday. In some sectors, such as restaurants, such contracts are even considered as in "regular use," so there is no constraint on successive contracts.

10. See for example Olympia Bover, John Muellbauer, and Anthony Murphy, "Housing, Wages and UK Labour Markets," *Oxford Bulletin of Economics and Statistics* 51, no. 2 (1989), 97–136.

11. Philippe Askenazy, "Capital Prices and Eurozone Competitiveness Differentials," IZA Discussion Paper no. 7219 (2013).

12. At the Dublin summit, November 30, 1979, Thatcher asked for and obtained a massive rebate for the UK's participation in the European budget.

CONCLUSION

France furnishes a remarkable laboratory in which to study political trouble in the face of transformations in capitalism and paradigm changes in economics. Since 1974, the country has never been able (unless for a transitory moment) to escape from mass unemployment. It has proven incapable of maintaining durable growth or of fully grasping the opportunities implicit in the regular reconfigurations of the world economy. Yet, at the same time, France has maintained from year to year its status and its credibility, even amid the Great Recession and the European sovereign debt crisis.

The step-by-step analysis developed in this book has allowed us to isolate the sources of this mediocre (yet never catastrophic) condition. Government activity has been the victim of recurrent errors in diagnosis and in expectations, inducing policies that were often counterproductive. The structural character of the crisis of the 1970s was not accepted until the very end of the decade. The Fed's change in monetary policy, designed by Volcker, was not understood until 1983. And the revolution of the "new economy" was not perceived until the twentieth century was closing. Most countries endured governments that committed major errors, as well. But unlike in numerous countries, no French administration, of whatever political complexion, has offered a structuring project to build the France of the future.

This absence contrasts with the constant efforts to construct an economic and then a political Europe. In a France integrated into the continent, the obsession with a "foreign model" ended up filling the whole political and social field. These models were comforting and convenient. They gave intellectual laziness an excuse for curiosity about the world outside. Yet, concerning France, the conclusion of their lessons was remarkably constant: if unemployment persisted, if growth remained hesitant, it was almost always the fault of the French people and their institutions. The people, especially: sometimes the majority of them (if not all) were alleged to be barely employable, and sometimes they were presumed to be pusillanimous in the face of change. And then, the institutions: their maladjustment—necessarily so, since they differed from the model of the moment—seemed to authorize those in power to modify them with scant consideration.

But in either case, as this book has shown, decade after decade, this double critique has too often led to the whims of a sorcerer's apprentice. Despite their ideological differences, governments on both right and left have followed the same methods and obtained the same paltry results. As a consequence, France has always lagged behind or run out of step with other countries. It imposed a budgetary cure in 1976 but stimulated its economy in 1981 at the very moment the United States was plunging into recession. Its educational democratization did not begin until the mid-1980s, and it took two decades to reach the level of higher education graduates enjoyed by the major developed countries. In the 1990s, its whole economic policy turned on the development of low-skilled employment, just when the global Internet and the knowledge economy were making their effects felt. In parallel, the economic and social situations of stigmatized groups (young people, immigrants) and of whole geographic zones (the housing estates on city peripheries) were deteriorating, feeding both permanent unemployment and inequality.

However, neither French society nor the French economy has crumbled. Public services—often presented as costly and hence a weakness—are more probably an element of stability, even if access to them remains inegalitarian. The French economy remains strongly diversified, at the heart of Western Europe; and its labor force is diligent, in a society that gives a central place to work.

Moreover, successive governments have not remained inert. Perhaps not *everything* has been tried (as François Mitterrand claimed in 1993), but surely *almost* everything has been tried—even schemes that ran counter to France's international commitments, under the Villepin government from 2005 to 2007. Without a political compass, at the whim of trends in economic science, at the mercy of the winds of company lobbying and the reefs of European affairs, those in power have sought among experts some direction for recovering growth and full employment. Various recipes and divergent measures have been piled on top of each other. Reform measures, even the most emblematic of them, have been essentially parametric; the complex laws on the 35-hour week—the shift to annual accounting of work-time, changes in how work-time is defined, modification of vacation allowance, financial aid, various kinds of minimum wages—and then their dismantling—all are emblematic of this. Measures have cannibalized each other, as have the multiple exemptions from social-welfare contributions. And in fact they were usually ineffective. But their number is so large that adding them all up has fended off deep recessions and contained unemployment, even during the Great Recession that began in 2008. Even apart from specific tools used in regions, *départements*, and *communes*, we can count (at the end of 2013) 160 simultaneous measures "in favor" of employment and of business, for a total cost of 8% of the French GDP. Additional decisions by the Valls government in 2014 will push this up to 10%.

My reading of recent French economic history is paradoxically optimistic. The French economy and French society have shown remarkable resilience, despite the decades of blindness I have documented. Revamping costly but inefficient tools could provide plenty of room to maneuver for any government that projects and prepares for a long-term horizon. Constantly running to catch the train of growth, France cannot be unlucky enough to miss it forever. The Great Recession probably marked the culmination, over four decades, of a transition from one industrial revolution to another. New opportunities will open up—if the uncertainty regarding the future of Europe vanishes. The state of France is far from justifying its image as the weak link in Europe.

INDEX